THE WORLD AT YOUR FEET
THE FUTURE IN YOUR HANDS
WITH SYD[illegible]HE

All of us war[illegible]ow, as we approa[illegible] the advent of suc[illegible]re-dictions, soci[illegible]ans and politicians debate about what it all means. From an astrologer's point of view, however, it's all about the planetary patterns that ultimately shape our lives. But any prophecy or prediction only depicts the pattern that prevails *at the moment.* Free will can alter any pattern.

A prediction, then, is merely a kind of mirror that reflects what's going on in the deeper levels of ourselves. Once that internal pattern is made visible and conscious, we can bring our will, desire, and intent to bear against the pattern and enhance it or change it. So where does all of this leave you and your sun sign in the millennium?

In this illuminating guide, world-famous astrologer Sydney Omarr helps you find out. . .

SYDNEY OMARR'S

NEW MILLENNIUM GUIDE

A SIGNET BOOK

SIGNET
Published by New American Library, a division of
Penguin Putnam Inc., 375 Hudson Street,
New York, New York 10014, U.S.A.
Penguin Books Ltd, 27 Wrights Lane,
London W8 5TZ, England
Penguin Books Australia Ltd, Ringwood,
Victoria, Australia
Penguin Books Canada Ltd, 10 Alcorn Avenue,
Toronto, Ontario, Canada M4V 3B2
Penguin Books (N.Z.) Ltd, 182–190 Wairau Road,
Auckland 10, New Zealand

Penguin Books Ltd, Registered Offices:
Harmondsworth, Middlesex, England

First published by Signet, an imprint of New American Library,
a division of Penguin Putnam Inc.

First Printing, September 1999
10 9 8 7 6 5 4 3 2 1

Sydney Omarr is syndicated worldwide by
Los Angeles Times Syndicate.

 REGISTERED TRADEMARK—MARCA REGISTRADA

Printed in the United States of America

Contents

Preface to the Twenty-first Century

For many of us, our concept of the new millennium has been molded and defined by the media. From the prophecies of Nostradamus and Edgar Cayce, to movies like *Deep Impact* and *Armageddon,* the dawn of the twenty-first century looks like it's going to be a chaotic, dangerous time. Movies such as *Twister* and *Volcano* depict violent weather and natural disasters that bear eerie parallels to predictions about massive earth changes.

Other scenarios, depending on who is talking, include the appearance of the anti-Christ, who takes over the world; a huge meteor that strikes Earth; economic ruin and a worldwide depression. All of this has contributed to an undercurrent of hysteria about the approaching millennium and should be placed in the proper perspective.

Any prophecy or prediction, whether it's done through astrology, clairvoyance, or soggy tea leaves at the bottom of a cup, only depicts the pattern that prevails *at that moment*. Free will can alter any pattern. Nothing is set in stone. Our point of power always resides in the present. Change your deepest beliefs, and your experience eventually reflects it.

If enough people experience a radical change in consciousness as a critical juncture is approached, the *predicted patterns* are changed. Disaster may be delayed or averted altogether. Perhaps that's part of the reason why California hasn't split away from the continental U.S., why the Mississippi hasn't flowed backward, why Florida hasn't broken up into tiny islands, why Atlantis hasn't risen. On the other hand, it's possible that Nostradamus, Cayce, and other psychics were simply wrong.

Astrological Patterns

At the advent of a new decade, century, or millennium, futurists make predictions, sociologists slap on labels that describe the period we've just left or are about to enter, and historians and politicians debate about what it all means. From an astrologer's point of view, however, it's all about patterns, specifically the pattern of planetary alignments. These alignments coincide with grand historical events that ultimately shape our lives and deepen our understanding of who we are. They also broaden the astrologer's knowledge about what these alignments mean.

Take the 1890s, the gateway to the twentieth century. Among the inventions of that era were the movie camera, telegraph, telephones, radios, planes, cars. Artists like Van Gogh, Cezanne, and Gauguin broke away from the pack and blew apart the Renaissance traditions of realism. Freud split open the unconscious and gave birth to contemporary psychology. Jazz and ragtime emerged, Russia headed toward revolution, Nietzsche turned the traditional view of science and religion on its head. The *energy* was changing, the new paradigm was being born.

All of this occurred when Pluto and Neptune linked up in Gemini, which rules communication, travel, thoughts and ideas, and education. Due to the nature of these two planets, the conjunction represented a particular *pattern* under which certain events unfolded.

Even though Pluto hadn't been discovered in the 1890s, astrological research has shown that whenever it linked up in the past with Neptune, old paradigms collapsed and new ones were born in the rubble. Even if you leave Pluto out of the equation, Neptune in Gemini represented the opportunity to transcend the established modes of communication, travel, and ideas of the 1800s.

Neptune symbolizes transcendence, delusion, mysticism, escapism, and everything intangible. In the 1960s, it was going through secretive Scorpio. Under this influence, we witnessed antiwar protests, the Civil Rights movement, a burgeoning interest in the occult, a deepening connection between sexuality and spirituality, and the birth of the drug culture. Drop out and tune in: that's Neptune.

In 1993, Uranus and Neptune joined up in Capricorn, a conjunction that hasn't happened since the time of the Industrial Revolution in 1821. In 1995, Pluto, the planet of transformation, power, death and rebirth, went into Sagittarius, the sign of the philosopher and the truth seeker. In 1996, Uranus, symbolic of disruption, individuality, and the breaking apart of old structures, moved into Aquarius, the sign that it rules. In 1998, Neptune went into Aquarius. What all this means in practical terms is that ordinary life became quite extraordinary. And now, as we approach the millennium, the effects of these patterns are evident.

Every major institution, from government to health care, public education to religion, is locked in a power struggle between the old and the new. The parts of these institutions that no longer work are dying, and in their place will emerge paradigms that are more intuitive, holistic, and honest.

For you, this may mean that you find and live your bliss. Or perhaps dramatic changes are underway in your job, career, or intimate relationships. Your spiritual beliefs may undergo a complete metamorphosis. Your creative and intuitive abilities can be greatly enhanced and deepened. However it shows up in your own life, be assured that we're all in the same boat.

Neptune in Aquarius is rather like marriage: you're committed, for better or worse. So from 1998 to 2012, we'll be committed to understanding how we create our own realities through our deepest beliefs. Even better, we'll realize that we can change that reality with a single thought or desire that is backed by intense emotion and intent. We'll become more psychic, more receptive to subtle energies, more yin. We'll be better able to perceive the larger patterns in our lives, the big picture. We won't be stuck in the trees anymore; we'll be forced to see the forest.

The bottom line, naturally, is what this means for you in terms of your daily life. Your family. Your business concerns and finances. Your friendships and health and romances. How can you facilitate the process? How easy or difficult will it be for you to keep pace with impending changes? The answers are as close as your sun sign.

Your Sun Sign & Natal Chart

When you breathed for the first time, the sun was located in a particular area of the zodiac. Your sun sign is the most powerful indicator of your overall personality, the primary color of who you are, the brightest light in your horoscope. It's your astrological DNA.

If you were born between May 21 and June 21, for instance, you're a Gemini. Your mind moves at the speed of light, and the rest of you probably does, too. If you're a Leo, you love being on center stage and live with a dramatic flourish that leaves Taurus gasping in the dust. Any of these traits are altered if you've got a moon in Pisces or seven planets in Aries. Certain aspects—angles between the planets—can also play havoc with your sun, but generally, the sun's brilliance is never dimmed.

If you know your exact time, date, and place of birth, then it's to your advantage to have your natal chart drawn up. Most New Age bookstores have computer services that can do this for about $5, in under fifteen seconds. Think of your natal chart as a schematic, a blueprint for a house. You're the architect and your life is the house. Doors are drawn here, windows there, the rooms are certain dimensions and shapes. But as the architect, you can alter the details. Maybe you add a porch or a swimming pool. You might knock down walls to make the rooms larger. You're not locked into the blueprint of your birth chart any more than you're locked into the blueprint of the house.

Free will prevails.

You're free to create the reality you want, based on the broad patterns that you chose before you were born. Your natal chart merely indicates talents and characteristics—the basic structure of your personality. Its value lies in the overall *patterns* of the house placements of the planets and the aspects they make to each other.

Your time of birth has to be exact because this is what determines your ascendant—the sign and its degree that were rising when you drew your first breath. The ascendant sets up the houses, which represent twelve different areas of your life. Along with your sun and moon signs, your ascendant has a lot to say about your personal appearance, health, early childhood environment, and the self that others see.

If your ascendant is in Virgo, it would explain why you're outside every morning, sweeping leaves off your driveway, an activity that doesn't fit into descriptions of your Gemini sun. That Virgo rising can make you so picky at times that it drives your Gemini sun absolutely nuts.

The three most important factors in your natal chart are the signs of your sun, moon, and ascendant. If you have any of the three in Sagittarius, then you're going to feel the impact of Pluto in that sign through 2008. Or if your significant other or one of your kids has an Aquarian sun with a moon or ascendant in either Aquarius or Sagittarius, then the impact of Neptune and Uranus in Aquarius and Pluto in Sagittarius is going to deliver a triple whammy. So if you know your moon and rising sign, then read the descriptions for those signs as well.

Be prepared. Self-knowledge empowers you. That's the motto for the new millennium.

The Outer Planets

This book focuses on three of the "other planets"—Uranus, Neptune, and Pluto. They are the slowest-moving planets, so they exert considerable influence over a prolonged period of time. When they transit or move through the same slice of sky as your sun, moon, or other planets in your birth chart, new *patterns* are formed.

All three of these outer planets were assumed to have existed since the invention of the telescope in the early seventeenth century. However, when astrologers discovered Uranus in 1781, the new planet rocked the boat, which is precisely what Uranus is good at. In 1846, Neptune was discovered and the discovery of Pluto followed in 1930.

These three planets represent the outer boundaries of human experience and consciousness. Think of them as the larger perspective, our connection to the transcendental. They allow us to look at the less conscious aspects of ourselves, the parts that are hidden, locked up, stashed away. They expose us to possibilities we would rather avoid, but in doing so, we're able to use strengths and talents that we may not have known we possessed. They tend to shake up our normal view of reality and demand that we change accordingly. Their lessons are rarely easy, but their benefits can be enormous.

Since these planets move so slowly, their influence affects entire generations. Each of these planets and the aspects they make to each other will have a tremendous impact on the new millennium.

How to Use This Book

The first part of this book provides general astrological information and touches on some of the dramatic changes that the outer planets may bring about in the millennium. These are viewed in light of some of the millennial predictions made by Nostradamus, Edgar Cayce, and Jane Roberts, as well as those of other cultures.

The second part of the book is arranged by sun signs. Each section provides a general description of the sign, which can apply to a sun, moon, or a rising in that particular sign, and how the millennium will affect each sign in various areas. It's not necessary that you have your natal chart for this section of the book. But if you do, then read the sections that apply to your moon and rising sign as well.

Each sun sign section includes specific methods for tapping and enhancing intuitive abilities; for recognizing and following synchronicities to create the kind of future you need and want; and for cultivating conscious awareness. As you read through the descriptions, keep in mind that the future isn't destined. If you read something you don't like in your sun sign section, use your point of power in the present to make the necessary changes in your life *now*.

PART ONE

The Three Musketeers

Chapter 1

Who's in Charge Here?

The Future

All of us want to know the future. Are we going to meet the right person, find the right job, win the lottery? We want to know what's going to happen tomorrow or next year, and we hope the news is, well, good. If it's not, we would rather not hear about it.

But if the future is malleable, if it's open-ended, then a prediction is merely providing information about the prevalent patterns in our lives. It's a kind of mirror that reflects what's going on in the deeper levels of ourselves. Once that internal pattern is made visible and conscious, we can bring our will, desire, and intent to bear against the pattern and enhance it or change it.

Suppose you dream that you're in a car accident. The dream is rich in detail—the yellow bus that races toward you through the intersection, the line of cars that block you on either side, even the particular buildings around you. For a few days, you're uneasy every time you're in the car. But you never see a yellow bus or the intersection from the dream and you forget about it. Then, a month later, you're in another city on a business trip, stuck in traffic, and see a yellow bus barreling straight toward you. The memory of the dream suddenly kicks in and you don't even hesitate. You scramble out of the car and a heartbeat later, the bus slams into the car you just vacated.

If you hadn't recalled the dream, would you have survived? Would you have survived if you hadn't had the dream at all? *Did the dream save your life?* This type of prophecy is actually common and has appeared in many forms over the centuries and has involved various types of transportation. You trust it because it originated in you. But suppose the prediction comes from a stranger who reads your cards? Or your horoscope? Or stones tossed on the ground that form a seemingly random pattern? Does that make the prediction less valid? Would it have the same impact on you?

Prophecies and predictions raise important questions about destiny versus free will. Is the future, both personal and global, already a done deal?

Recent discoveries in quantum physics indicate that the future may be like a script that each of us writes, based on the choices that we make, within the broad strokes of our lives. In other words, tomorrow doesn't just follow today. Tomorrow may be a multidimensional smorgasbord with a dizzying array of possibilities that arise out of the choices we make now. *At this moment.*

If we become aware of a particular pattern through prediction, divination, or any other method, and we don't like what we see, then we can change it. This seems to apply whether the prediction is personal or global. If enough people believe in something, that belief builds momentum until it crashes through the established paradigm and becomes a reality. If you pay attention to that dream about the future car accident and are able to alter the actual event so that you aren't killed, then why can't the same thing happen on an even larger scale?

Perhaps it already has.

The French Prophet

Prophecy is hardly the new kid on the block. It has been around as long as we have and its history is rich with both hits and misses. In the twentieth century, the hits have invariably involved dramatic historical events—the sinking of the *Titanic,* the stock market crash in 1929, the Kennedy assassination, the explosion of the *Challenger,* the collapse of the Berlin Wall, and the end of the Cold War. These hits have come about through dreams, clairvoyant and precognitive visions, various kinds of oracles, and of course, through astrology.

None of these tools is accurate all of the time. They are subject, after all, to the skills and interpretation of the seer, the mystic, the astrologer. Even Nostradamus, undoubtedly one of the greatest and most controversial prophets, gave conflicting interpretations of his visions.

Born in France in 1503, Nostradamus was a Sagittarian with a Scorpio moon. He showed an early aptitude for math and astrology, but at his family's insistence went on to become a physician. Much of his adult life reads like a Shakespearean tragedy. His wife and children died in a plague, he was accused of heresy, and he had to flee the church inquisitors. As a result of the religious superstitions of sixteenth-century France, Nostradamus's prophetic talent didn't reach fruition until after he turned forty. He didn't begin writing the quatrains, for which he is famous, until he was fifty-one, and he continued writing them until his death at the age of sixty-three. The final dozen years of his life encompass his legacy that we know today. And what a legacy it is—obscure, open to wide interpretation, but eerily accurate in many instances.

Astrology was one of his tools, for there are many references to it in his writings. His other tool was a bowl filled with water. Many nights Nostradamus stared into this bowl of water until his immediate surroundings fell away and the waters parted to reveal visions of the future. The visions were often vivid and terrifying. Nostradamus, fearing that the inquisitors would find and persecute him if he recorded the visions exactly as he saw them, wrote his predictions in quatrains that read like a Tower of Babel cookbook. A glob of French, a dab of Italian, some Latin and Hebrew, some Arabic and Greek: translators and interpreters have been puzzling over these quatrains ever since.

Nostradamus's predictions about the latter part of the twentieth century are about as dark as it gets. Interpreters of the quatrains seem to agree that he not only foresaw Kennedy's assassination, but also foresaw that Oswald didn't act alone. While other people predicted the assassination as well, none did it four hundred years before the actual event. He also predicted the fall of the Berlin Wall, the end of the Cold War, the beginning of AIDS and its insidious spread, the *Challenger* explosion, famines, earthquakes, natural disasters of every conceivable shape. At a time when the general belief was that Earth was the center of the universe, Nostradamus predicted that man would walk upon another planetary body. *"He will come to take himself to the corner of Luna, where he will be taken and placed on alien land . . ."*

Nostradamus had some notable misses, however. According to some interpretations, the British Isles should have sunk in 1993. By the mid-1990s, the western U.S. should have broken into small islands. New York and Florida should be flooded. Eastern Africa should be split into three pieces. In 1997, New York City should have been under some sort of catastrophic attack. *"The sky will burn at forty-five degrees; Fire approaches the New City; In an instant a huge scattered flame leaps up . . ."* None of this happened. Why not?

The obvious answer is that he wasn't always right or that his timing may have been off. His own interpretation of the visions may have been flawed. He was trying to interpret information that related to a future he couldn't even imagine. The burning sky over Manhattan might have been nothing more than a Fourth of July celebration. Maybe the flooding in Florida that Nostradamus saw was due to Hurricane Andrew, not the end of the world. To a man in the 1500s, the devastation of Homestead and certain areas in Miami might have looked like the end of the world.

Another explanation is that these visions related to what might have happened if we hadn't started waking up as a nation, a world, a global community. Nostradamus himself seemed to envision at least two possible scenarios as we headed into the millennium—nuclear annihilation in 1999 or the dawning of a golden age of enlightenment. Is it possible that we raised our collective consciousness sufficiently so that we leaped from one probable track into the future to the other? Is such a thing even possible? Recent discoveries in quantum physics suggest that it's not only possible, but that it happens more frequently than we can imagine.

Eerie parallels to Nostradamus's predictions persist. One of his predictions about a blood plague (AIDS) was that the cure lay in "space grown" crystals. In 1988, astronauts on the first post *Challenger* flight planned to grow crystals of a protein taken from the AIDS virus.

"Researchers want to grow the crystals of reverse transcriptase to decipher its structure," reported the *Fort Lauderdale Sun Sentinel* on August 1, 1988. "Crystals grown in space are not distorted by gravity while they form. Scientists hope to learn how the AIDS virus takes over the genetic machinery inside a cell and use that knowledge to develop a drug to conquer AIDS."

Perhaps these parallels serve as reminders that we're not completely in the clear yet.

The Sleeping Prophet

Edgar Cayce, a Pisces with a Taurus moon, is probably the most documented psychic and greatest seer of the twentieth century. While asleep, he gave more than fourteen thousand psychic readings on topics that ranged from health and homeopathic remedies to reincarnation, astrology, Atlantis, and of course, "coming earth changes."

Many of Cayce's predictions have panned out, others have not. Atlantis, for instance, didn't surface in the late sixties. But in 1968, a diving expedition off the shores of Bimini discovered what looked like marble pillars and a great road fashioned out of huge blocks. Since then, other discoveries have been made in the same area—towers, stairways, walls, even pyramids. Was this what Cayce meant by Atlantis rising?

A repetitive theme in his readings was a pole shift, the ultimate climax to a series of increasingly violent natural disasters. According to Cayce, pole shifts had happened in the past and this one would occur within three months of the eruption of Mt. Vesuvius in Italy and Mt. Pelee on Martinique. Japan, he said, would slide into the sea. Coastal regions would vanish. *"The earth will be broken up . . . the upper portion of Europe will be changed in the twinkling of an eye . . . the earth will be broken up in the western portion of America . . ."* Cayce placed the shift at around 1998, which would usher in the Aquarian age, but saw it happening in gradual stages. Nostradamus, however, predicted that the axis shift would happen by October of the seventh millennium (2000), and that there would be signs of its approach in the spring of that year.

On May 3, 2000, seven planets will line up in the sign of Taurus, converging within 30 degrees of the sky. Taurus is a fixed sign that resists change and with Saturn and Jupiter involved in the alignment, the result is likely to be economic rather than seismic. Perhaps it relates to the Y2K bug. But whenever so many planets line up together, an imbalance is created. How this imbalance affects you depends on how prominent Taurus is in your chart and the angles this lineup makes to other planets. In 1994, the Northridge earthquake happened during an alignment in Capricorn. The alignment in May 2000 will catalyze a twenty-year Jupiter/Saturn cycle, the first of the millennium. Benefic and expansive Jupiter will be pitted against Saturn's need for structure and form.

Even more important than the seven-planet lineup is the total solar eclipse in Leo less than a year earlier, on August 11, 1999. It's been called the "eclipse of the century" and the "crisis eclipse." It could result in political terror, eruptions in Russia and the Middle East, and various types of power struggles. Then again, nothing like that may come about.

Cayce knew virtually nothing about astrology in his waking state. But while asleep, he made numerous references to it. "The strongest power in the destiny of man is the sun, then the closer planets of those coming into ascendancy at the time of the birth of the individual. But let it be understood, no action or any planet or any phases of the sun, moon, or any of the heavenly bodies surpass the rule of man's individual will." In other words, planets lining up in a particular way or the sun's total eclipse in a particular sign doesn't have to spell the end of anything if our will is sufficiently developed *to change the inherent pattern.*

The Reluctant Prophet

In the fall of 1963, writer Jane Roberts was sitting in her apartment in Elmira, New York, working on her poetry, when her consciousness suddenly rushed out of her body and astonishing ideas flooded her mind. When she returned to her body, she discovered that she'd written down many of the concepts she'd received and had entitled it *The Physical Universe as Idea Construction*. The ideas were so evocative that she began researching psychic phenomena and planned a book on the topic.

Several months later, she and her husband, artist Robert Butts, experimented with a Ouija board, and eventually the pointer started spelling out messages from a personality called Seth. When Roberts began to anticipate the board's replies, she assumed the responses were coming from her own subconscious. Within a month, she was speaking for Seth while in an altered state of consciousness.

Seth described himself as "a personality essence no longer focused in physical reality," a description with which Roberts generally agreed. Whatever he was, his relationship with Roberts continued until her death in 1984. Together, they produced ten Seth books and more than six thousand pages, some of it still unpublished, on the nature of reality. All of the notebooks and materials related to the Seth material are now on permanent file at the Yale University library.

Roberts never considered herself a prophet or even a psychic. She rarely did readings for other people, and when she did, it was with great reluctance. She was first and foremost a writer who published a number of books under her own name. But the core of her life was the Seth material. Twice a week for twenty years, she went into a trance, Seth spoke through her, and Butts wrote down the sessions in a kind of shorthand. Regardless of whether Seth was a part of Roberts's higher consciousness or a separate personality, the material has greatly influenced New Age thought.

Seth, like Roberts herself, rarely gave predictions,

either global or otherwise. "When you understand the nature of reality, then you realize that predictions of future events are basically meaningless. You can predict some events, and they can occur, but you create the future in every moment." The fundamental tenet of the Seth material, in fact, is that each of us creates our own reality, according to our most deeply held beliefs, and we do it from our power point in the present. "This is one of the reasons why psychics' predictions often do not seem to bear out, for at every point you do indeed have the free will, through your beliefs, to alter your experience."

So, according to Seth, the earth changes foreseen by Nostradamus, Cayce, and other psychics through the centuries, aren't predestined. Nothing is fated. In this belief system, natural disasters aren't thrust upon us by some external force; they are reflections of the mental properties of the people who live in those particular areas. If the level of consciousness is raised, it's reflected in the environment. A change in our collective beliefs, then, brings about a change in our experience.

Seth saw us as multidimensional beings, living but one possibility among many. With each choice that we make, he said, the road not taken continues along its own lines of development. To us, though, it is just a path that didn't pan out.

If, for instance, you're an art teacher with a passion for aviation, then perhaps in one probability you're a pilot with a passion for art. Each *you* lives out his or her life. Taken a step further, think back to a relationship that didn't work out. In some probability, the relationship *did* work and a probable you is living that relationship. Now apply this to all the major decisions you have made in your life—a move, a career change, a marriage or divorce, children—and it gets complicated very quickly. Yet, according to Seth, each self is equally real within its own system and is able to draw on the abilities and talents of the other.

This theme has appeared in novels, in movies, and may have a basis in scientific thought, in the Many Worlds Theory of quantum physics. The hypothesis echoes Seth. In every road not taken, reality splits off and continues toward its own completion. If all possible universes exist, then how does astrology fit into Seth's view of things?

"Using conventional astrology, you will find certain correlations, because of particular events occurring, that are indeed interrelated. Yet many individuals will not discover semblances of themselves in the charts of astrology simply because their chosen probabilities are . . . so different from the norm," says Seth.

In Seth's scheme of things, a birth chart depicts only one probability. People born on the same day, at the same time, in the same city, have identical charts. But their experiences of the *birth pattern* may be totally at odds. The litmus test in astrology is that of identical twins, born only minutes apart. Why does one twin battle alcoholism and cancer while the other twin lives an ideal existence? The patterns in the chart vary so little they are virtually identical. The reason, in Seth's world, lies in the individual's inner reactions, which may vary greatly. When astrology works, he says, it does so because the astrologer uses his or her creative and intuitive abilities; the chart, the symbols, are just another tool.

Both Roberts (a Taurus) and Butts (a Gemini) felt that astrology, as it is practiced now, is too limited in conception to accommodate the idea of a multidimensional self living in a multidimensional universe. "Jane and I," he wrote in a footnote, "appear to be two of those individuals who follow a different order of probabilities as far as astrology is concerned." Their birth charts didn't seem to describe the selves they had become. *The pattern didn't fit.*

So where does all of this leave you and your sun sign in the millennium?

You, the Prophet

Astrology has been called an art, a science, an oracle. But it may be all three. The sign of your sun, moon, and ascendant may have a lot less to do with who you are than how you react to the pattern under which you are born. You're the captain of the ship, the writer of the script, the director of the movie. You're the one in charge.

Chapter 2

It's About Time

Astrology & the Ancients

Astrology has been practiced, in one form or another, since 25,000 B.C., when the ancients kept track of time through the phases of the moon. But it was in Mesopotamia in the fourth millennium B.C. that astrology was practiced as a science and had a religious foundation, a glaring dichotomy by today's standards. And yet, nearly every religion of the world holds traces of astrological influence.

Astrological allegories are found in mythology of ancient Greece and Rome and in the Jewish Old Testament. One theory says that the original twenty-two letters of the Hebrew alphabet were derived from groups of stars. This theory compares the fixed stars to consonants and the planets to vowels and says that when this "language" is properly interpreted, it foretells the future.

In the ancient world, the measurements of a year were based upon the equinoxes and the solstices. The vernal equinox, celebrated March 21, marked the advent of spring, when the sun crossed the equator.

June 21, the summer solstice, was when the sun reached its most northerly position. The autumnal equinox on September 21 marked the point when the sun descended and crossed the equator again. And on December 21, the winter solstice, the sun reached its most southerly position once more. These dates are still in use today.

Sun worship was one of the earliest forms of religious expression. The pyramids of the Yucatan and Egypt, the ziggurats of Babylon and Chaldea, and the stone structures found throughout England were temples to the sun god. No surprise, then, that the sun came to symbolize God. In Egyptian ceremonies, the priests wore lion skins, which symbolized Leo, in which the sun was considered to be exalted. In contemporary astrology, the sun still rules Leo and is considered exalted in that sign.

For the pagans of ancient times, the stars were alive. They were divine beings, entities with power and will that could influence life on Earth. This belief was shared by the Chaldeans, Phoenicians, Egyptians, Persians, Hindus, and Chinese. The Chaldeans of Mesopotamia built watch towers from which their priests could observe the movements of the stars and planets. They eventually were able to predict eclipses with great accuracy, but personalized birth charts were confined to the kings. At this time, astrology was considered a sacred art, and those who practiced it were revered.

Astrology was practiced with the belief that the future wasn't determined and that omens could indicate which way to turn, what choices to make. By the first millennium B.C. astrology was the favored divination technique, used by the rulers to expand their domains and protect their kingdoms.

In the fifth century B.C. Chaldean astrology landed

on the shores of Greece and greatly influenced Plato, Aristotle, and Democritus. Greek astronomers used this new astrological information to construct laws about planetary motion and how the cosmos worked. It was in ancient Greece where the zodiac was first divided into twelve sections or houses. As the sun traveled through the sky, it passed through each of these houses, illuminating them, filling them with vitality.

There's some evidence that before the Greeks, the zodiac was originally divided into ten houses. This would reflect the division of the solar year in earlier times into ten months of thirty-six days each, with five sacred days reserved for the gods. The ancients thought of these ten sections as ten divine orders, each one representing particular qualities and characteristics. This may have followed Pythagoras's belief that ten was the most perfect of numbers. The ten signs were eventually changed when the constellations of Virgo and Scorpio were divided and Libra was inserted between them.

There was also a lunar standard in early times that consisted of thirteen months of twenty-eight days each, with one day left over. This standard has carried over, somewhat altered, into certain practices among pagans and Wiccans today.

The origins of astrology that bear the closest resemblance to what is practiced today began after the death of Alexander the Great in 323 B.C. At this time, Alexandria, Egypt, became an international hot spot and center of learning. Over the next few centuries, astrology became a curious meld of Babylonian divination, Egyptian astronomy and physics. At some point in the subsequent centuries, astrology took on a deterministic air that eventually spelled its demise as part of religious practices and beliefs. By Nostradamus's time, the practice of astrology was something to be hidden, to be practiced in secret. And it didn't get any better until the nineteenth century.

The Mayans

Despite the lack of technology, the ancients seemed to understand the precessions of the equinoxes. Every year, the sun moves entirely around the zodiac and returns to the vernal equinox, where it started. But each year it falls a little short of making the complete circle in the allotted time. So the sun loses about one degree every seventy-two years, which means that it regresses through an entire constellation or sign in 2,160 years or through the entire zodiac in 25,920 years. At the end of this period, it goes into the sign before it. In other words, after the age of Aries, we entered the Piscean age, the sign before Aries. When the Piscean age is over, we'll enter the Aquarian age, and so on around the zodiac.

Part of the problem in determining exactly when one age ends and another begins is due to the discrepancy about how many years constitute an age. Is an age 25,000 years? 25,920 years? Or 26,000 years? Astrologers generally agree that the Piscean age began around the birth of Christ and that the Aquarian age will begin around A.D. 2000. But the exact date is open to debate.

The Mayans, however, arrived at a date through another method. Even though they don't appear to have been astrologers, they studied celestial cycles and used them in constructing their calendars. Their calendar, in fact, lies at the heart of Jose Arguelles's book, *The Mayan Factor*.

According to Arguelles, the complex code of the Tzolkin is actually a system of knowledge that has been "written" both mathematically and symbolically by the Maya. This system explains that human history is largely shaped by a galactic beam that the earth and the sun have been going through for the last five thousand years. We reach the end of this beam in 2012, which is, in fact, when the Mayan calendar ends.

Arguelles sees this moment as an evolvement in human spirituality, a spiritual awakening, a radical shift to a new paradigm, the "path beyond technology." He referred to a 26,000-year cycle, which echoes the precession of the equinoxes, and said the last twenty-six years of the cycle would be crucial. He saw August 17–18, 1987, as a turning point in this 26,000-year cycle, the elimination of any sort of Armageddon at the end of that beam in 2012. He called it the Harmonic Convergence, a "re-impregnation of the planetary field with archetypal, harmonic experiences of the planetary whole." The term and the idea took root, and so many people celebrated the Harmonic Convergence that it made the national evening news.

What's particularly interesting about 2012 is that in February of that year, Neptune will enter its own sign of Pisces for only the second time since its discovery in 1848. This could very well signal the beginning of our global unity and an emergence into a higher state of consciousness.

The Modern World: Quantum Leaps

For centuries, our predominant view of the universe was that it functioned like a giant machine made up of independent parts that followed predictable movements. Yes, some of the parts were missing, this view said, but once we found them, we would be able to predict anything because nature's laws were inviolate.

Then along came Einstein's theories of relativity. In his special theory of relativity, Einstein concluded that time isn't absolute everywhere in the universe. As a clock *approaches* the speed of light, Einstein said, time moves more slowly than a clock, which is stationary. As a clock *reaches* the speed of light, it grinds to a halt. Therefore, nothing can travel beyond the speed of light because the structure of time itself breaks down. All the rules go out the window. In Einstein's general theory of relativity, he stated that space and time aren't separate entities at all; they are part of a larger whole that he termed the space-time continuum. These two theories rattled classical scientific thought that says the parts of a given system create the whole.

Physicists David Bohm and Karl Pribram delivered a potentially fatal blow to the notion that the universe is a machine. Working independently of each other, they theorized that the whole is actually greater than the sum of its parts, that there is a hidden order in the universe, a deeper level of reality, an *implicate* or enfolded order. Bohm referred to our level of existence as the *explicate* or unfolded order.

In this view, everything is connected and the universe bears an uncanny resemblance to a giant hologram rather than a giant machine. We, each of us, are a part of the whole and also contain the whole. This concept echoes Seth's views of an invisible (implicate) universe from which the visible (explicate) universe is born. In quantum thought, what we think of as the world *out there* is a vast ocean of wave probabilities and frequencies. This also sounds like Seth, who contends this ocean of possibilities is the framework from which we create our lives. He calls it "framework two," a sort of etheric place where all is probable and, therefore, possible.

In the quantum universe, these wave probabilities or functions are collapsed to a particle as soon as they are observed. In other words, as soon as consciousness enters the picture, the wave becomes something else. In Seth's view, this "collapse" happens when our beliefs and intents "pull in" the desired wave or pattern.

The idea of a universe as a hologram, a pattern of unbroken wholeness, lies at the very heart of the Mayan cosmology and at the heart of astrology. The birth chart is the visible pattern of a hidden (implicate) order, the soul's intent in this particular life. How this hidden order unfolds is the explicate order.

In a broader context, when we say someone is a Pisces, this indicates a broad gestalt of characteristics and traits. A certain personality pattern emerges, a holographic picture that creates the concept of "Pisces." Yet, not every Pisces is mystical, dreamy, moody, or enamored of the sea. Not every Pisces experiences a tug of war between mind and heart. To get an accurate picture of a Pisces or any other sun sign, it's necessary to look at the entire birth chart, the whole holographic snapshot.

Transits, the movement of the planets, act as triggers that set certain proclivities and patterns in motion. If we're aware of an approaching transit, we're suddenly in a much stronger position to take advantage of the opportunities to change our existing patterns by "pulling in" new waves of probabilities. The transit of Pluto in Sagittarius is likely to have an impact on a person whose sun is in that sign. But if the person is *aware* of what it may mean to his life, then he's better equipped to direct the energies in a positive way, to take advantage of the opportunities. With an awareness of the hidden order, he may recognize synchronicities related to this transit that urge him in one direction or another.

Synchronicities tend to happen in clusters, usually during intense periods when our lives are in a state of flux. They are the types of experiences we can dismiss as coincidence—or we can try to place them within the larger context of our lives. What is the experience attempting to convey? Is it a prompting to try something different? To move in a new direction? To release something or someone? Sometimes, a synchronicity happens to confirm something we already sense, as in the following example.

A woman and her family were traveling across the country on a combined pleasure and business trip. The number 33 kept cropping up. Aisle 33, seat 33, gate 33. It happened so many times that she couldn't ignore it. She finally consulted the *I Ching,* a Chinese divination system based on sixty-four hexagrams. Hexagram 33 was called *Retreat*. She and her family recently had put her mother in an Alzheimer's unit, so the hexagram seemed to fit in that the trip was a retreat from that situation. But she sensed there was more to it than that. When they returned from the trip, she went to visit her mother and realized her room number was 33. This tied the recurrence of the number directly to her mother. The trip was a retreat from the situation with her mother.

A synchronicity unfolds from the implicate or hidden order of our lives. It may involve numbers, names, times, animals, people, virtually anything. It can be dramatic, is sometimes amusing, and is always intended to seize our attention. Sometimes, synchronicities are signposts that indicate we're on the correct path or in the right job or with the right person. They are always significant in some way, but only if we *recognize* them as part of a pattern that relates to our lives in this *moment*.

The recognition itself seems to be an important element in synchronicities and also has a parallel in quantum physics called Bell's theorem. Ultimately, this theorem may explain the very phenomenon that skeptics now attack—telepathy, clairvoyance, precognition, and telekinesis. Imagine two Ping-Pong balls released from a slingshot or similar mechanism, at exactly the same moment, with the same force, in the same direction. Everything concerning these two Ping-Pong balls is equal, so they should continue along the same trajectory, at the same speed. You touch one of the balls and it changes direction. The other Ping-Pong ball changes direction instantly.

This happens at a quantum level with particles, which suggests that something is seriously amiss in the classical scientific view. It implies instantaneous communication between the particles (telepathy?) and also indicates that the observer is critical to the process. Brian Josephson, who won the Nobel prize in 1973 for his work on quantum tunneling and superconductivity, said: "It raises the possibility that one part of the universe may have knowledge of another part—some kind of contact at a distance under certain conditions."

This brings us back to the hologram, where every part not only has knowledge of every other part, but contains it as well.

Bell's theorem raises certain questions about astrology. If we seek to understand the inherent patterns that operate within a birth chart or even just within a particular sun sign, does our participation in this process alter it somehow? Perhaps our openness to such ideas creates a fertile atmosphere for the proliferation of synchronicities—and for our eventual recognition that synchronicity may well be the connecting thread between the hidden order and its unfoldment.

Myths, Skeptics & Debunkers

A skeptic is different from a debunker. The first says, *Prove it to me.* The second says, *You're wrong, and I'm going to make it my personal mission to discredit you.* Religious fundamentalists and debunkers who call themselves scientists are a growing threat to astrology. In essence, they are saying that we shouldn't be allowed to make up our own minds about astrology or any of their other pet peeves. They have appointed themselves watchdogs of truth, and their truth doesn't include astrology or alternative healing, or anything paranormal.

During the last twenty years, psychology journals have published an average of eight studies a year that refute astrology. In 1995, the *New York Times* reported on a major scientific convention in which debunkers were urged to attack the "enemies of science," which included astrology, alternative healing, and the paranormal.

Their bias has permeated schools and learning, as well. According to a recent article in *Mountain Astrologer* by astrologer Valerie Vaughn, an organization called Project ASTRO provides schools with materials for debunking astrology. In their activities for grades seven through nine, they have compiled ten questions to ask supporters of astrology. This activity, entitled, "Ten Embarrassing Questions," has only one thing in its favor—its transparency. But there are far more insidious debunking schemes in the works.

Vaughn notes that in 1993, the American Association for the Advancement of Science created benchmarks for "science literacy," which were incorporated into guidelines set by the National Science Education Standards in 1996. Basically, these standards outline what students should learn about science between kindergarten and graduation from high school. These standards naturally result in curriculum reform, which is ultimately reflected in textbooks. As a result, many textbooks for every facet of science now boast entire units designed to teach students the difference between science and "pseudoscience." Astrology is lumped under "pseudoscience" and is the primary target for teaching that pseudoscience isn't just ineffective, but "wrong" and "dangerous."

This particularly vile form of censorship is done in the name of science. It reveals the fundamental fear that mainstream scientists seem to have about the new paradigm that is being born with the millennium.

Debunkers even have their own organization, appropriately called CSICOPS. They frequently target astrology and those who practice it. At one point, they focused their attacks on horoscope columns in newspapers. Their attacks were so virulent that some newspapers actually dropped their horoscope columns. With the expansion of the Internet, however, this hasn't been a problem. Most of the search engines offer daily horoscopes. But the debunkers don't give up easily.

Carl Sagan was probably CSICOPS' most renowned member. When he gave his opinion on something, whether it was the impossibility of life on other planets or the level of water at the Hoover dam, it made news. He was a strident defender of *his* views. He understood that the real battles concern belief systems. If enough people believe in something, it creates enormous momentum for that viewpoint, which gives people with that viewpoint considerable power and influence. Politicians and religious leaders have known this for centuries.

So when Sagan announced that astrology was unscientific (and therefore without merit), it made an impact. But Sagan, like most people with a vested interest in a consensus belief system, missed the point. Astrology doesn't conform to the rules of science *as it exists now*. It is holographic, the unfoldment of the implicate. It is intuitive, a seamless whole that engages both hemispheres of the brain.

As psychologist Rollo May pointed out, astrology is like myth. It's a story that has gone through countless permutations in its retelling over the centuries, and yet it retains its essential truth. To be personally significant or meaningful, May says, astrology has to be viewed in light of the language of myth. A Pluto transit, for example, might be seen as analogous to Persephone's archetypal journey through the underworld (personal unconscious) and her subsequent return to the surface of the world (transformation). A transit of Pluto through Sagittarius would have Persephone shrieking her truth as she emerged from the underworld.

When we navigate these myths with conscious

awareness, then we harness their archetypal powers and can use them to empower ourselves. And maybe that's what the fracas is really about. Perhaps science, after all, shares a need with religion and medicine and education to perpetuate its own narrow view so that we remain isolated and alienated from our own power as human beings. If too many of us seek our own answers and refuse to allow others to think for us, then the structure of power will shift.

As we enter the millennium, the mainstream perception of astrology will undergo a metamorphosis. But any such change has to begin at the individual level. Think of it as a grass roots acknowledgment that we don't have all the answers, that we may never have all the answers, but that the mysteries we live hold hints about the true nature of reality. Perhaps the new paradigm emerging in science will be more tolerant or less threatened or both by astrology. Perhaps, as Thomas Moore wrote, there will be a realization that "the advantages of an astrological viewpoint begin with living in tune with nature rather than in alienation from it."

Twenty-first Century Stuff

Okay, so you've had a rotten day. You're bushed. You're irritated. You're hungry. You're stressed. You need some downtime. Instead of reaching for a bottle of wine or popping a valium, instead of cranking up your stereo as high as it will go, you pull out a Jupiter tape. As soon as its music filters through the headphones, everything melts away. Your dark mood lifts. Your body feels better. You feel more expansive. You begin to feel, well, great. Optimistic.

Lucky. You start to feel as if your world is on the right track again.

This technology already exists. As the positions of the planets in the solar system change, they affect the magnetic atmosphere of Earth. Human cells are sensitive to these magnetic changes. In magnetic therapy, magnets are attached to acupressure points or around the body to alter the magnetic field. This, in turn, produces beneficial physical effects. This same idea would be operating with "magnetic music."

Recordings can be made of the changes in the Earth's magnetic fields, which relate to planetary positions, and are fed onto an audiotape, and played through a speaker. You could either put on headphones and listen to this magnetic music or attach a magnet to your body and listen to it through the speaker. Either way, the magnetic music affects how you feel physically, emotionally, and spiritually, and may hold important implications for health and medicine.

Suppose, for instance, that the magnetic music of certain aspects (angles) between planets could accelerate healing after surgery? Or mitigate the confusion of Alzheimer's patients? Or bolster the immune system of AIDS patients? This is the type of celestial technology that we can expect with Uranus and Neptune in Aquarius. With any luck at all, the possibilities won't stop here.

The millennium is a threshold, a demarcation between the old way of doing things and the new paradigms. Our success in crossing it depends on our awareness, on how *conscious* we are individually and globally. Let's embrace it.

Chapter 3

•

Uranus, Genius & Revolution

A Bit of History

If you've ever gazed through a telescope, you may have seen Uranus, that gaseous wonder that lies more than one and a half billion miles from your backyard. It has five moons, a day that isn't quite eleven hours long, and a year that lasts eighty-four of ours.

Uranus, ruler of Aquarius, was discovered in 1781, a time of enormous upheaval. The American Revolution was in full swing. The French Revolution lay just around the corner. Kant published *Critique of Pure Reason,* the basis of modern philosophy. The era of scientific enlightenment had begun. The planet was discovered with a Uranian kind of instrument, the telescope, which was developed by Galileo, an Aquarian. The man who saw it first, the Englishman Sir William Herschel, wanted to name the planet in honor of King George. He came up with a name that echoes Dr. Seuss: Georgium Sidus or George's Star. Fortunately, that name didn't stick.

If you live in a rural area or someplace that isn't flooded by city lights, it's possible to detect Uranus with the naked eye. Without a telescope, it won't look like much more than a distant twinkling. But the point is that if it's possible to detect it now, how did the ancient Egyptians miss it? Or the Chaldeans, who were accomplished astronomers and astrologers? Astrologers tend to believe that the discovery of Uranus, like the discoveries of Neptune and Pluto, happened when man's consciousness had evolved sufficiently to deal with the planet's energy.

Uranus represents disruption, sudden and unexpected change that frees us from restrictions, and individuality in its highest and most eccentric form. It's about breaking rules to follow your own bliss. It's the unemployed workers in *The Full Monty*, who turned sudden unemployment to their advantage. It's the volcanic eruption in the movie *Volcano* and the violent weather systems and tornadoes in *Twister*.

Without Uranus, we might all be drones cast in a mold of sameness. We would be terribly boring. Without Uranus, there would be no civilization as we know it. We would still be cavemen, stuck in time, with not a single original thought in our heads. Even if originality and creativity managed to creep in, a mutant in our midst, we wouldn't know what to do with it.

Uranian Energy

Uranus governs astrology, electronics and electricity, computer sciences, aeronautics, chemistry, physics, mathematics, and natural disasters. Its influence is felt in the areas of our lives where we experience sudden, brilliant flashes of intuition. Its manifestation is the sixth sense—clairvoyance, telepathy, telekinesis.

When you're trying to comfort a sick child or a sick pet and feel a surge of warmth in your hands, this is Uranian energy, an electrical vibration so intense it's like being struck by lightning. It's the epiphany you have in the middle of the night when you wake from a startling dream and understand, in a flash, its message. It's your marriage collapsing, the bank foreclosing on your home, The Tower card in the tarot, or *Hagalaz*, the rune of disruption. It's about change that slams into your life and rearranges it.

Uranus is rarely concerned with feelings. This is a mind planet and proud of it. This makes the planet seem, at times, utterly cold, almost inhumane, a devil in a red dress that tosses a heavy wrench into the scheme of things. Uranus is about chaos.

The problem with Uranus is that most of us aren't prepared for it. We're so accustomed to living within our prescribed systems of reality that when chaos sweeps into our lives, we cling to what we have, to what's familiar. This only makes the journey more difficult.

In 1996, Uranus moved into Aquarius, the sign that it rules and the sign which best expresses its energy. It hasn't been there since 1912, when the planet was primed for the First World War. This was also the year that Carl Jung published *Psychology of the Unconscious*. Photons and electrons were first detected, and cosmic radiation was discovered. The *Titanic* sank. You get the general picture.

With Uranus moving through its home sign, structures that no longer work suddenly collapse so that something new can be rebuilt from the rubble. Upheavals are abrupt and powerful. Changes and discoveries are momentous and often miraculous. And amid the chaos is an acceptance of humanitarian ideals.

With Uranus in Aquarius, the general thrust of things will be toward implementing these humanitarian ideals. This means that the evening news about flooding and starvation in Bangladesh or the AIDS epidemic in Africa may prompt you to get involved. Maybe you make a monetary contribution to the Red Cross. Maybe you're a physician and head to the center of the chaos to help. In short, "global community" is no longer just a buzz word; it's a concept that you live.

On a personal level, the energy of Uranus in Aquarius is likely to hit you in the area of your life that is most inflexible, where your beliefs have calcified, where you have ceased to grow and evolve. Wherever you've gotten stuck, Uranus zooms in on it and uproots you. Think of it as a cosmic kick that gets you moving again.

You may seek the support of groups of like-minded individuals or you may pen the next great American novel. You may fail completely at what you're doing now, only to slap your life back together in a way that is more personally satisfying. One way or another, the Uranian energy makes itself known. It isn't shy. It doesn't give a damn what you think. It merely forges ahead, one eye on the future.

It takes Uranus about seven years to go through a sign and eighty-four years to travel around the zodiac. In 1988, it went into Capricorn, a sign ruled by Saturn, which is the very antithesis of Uranus. Think of these two in terms of polarities: restriction versus freedom, structure versus a free-for-all. In this sign,

Uranus chafed like a horse at the bit. When it finally went into Aquarius, the transition may have marked a turning point of some sort in your personal life. Maybe you got married or divorced. Perhaps your career bottomed out, or you went back to school. Maybe you had a heart attack. Whatever your crisis, you had to reevaluate where you had been and where you wanted to go, and you had to do it in the most basic sense. You had to change something fundamental to your existence.

In 2003, Uranus enters Pisces, where it will be for about eight years. Pisces will bring harmony, mysticism, escapism, and a profound need to pierce and understand deeper truths. Some aspects of the 1960s may show up again—drugs, music as a unifying cultural force and the language of rebellious youth, and a fascination with anything in occult. In 2011, Uranus goes into Aries, stays for about seven years, then moves on through the subsequent signs.

At each juncture, the planet's nature is colored by the sign in which it falls. A Uranus in Taurus, for instance, expresses its freedom through the earth, through possessions, finances, and other areas that are Taurean-ruled. Ecology and stability are its theme songs. Uranus in Gemini, where it was when it was discovered and its location in 2025, will bring about momentous changes in communication and travel. Extraterrestrial contact is a distinct possibility. The Internet in 2025 will bear little resemblance to what it is now.

Uranus always symbolizes a revolution in our thinking. On a personal level, this planet usually stirs up that part of us that is rebellious, that seeks independence from the constraints and restrictions that society imposes on us. It's the outlaw, the eternal rebel, the James Dean of the zodiac. And yet, when its energy slams into your life, it seems to have come out of nowhere, suddenly and precipitously, an unwelcome intruder. But if you can navigate the chaos, the benefits you reap are considerable.

Suddenly, you're aware of subtleties and nuances that eluded you before. Your intuition is sharper. You notice that what you called "coincidence" is actually an inner nudge, a voice from the deepest levels of yourself that has been trying to get your attention. Take an incident, any incident. Let's say you're out hiking and get stung by a bee. Instead of getting angry about it, instead of panicking and running for the Benedryl, you listen to the voice, you interpret it. Who or what in your life is going to "sting" you? What's the voice trying to tell you or warn you about? Sometimes, the answer will come immediately to mind. Other times, you may have to wait awhile before the answer is clear. The difference, though, is that now you're *aware* of the connection between an external event and the inner you.

Imagine a man who, as the millennium approaches, is a physician from a family of physicians. His practice is thriving, money is pouring in, his family life is stable. But inside, he feels restless, vaguely dissatisfied. He doesn't sleep well at night, he begins to dread getting up in the morning and going through the whole grind for another day. What he really wants to do is paint, a childhood dream that was squashed by parental and societal pressure to conform because, after all, "no one can make a living as an artist."

But now the physician is pushing forty, and the old dream returns. Uranus is urging him to break free of everything he has created for the last twenty years. His internal revolution demands that he change the way he has been living. Tough? You bet. But he if rises to the challenge, the eventual benefits far outweigh the journey through chaos.

Best & Worst

Genius, liberator, awakener, spiritual entrepreneur, a psychic wake-up call: these words describe Uranus at its best. Its shadow side is that it can heighten tensions that lead to wars, rebels without quite understanding why, and acts out impulses that are often destructive. At its worst, it's the scientist who seeks to advance his technology at the expense of everything and everyone else.

In actuality, though, adjectives like "good" and "bad" don't apply to planets. A planet's energy is only a *vibrational pattern,* and how it affects you depends entirely on how well you're able to integrate it into who you are.

Think of music. Jazz, rock, rap, blues, classical, country: what's your pleasure? The music of Uranus is fast and strange, erratic and dynamic, and always original. Its pitch may be so shrill that it shatters crystal. But once you hear it, your life is never the same.

Going with the Flow

Ultimately, the message of Uranus is to go with the flow. Trust the process. Trust that the disruptions in your life are intended to take you somewhere new. If you go with the flow, releasing the people, situations, and beliefs in your life that no longer work, your life improves dramatically.

If you resist, then an internal tension builds. You encounter one obstacle after another. Nothing seems to work out the way you envision it. That bee sting on the hike explodes into a full-blown adrenal shock, you end up in ER, and are terrified of bees for the rest of your life. If you resist, the tension builds to such an impossible level that you eventually explode. You suddenly get sick, you're fired from your job, your intimate relationships collapse. It seems, then, that the change is thrust upon you from an external force, and you begin to feel that you are utterly powerless in your life. Resentment deepens, bitterness takes root.

Regardless of whether you resist the change or go with it, you discover intuitive and creative reservoirs in yourself that you weren't able to tap when you were younger. Your individuality becomes more pronounced, you find your true voice. There may be people around you who don't like the new you, but you don't change to suit them. You become a new and improved version of your own potential.

The best news is that even if you're bankrupt and your spouse has walked out and the bank has foreclosed on your house, you're able now to make conscious choices that reflect who you really are. Like the physician who wanted to be an artist, the end result is that you're fully equipped to reach and fulfill your potential. That's the gift of Uranus.

Chapter 4

•

Neptune, Inspiration & Illusion

A Faint Twinkle

Imagine, if you can, the almost three billion miles of black stillness that lies between you and Neptune. Scary, isn't it? Even the most powerful telescopes can detect only a faint greenish twinkle, pale at the polar ice caps, darker at the equator. Neptune's orbit is so large that one year there is equal to a hundred and sixty-four of our years. It has two moons, and a day lasts only fifteen hours.

Neptune was discovered because of Uranus's erratic orbit. When mathematicians calculated where Uranus was supposed to be at a given time, it sometimes arrived too early and other times arrived too late. Astronomers felt that another planet, yet undiscovered, might be the cause of the disturbance.

In 1846, a German astronomer, Johanne Galle, discovered the offender, and once again, astrologers were thrown into a panic. They'd had only sixty-five years to figure out how Uranus fit into the scheme of things and now along came Neptune.

Neptune was in the sign of Aquarius when it was discovered. Humanitarian ideals were catching on, notably in the struggle against slavery. Romanticism had seized the collective imagination, Chopin and Liszt ruled the world of music, and the Fox sisters were stirring up interest in spiritualism. Neptunian stuff, for sure! In science, Howe patented the sewing machine, ether began to be used as anesthesia, and film was used to record images. This was also the time when Morse code started connecting people in the same way that the Internet connects people now. This was the year the Smithsonian was founded, protoplasm was identified, and John Deere constructed the first plow.

Howe's sewing machine was completed in a Neptunian way, through a dream that showed him the needle needed an eye at the end of it. The use of ether is also very Neptunian, since the planet rules drugs. Neptune governs the heights of imagination, so it's fitting that its discovery coincided with the publication of Hans Christian Andersen's autobiography, *Fairy Tale of My Life.*

Neptunian Energy

Neptune's energy is elusive, vague, unreal, nebulous. Quite often, it is felt as a disturbance in the deeper layers of the self, a sense that things aren't as they seem, that something is amiss. Last night's dream clings to you throughout the next day. Strange images dance across your eyelids as you fall asleep. Poetry rises from your soul. You see ghosts. You feel a psychic and spiritual connection to a larger universe.

As the natural ruler of mystical Pisces, Neptune dwells in the hidden, the shadowy, the surreal, the etheric. It is numinous, connecting us to the divine, and yet it often seems to be the psychic garbage pail of the zodiac. This isn't a contradiction. It's simply Neptune's nature. Nursing homes, hospitals, Alzheimer's units: these are Neptunian. Environmental toxins, oil spills, mysterious diseases that are difficult to diagnose, slippery viruses that mutate and remain elusive are part of the Neptune contradiction. AIDS, Epstein-Barr, Chronic Fatigue Syndrome, Lyme Disease, and the Ebola virus are examples of Neptunian types of ailments.

The diseases that break down the human immune system bear disturbing parallels to the breakdown in the planet's immune system through pollution, the depletion of the ozone layer, and global warming. And yet, viewed in terms of a "Sethian" universe, this parallel isn't strange at all. It reflects our collective beliefs.

You're probably saying that *your* beliefs don't encompass any of those things. You don't believe in global warming or famine and starvation or human rights violations or in animal abuse. When the nightly news beams vivid scenes of starvation into your living room, your heart breaks.

But what's at work here are invisible beliefs, the core of who we are, beliefs that were formed in early childhood, the consensus beliefs that we share with everyone else in this reality, on this planet, at this point in history. These consensus beliefs create the paradigms that we live by.

Uranus comes along and shatters the paradigms that no longer work. Neptune hovers over the rubble, making us aware that we have the innate power to create our own realities through what we believe. This awareness is intuitive, psychic, spiritual.

New Paradigms

A woman believes that people are stealing her clothes, her jewelry, her money. She holds conversations with her mother, dead now for thirty years, and sometimes thinks that her son is a distant cousin and that her husband is her father. She hears voices and sees things and people that aren't there.

Another woman also holds conversations with the dead, hears voices, sees things that aren't there, and knows that her son was her husband in a previous life. People seek her out for precisely these reasons and pay her handsomely for the messages she brings from the dead.

The first woman is an Alzheimer's patient; the second woman is a psychic. Both illustrate the elusive nature of Neptune, its ethereal veil, the way it dissolves the barriers between realities. Think of Neptune as a tuning fork. Tap it. It hums. But no two people hear that hum in exactly the same way. Neptune transported Edgar Cayce into other realms and swept Einstein into the very heart of scientific truth. It gave diarist Anaïs Nin (a Pisces) penetrating insight into other people. But it can also lead into the basest escapism through alcohol, drugs, sex, and the darker side of the occult.

Neptune's placement in your chart indicates the area where you can transcend the parameters of consensus reality. It's the place where you can tune in to the hum of the tuning fork and experience inspiration, illumination, enlightenment. It's where you're most vulnerable to escapism and illusion and delusion. How it shows up in your life is, of course, entirely up to you.

In 1998, Neptune returned to the sign it occupied when it was discovered, and will remain there until 2012. In Aquarius, Neptune is the call of the spirit, the burgeoning of the psychic, the intuitive. Barriers between the conscious and the unconscious become progressively thinner and, in many cases, dissolve altogether. As a result, much of the wisdom in our personal and collective unconscious becomes available to us. We tap the divine for our answers.

Medical breakthroughs are likely, but not in the ways we expect. Instead of finding a miracle drug for diseases like cancer and AIDS, we reach a deeper understanding of the intimate connection between body and mind, and how emotions and beliefs create health or *dis-ease*. The stage for these types of realizations already has been laid by medical intuitives like Carolyn Myss (*Anatomy of the Spirit*) and Mona Lisa Schultz (*Awakening Intuition*). Deepak Chopra brought us the medical wisdom from the East. Andrew Weil's *Spontaneous Healing* bolstered the voice of alternative medicine in the nineties, and in the millennium the entire field is likely to flourish beyond even his wildest expectations. During Neptune in Aquarius, we'll witness the birth of a new medical paradigm.

The old paradigm, the medical establishment, won't slip quietly away. Already, they feel threatened by the fact that in the U.S. alone, more than a billion dollars a year is spent on alternative medical treatments. They debunk alternative medicine at every opportunity, calling for more government control over vitamins, herbs, and treatments like acupuncture.

The best outcome of this struggle between old and

new would be a melding of the two. Medical intuitives would work alongside MDs. Doctors would treat the whole person, not just a set of symptoms. Patients would become educated partners in their treatments. Vitamins, herbs, acupuncture, yoga, massage therapy, and other types of body work would be used in conjunction with more conventional treatments. The emotional and spiritual causes of disease and illness would be addressed, studied, and patients would be educated in this area. It sounds like utopia. And yet, all of this is possible with Neptune in Aquarius.

The spiritual enlightenment that is possible with Neptune in Aquarius has been growing steadily since the early eighties. Dr. Elisabeth Kübler-Ross woke us up with her landmark work, *On Death and Dying,* and Dr. Raymond Moody shook us up with his book *Life After Death.* These two individuals, both of them traditionally trained MDs, deepened our understanding of the continuity of life. Their works were followed by a spate of personal stories by people who died, then returned, only to find their lives irrevocably changed.

Movies like *Jacob's Ladder, Brainstorm, Flatliners, What Dreams May Come,* and *Siesta,* with their Neptunian themes about what may happen after death, are perfect examples of the spiritual search that will characterize the millennium.

The idea of reincarnation will be more readily accepted in the Western world. Again, the stage for this acceptance has been set by luminaries like Dr. Ian Stevenson and physician Brian Weiss. Carol Bowman's book *Children's Past Lives* taps an area that has barely been explored. We're primed for this stuff. We desperately need a new paradigm for our evolving spiritual beliefs about the big cosmic questions. Who are we? Who or what is God? Where have we been? And, more to the point, just where are we going when we leave *here*?

Religious institutions are likely to go through the same type of radical change as the medical establishment. If our spiritual needs aren't being met by our churches, our synagogues, our Bible groups, then we'll go elsewhere for answers. The old religious paradigms won't succumb without a fight. They have too much to lose. But they *will* change. They have to. It's time.

The flip side, of course, may lead to more tragedies like Heaven's Gate, the mass suicide in California. Our forays into the unseen, the unspoken, the barely imagined, can drive us off the deep end. In this scenario, we see conspiracies to rival those in the *X-Files*. We believe we are chosen or doomed. We forget that we have the power to change anything. We forget that one individual, infused with passion and intent, can literally change the world.

Keep in mind what has happened in the past with Neptune in Aquarius. Spiritualism took off, a wild, brilliant star that opened up the possibility that life really does continue after death. Mystical groups like the Theosophical Society were formed. Buddhism reached the West. Social awareness zoomed in on humanitarian ideals: the rights of women, the morality of child labor and slavery, and the issue of poverty. In short, Neptune was discovered when we were ready, when we needed new patterns for growth.

Neptune in Aquarius can lend itself to millennial hysteria, as well. Widespread fear about the collapse of society, of the global economic structure, and of the Y2K glitch is the kind of energy that feeds Neptune's darker side, where confusion is the MO of the new society. This confusion and fear can run through such diverse areas as cloning, so-called miracle drugs (Viagra, for instance), and mind control (as in remote viewing). But it doesn't have to be that way. If we pour our energy into the positive opportunities that Neptune in Aquarius offers us, then the *pattern* changes.

The Uranus/Neptune Connection

A conjunction means chemistry, an infusion of energy. It's like a marriage. Two planets link up in the same sign, at a wide orb of ten to twelve degrees, and bolster each other's power.

Uranus, which symbolizes our individual thrust for freedom, joins with elusive and mystical Neptune to create a unique experiment. We seek peace, harmony, and spiritual satisfaction. We are pioneers, entrepreneurs of the weird and the strange, borderline nomads, innovative geniuses who seek *a new reality*. We have a few tools, a little knowledge, and a desire so vast and powerful that we make the leap.

Cultural and racial differences won't matter anymore. Walls between people will dissolve, and this, in turn, will dissolve walls between nations. On a personal level, the neighbor you haven't spoken to for five years will suddenly and inexplicably greet you out by the mailbox one morning. Your curiosity about the world beyond your backyard will be almost overwhelming at times, urging you to travel and experience other cultures. You may do this in the literal sense or through the rapidly changing and expanding Internet. The global community will become more of a reality.

With Uranus and Neptune joining up in Aquarius,

even at a wide orb, areas like telepathy, clairvoyance, remote viewing, and precognition will be seen as abilities that we all have. We'll learn to tap these resources in ourselves as the left and right hemispheres of our brains come into synch. We'll find a balance between intuition and logic, instinct and reason, yin and yang.

Communication between species will awaken intuitive skills that we've forgotten. The role that animals play in our lives will change. Once we no longer see them as "beneath" us, animal experimentation and other abuses will stop. People who have profited from experimentation and abuse may resist the change. But eventually they'll want to change as well. This is the nature of a paradigm shift.

The nature of oracular knowledge will transform during this shift. We'll learn how to listen to our own bodies for clues about what's ailing us. We may be confused initially about some of the messages, but there are experts around who speak that language and can educate the rest of us. We'll be better equipped to interpret external events as hints about our internal lives. Our understanding of synchronicities will deepen and expand. New myths and archetypes will emerge, breathed into being, perhaps, by our collective need for guidelines. The information explosion won't be accessible to us just through the Internet; we'll be more aware of the subtle energies around us. Through this growing awareness, our creative abilities will blossom.

Surrender & Spiritual Expansion

If the message of Uranus in Aquarius is to go with the flow, then the message of Neptune in Aquarius is to surrender to the process and seek to expand our spiritual beliefs.

This doesn't imply passivity. It means living honestly, authentically, closer to the bone of what matters. If we encounter obstacles or resistance, we work to change our beliefs. At every step, we consciously construct our reality through our deepest beliefs and attempt to live with an awareness of the larger picture.

Neptune, symbolized by the trident, represents the vast ocean of our personal and collective unconscious and the deepest levels of our emotions, our compassion for others. Compassion connects us as human beings, without regard for cultural, racial, and personal differences. With Neptune in Aquarius, this compassion is likely to become a major force in our lives. If we follow the promptings of our hearts, we will come to understand the slogan of the sixties: that we are all connected, animal and human alike, and that the planet itself is conscious. What affects one, affects all.

Chapter 5

•

Pluto, Power & Transformation

Power

At the outermost edges of our solar system, some four billion miles from the sun, a faint yellow light orbits in utter solitude. It has at least one large moon and perhaps others, yet undiscovered. Its density and size are still debated. Its orbit is so erratic that it takes Pluto two hundred and forty-eight years to travel through the zodiac, spending as little as twelve or thirteen years in Scorpio and more than thirty years in Taurus. It is the ruler of Scorpio and is nearly as mysterious now as when it was discovered in 1930.

When Pluto was discovered, the world was staggering along in the aftermath of the 1929 crash. The Roaring Twenties had died, the Nazis were gaining power in Germany, existentialism was on the rise. Chaos was planting the seeds that would ultimately take root in the discovery and use of nuclear power. Pluto was discovered when we were primed to understand our relationship to power on a personal and a collective basis.

Power: that's it in a nutshell for Pluto. And yet, nothing is quite that simple about Pluto. Pluto represents personal power and the power of the collective; the power we hold over others and the power they hold over us. Birth, death, rebirth, regeneration, and transformation are powers that Pluto emulates. Pluto stands for sexual power, occult power, the power of taboos, of the forbidden, the power of religion and politics. Also represented are power issues we bring with us from previous lives, the soul's "karma," better known as the power of the unconscious.

Due to Pluto's very slow movement, an entire generation is affected by the sign in which it falls. In a sense, then, Pluto's sign can be viewed as our soul's tribal connections. The house placement in an individual's birth chart indicates the area of life in which the person experiences the deepest transformations through his or her confrontation with power issues. Much of this transformation process occurs on an unconscious level. But when we become aware of Pluto's power in our own lives, we realize that we have something special to offer others. Through our awareness of this gift, whatever it is, and offering it to others, we are better equipped to claim our power in a positive way.

Pluto's Doors to Perception

Astrologers have various ways of reading past-life themes in a natal chart. Some use the sign, placement, and aspects of Saturn or the moon's nodes. Others focus on the rising sign and aspects made to the ascendant's ruling planet. And other astrologers focus on Pluto.

The reality is that whatever system an astrologer uses is only an intuitive trigger. It's difficult to confirm a past life unless very specific information is provided under hypnosis or through some other means. Even then, absolute confirmation is often impossible. Records may have been destroyed, families may have died, cities may have been destroyed.

Sometimes, though, when you're told about a past life or a past-life theme that affects your life now, you experience a particular inner resonance. Goose bumps may erupt on your arms. The hairs on the back of your neck may rise. You may feel a tightness in the pit of your stomach. However you experience the resonance, you usually recognize it immediately for its *rightness,* its *truth.* That's how Pluto works in our lives, by opening doors we haven't walked through before.

This process began with Uranus shattering the structure of our personal paradigm, continued with Neptune urging us to transcend our loss of the old structure by exposing us to what is ultimately real and timeless, and ends with Pluto leading us toward the transformation of consciousness we need to complete the process.

The door to past lives might be one that Pluto will hurl open. A new career might be another. A marriage, a divorce, the birth of a child, illness or remission, an inheritance: the door that opens is whatever you need at the time to fulfill your potential. This isn't to imply that any of it is fated. Always, free will and your deepest beliefs are the keys that unlock the door. As your beliefs change, your options change.

And none of it happens with the abruptness that characterizes Uranus.

When Pluto's power is unleashed, we may feel, at first, that we're losing control. And we are, make no mistake about it. In the middle of a Pluto crisis, we come to understand what Carl Jung meant when he said that archetypes don't merely *happen* to us; they *seize* us. We feel as if everything in our lives has been turned inside out like a dirty sock. And then something happens, some magical moment when it all clicks, when we *get the message*. After that, Pluto becomes easier to live with. It becomes our ally, our cheerleader. Ultimately, it becomes the giver of new life.

Pluto's Signature

Every planet has a signature, a particular way in which its energy pattern influences our lives. Pluto's signature begins with rumblings in the deepest reaches of our lives, the cellars where we've shut away things we don't want to confront.

It feels, at first, as if furniture is being rearranged somewhere inside of us. It's annoying. We know something is going on, but aren't sure what it is. We hope that whatever it is will go away. But it doesn't. The rumblings get louder, more difficult to ignore.

One woman, a sixty-year-old Aquarian, had been studying metaphysics for most of her adult life. She had been an astrologer, a tarot reader, a past-life regressionist. She'd taken every conceivable course and workshop and had worked with some of the best known experts in various fields. She lived according to her spiritual principles. She began writing about metaphysics and sold her first book to a major publisher and launched a new career.

The one area of metaphysics that never interested her was health. "I'm an Aquarian," she would say when someone handed her a book on the mind/body connection. "I'm interested in the mind, not the body."

Then, during a Pluto transit to the fourth house of her natal chart, which symbolizes the home, your very roots, and your immediate environment, her husband was diagnosed with cancer. At first, she believed that he would survive the illness, that the power of her beliefs would help carry him through it. But for six months, the news got progressively worse and challenged every belief she held. *She was brought into direct contact with the health issues that had never interested her.* While he went through the traditional medical treatments for cancer, she learned Reiki healing, had an acupuncturist work on her husband, tried herbs and vitamins and homeopathic treatments on him. She realized that her belief that she created her own reality was not her husband's belief.

Even though she was an astrologer, she didn't see any astrological patterns that indicated his illness. In the midst of crisis, she couldn't see the obvious possibilities of the Pluto transit.

After her husband's death, she understood that even though her mate of thirty years had died under the Pluto transit, it hadn't left her completely stranded; she now had a new career.

This isn't to say that every transit of Pluto through the fourth house of the natal chart or any other house, for that matter, results in the death of a spouse or significant other. But it does spell transformation and awareness at the deepest levels.

For this woman, her husband's death had made her realize that although she creates *her* reality, she shares that reality with other people who have their own take on how things work. Their ideas may not coincide with hers. But because they share the same corner of the cosmos, and because, in her husband's case, she agreed at some level to participate in his soul's choices, her life was dramatically altered.

Pluto rules the eighth house in a natal chart, which reads like a Woody Allen movie: death, sex, and taxes. F. Scott Fitzgerald called this the "dark night of the soul." It's that phone call that comes at four A.M. with bad news. But it's also the light on the other side of that call, the place you reach when you have placed the experience into some sort of spiritual context that works for you.

Pluto in Sagittarius

In 1995, Pluto moved into Sagittarius, where it remains until 2008. For many people, the initial transition period was a dramatic wake-up call. Whatever had been hidden or difficult to detect under Pluto in Scorpio, reared up and announced itself in the most unsubtle way. Even though the hidden element may have been embedded in your life for years, it seemed to appear suddenly. A health problem. A long-standing marital rumbling. A career glitch. Family secrets. Pluto ferreted out the hidden, and Sagittarius announced it to the world.

Pluto in this sign demands that we speak our truth. If we don't do it, if we resist rising to the challenge, then someone or something else will do it for us. President Clinton learned that. Until 2008, in fact, when Pluto goes into Capricorn, we're going to get an earful of truth from a number of arenas—higher education, the law, foreign governments, scientific institutions, religious organizations, the military. Many of these truths won't be pretty. But we need to hear them and hear them we will, through every media device possible, especially the Internet.

Sagittarius, like every sign, every planet, every type of energy, has its darker side. It can be bombastic and obnoxious in its endless pontificating about the cosmic questions, the big stuff. In Pluto, it could become incredibly opinionated and go on and on until no one listens anymore. Is there anyone on the planet who didn't get fed up with the endless versions of Clinton and Lewinsky?

The Musketeers & Time

From 1998 until 2003, Uranus, Neptune, and Pluto are lined up in Aquarius and Sagittarius, air and fire signs respectively. The last time this rare lineup happened was in the 1500s, before any of these planets had been discovered. It launched the Renaissance, the discovery of the New World, and momentous changes in every other facet of life at that time. This time, it presages changes that jolt and rearrange our individual perceptions of reality. Each of us is sure to become more deeply aware of the connection between belief and experience, that the first creates the second, not the other way around.

The outer planets allow us to see the bigger picture of our own lives. Quite often, they do this by exposing the shadow side of our personalities, the stuff that has gotten pushed underground over the years, the buried debris of disappointments and heartbreaks. They are the therapists of the zodiac, the collective force that urges us to examine the chinks in our present belief systems and to acknowledge that what we see isn't all there is. With these planets in active air (the mental process) and fire (action, movement) signs, we're compelled to *think* differently and to *act* upon those thoughts.

During the last cycle of these three planets, they were in earth and water signs. Earth grounds us, water flows through us. Earth is physical, water is emotional. When Uranus and Neptune were in Capricorn, from 1988 to 1998, the reality structures we took for granted were weakened. Part of this was the result of Pluto in Scorpio, a water sign, which brought hidden elements in ourselves to the surface. Now, with two of the planets in air signs and the third in fire, we will feel compelled to confront and deal with whatever surfaced.

One of the curious affects of these outer planets is that their powerful influence redefines our sense of time. Most of us live by clock time. Sixty minutes to the hour, twenty-four hours to the day, three hundred and sixty-five days to the year. This is the time that defines our lives within society. We eat and sleep and live according to the clock.

But the outer planets make us more aware of subjective time. A meditative walk on the beach may take twenty minutes of clock time, but by the end of the walk, it seems as if an hour or two has passed. During a peak experience, our senses are in a state of hyperalertness, and the passage of an hour on the clock seems like seconds. In both instances, the *pro-*

cess of the experience, whatever it is, dominates the awareness of clock time.

While we're in the midst of the influence of these three planets, our subjective time is likely to be influenced. Whether time seems to speed up or slow down, however, will depend on whether we resist the influence or work with it. Again, the choice is ours.

Chapter 6

•

Houses

Pieces of the Pie

A birth chart is divided into twelve houses that represent different areas of our lives. On the cusp or dividing line between each house lies a sign in a particular degree. Planets fall into these houses according to their degrees and signs, which is determined by your ascendant, the sign and its degree that were rising when you were born. This is why it's so important to have an accurate birth time.

Most charts use the signs and symbols for the planets and signs, which are found in Tables 1 and 2. Table 3 lists the signs with their planetary rulers.

Table 1: Signs & Their Symbols

Signs	*Symbols*
Aries	♈
Taurus	♉
Gemini	♊
Cancer	♋

Leo	♌
Virgo	♍
Libra	♎
Scorpio	♏
Sagittarius	♐
Capricorn	♑
Aquarius	♒
Pisces	♓

Table 2: Planets & Symbols

Planets	*Symbols*
Sun	☉
Moon	☽
Mercury	☿
Venus	♀
Mars	♂
Jupiter	♃
Saturn	♄
Uranus	♅
Neptune	♆
Pluto	♇

Other Points

North Node	☊
South Node	☋
Ascendant	Asc
Fourth house cusp	IC
Seventh house cusp	Des

Tenth house cusp	Mc
Part of Fortune	⊗

Table 3: Planets & Their Rulers

Each sign is ruled by a particular planet, which best expresses the nature of the sign.

Sign	***Planetary Ruler***
Aries	Mars
Taurus	Venus
Gemini	Mercury
Cancer	Moon
Leo	Sun
Virgo	Mercury
Libra	Venus
Scorpio	Pluto
Sagittarius	Jupiter
Capricorn	Saturn
Aquarius	Uranus
Pisces	Neptune

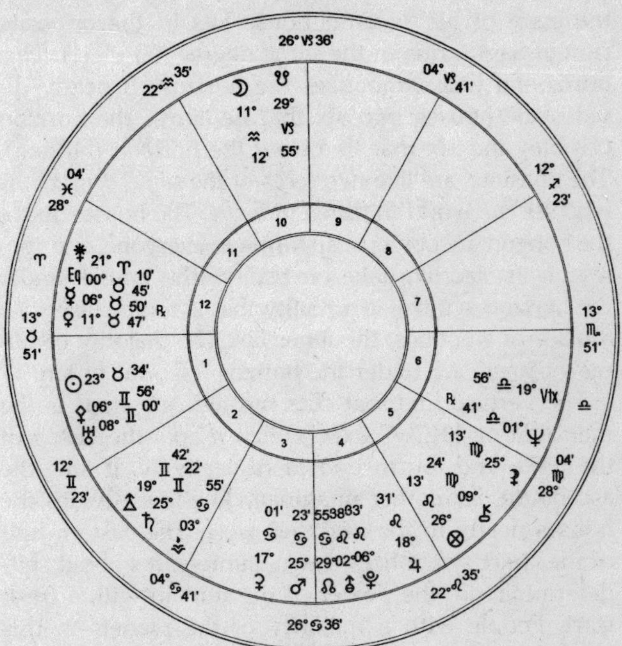

This chart was generated by the WindStar program. Used by permission of Matrix Software, Inc.

What a Birth Chart Looks Like

The chart above belongs to filmmaker George Lucas. The horizontal line that cuts through the center of his chart is the ascendant/descendant axis. Planets rise on the left or eastern side of this axis because here in the northern hemisphere we're "on top" of the planet. On the right or western side of the chart, planets set.

Lucas's rising sign lies in Gemini, at two degrees and forty-one minutes (02 II 41). His descendant or the cusp of his seventh house lies in the opposite sign of Sagittarius in the same degree (02 ♐ 41). This horizontal line symbolizes the horizon. It neatly divides the houses into six that lie above the horizon (visible) and six that lie below the horizon (hidden). The divisions are like two faces of the same coin, twins who see the world in different ways. The houses above the horizon are obvious, apparent to everyone, and represent an objective take on reality. The houses under the horizon symbolize a reality that is more subjective, a place of emotions, the inner life. The majority of Lucas's planets are under the horizon—six out of ten.

The vertical line that cuts through the chart is the meridian or MC/IC axis, which marks the cusps of the tenth and fourth houses respectively. It, like the ascendant, is another imaginary line that divides the houses neatly to the east and west. The eastern half of the chart symbolizes dawn, sunrise. It's about self-determination, the power of the human will, a fresh start. People with a majority of the planets in this hemisphere tend to make their own opportunities.

The western part of the chart symbolizes twilight and darkness. With a majority of planets on this side, the individual's freedom is limited somewhat by the society in which he lives. He has to bring his free will to bear against the challenges he brought into life with him.

The majority of Lucas's planets fall on the eastern side of the chart.

There are four important angles in a chart: the ascendant or the cusp of the first house; the IC or the cusp of the fourth house; the descendant or the cusp of the seventh house; and the cusp of the tenth house, the MC. These four houses are known as angular houses; any planet that falls in or on the cusp of one of them is called an angular planet and deserves special consideration. Quite often, a planet on or close to one of these angles is a dominant theme in an individual's life.

In Lucas's chart, notice the sun in Taurus in the twelfth house and the moon in Aquarius in the tenth house. Both fall on or very close to angles. The moon sits smack on his MC or the cusp of his tenth house and is the highest planet in his chart. His sun is quite close to his rising.

So what does any of that mean? Let's look at the houses first.

The houses, like the signs, are a baker's dozen and represent processes and stages that we go through, that we experience. They are our arenas of life, the places where we act out who and what we are. They include our attitudes, traits, and our experiences of other people. They cut up the circular pie of the horoscope. Some pieces are larger or smaller than others, some pieces may be totally empty of planets, others may have one or two planets, and still others may be packed to the brim, a full house.

Each house also has a psychological meaning. The traditional meanings of the houses relate primarily to the practice of astrology in the western world. Keep in mind, however, that astrologers expand and tailor the meanings of the houses to fit the kind of astrology they practice. An astrologer whose focus is Jungian may have somewhat different meanings for the houses than a humanistic or karmic astrologer.

Ascendant & First House

Who are we? What adjectives fit us? Are we defined by the color of our skin, hair, and eyes? Are we sickly or healthy, optimists or pessimists? What kind of self do we project to the world? These are some of the issues that are ruled by our rising sign and our first house.

Above all, we are creatures of dichotomy, haunted by what we don't understand, seduced by what we think we want. A part of us is forever seeking to bridge that contradiction by making it whole. The degree to which we succeed depends on how we deal with the issues of our first house.

The ascendant and first house represent the outward expression of our personality. It's the part that comes most easily to us, the part we don't really have to work for to achieve. Since the rising sign is the equivalent of the horizon, it represents our individual viewpoints in life. Too often, though, we hide behind the mask of our rising sign. We hide within our viewpoints. We become myopic and begin to believe we are only our viewpoints and our opinions. We forget to look more deeply.

The first house is also connected to our physical body and describes our general physical appearance. The overall state of our health and our abilities to cope also fall into the first house. The planet that rules the ascendant is usually considered the ruler of the chart. In Lucas's chart, the ruler of his ascendant in Gemini is Mercury, and Mercury lies in his twelfth house.

Here, too, we encounter oddities, eccentricities. The first house is all about the self—physical health, facial characteristics, attitudes, mannerisms, overall health. It's also about the beginning of life, the attitudes that surround our beginnings, and the kinds of memories and attitudes that we may bring in with us from previous lives.

Second House

Money, money, money. That's the bottom line with the second house. But it's not quite that simple. Money is never that simple. This house is also about our capacity to earn money, how we spend it, and how we meet our financial obligations. It's about debt and credit, about how we save and invest. It's the house our stockbroker should be most interested in because it describes our financial picture.

On a deeper level, the second house is about security. We feel secure when our bank accounts are padded. Or we feel secure with certain possessions, like our cars or our jewelry or prestige. We attach ourselves to these things and, to some extent, define ourselves through them.

Now look at Lucas's chart. The house is empty.

But this is the guy worth millions, which he made on two basic themes: good and evil in the far distant future and a hero's quest in the earlier part of the twentieth century. This is *Lucas,* who brings us archetypes. Darth Vader, Luke Skywalker, Indiana Jones, Princess Leia, Chewbacca, and Han Solo. His library at Skywalker Ranch was the spot from which Joseph Campbell spoke to us about myth. How come he doesn't have *any* planets in his money house?

Because money isn't the issue for Lucas.

With three planets, including Mercury, which rules his chart, sitting in the twelfth house and his moon on the midheaven, his issues are to illuminate the personal unconscious for the public. Lucas is the conveyor of a message, as witnessed by Mars (energy) and Pluto (transformation) in his third house. The North Node of his moon also lies there, so communication was part of his soul's agenda this time around. His Neptune is part of the fifth house's story.

Third House

We write, we speak, we read, we *communicate.* The third house is rather like a school where we learn to express what we feel and think, what we dream and what we despise, what we love, what we hope. But expression isn't just verbal or written. It's also in what we don't say, the language that our body speaks if we're angry or defensive, upbeat or sad. It's the sweet and the bitter thoughts we think.

In this house, information is culled and disseminated and acts as the Internet for the rest of the zodiac. If the first house needs a verbal boost, it goes to the third house for help. If the third house is fresh out of the verbal boost, then it finds another house that can do the job. The third house is the relay station, the clearing house, the neighborhood billboard. Therefore, it's hardly surprising that computers are ruled by the third house.

The third house necessarily involves other people. The neighbors with whom we share local gossip. The brothers and sisters connected to us through blood. Local clerks whose lives touch ours in small but consistent ways. This house doesn't symbolize the people themselves, but our experiences and perceptions of these people.

The third house is about daily life, its minutia, its nuances, the small but vital thoughts and events that comprise our lives. It's our personal slice of sociological history for future generations, the journal entries that might put everyone but our intimates to sleep. It's trips to the grocery store, carpooling for Little League or Girl Scouts, a weekend retreat at the beach.

To be successful in getting through the issues associated with this house, we need to define two things:

what comprises our immediate environment and what we're trying to accomplish in it. The rest pretty much takes care of itself.

Fourth House or IC

This house is midnight. Shadows eddy through the darkened corners, the towering eaves. Ghosts whisper. And yes, we hear them. The ghosts of the past, the ghosts of the distant future.

Sometimes, the voice of the ghost sounds like Mom. Other times, it's Dad. This house represents the parent who nurtures us, as seen through the eyes of a child. Our early childhood, the type of childhood we have, the kinds of early experiences that molded and sculpted us into who we are now are described in the fourth house.

This house represents our physical home, our personal slice of paradise, the place we park ourselves and put down roots. It's our retreat from the outer world and includes our family or the unit that we call family. The end of life is also represented, the last twenty years or so that we spend on the planet.

This is Jung's house of the collective unconscious, where psychic ties connect us to the larger family of man. Our shadow lives here, too, the Jungian shadow of obsessions and fears, and to get through this house successfully requires that we make our shadows conscious.

In Lucas's chart, Jupiter sits in the fourth house, within seven degrees of a conjunction to the cusp. Jupiter, as the planet of expansion and luck, indicates that his early childhood was financially secure and that the latter part of his life will be as well. Since the fourth house involves real estate, it's no wonder that, with Jupiter placed here, he owns several thousand acres that comprise Skywalker Ranch. Jupiter here would also indicate a good relationship with the nurturing parent.

Fifth House

What brings us the deepest pleasure? Creativity? Children? Sex? Nature? Gambling? Love affairs? All of these things fall into the fifth house. This is where we embrace whatever brings us joy.

Horse racing and gambling and sex are all external pleasures, but the pleasures of the fifth house are also internal. Artistic creation, for instance, rises from the deeper parts of our psyche and draws upon our individual visions, experiences, and perceptions. Meditation can be as joyful to one person as sex is to another. Yoga can be both a physical and an internal pleasure.

Pets traditionally fall into the sixth house, as chattel, but in the contemporary world, we generally have pets because they bring us pleasure. Pure, unadulterated fun belongs here, too, the things we do just for the zany, wild high that we get from it. Roller coasters. Water slides. Windsurfing. Sailing.

Children are part of this house, specifically our experience of our children and childbearing.

In Lucas's chart, notice Neptune in the fifth house. Neptune rules films. No surprise, then, that Lucas does what he does! But Neptune here also allows him to tap intuitive and psychic resources within himself that he then translates into film.

Sixth House

A woman gets sick, loses her job, and the bank is prepared to foreclose on her house. Friends and neighbors rally around her. They bring her food, pitch in to help however they can, and start a collection drive to raise funds so she'll be able to keep her home. This is service in its highest form, something we do without expecting anything in return.

Here, too, we find employees and our general working conditions, the daily tasks that we perform in our profession. Illness and health concerns are also found here. The type of illness related to this house is rarely life-threatening; that belongs to the eighth and the first. Here, there may be a clear concern with health issues and nutrition and the types of illnesses experienced may be connected to work issues. Do we find purpose in the type of work we do? Do we like what we do? Is our work more than just a means of paying bills?

To move successfully through the issues of the sixth house, we need to find a skill that we enjoy, that we can hone and polish. Then we need to ask ourselves if this skill is marketable. If it is, then pursuing it will bring the purpose that sustains and enriches us.

Seventh House or Descendant

We fall in love, we marry, we commit ourselves to a particular person. And commitment is really what this house is about. Intimate partnerships, whether for love or for business, require equality. No boss, no underling. Balance is the key.

But commitment can be a sticky proposition. In any partnership, we have to walk in our partner's shoes, experiencing the world as he does. If that world seems alien and strange to us, then perhaps the relationship is touching parts of ourselves that need to become conscious.

Traditionally, the seventh house is also associated with "open conflicts" and "open enemies." In this house, then, you aren't likely to encounter the close friend who gossips behind your back or seduces your spouse. Those types of experiences belong in the twelfth house. Here you know who your enemies are. They make no bones about it.

Eighth House

You walk through Edinburgh Castle as a tourist, eager to explore. But suddenly a door slams open in your head, and you see yourself in the clothing of that era, speaking as people did then. *You remember a life in this place.* That memory changes your present life. This is the stuff of the eighth house. Instincts. Deep memories. Weird experiences. Transcendence.

This house can also read like a Woody Allen movie: death, sex, and taxes. The death part, however, has more similarities with rebirth and resurrection than it does with dying. The sex isn't sex for pleasure; it's a form of transcendence. And the taxes . . . well, the taxes are taxes no matter how you look at it. Taxes belong to that part of the eighth house that concerns other people's money and financial resources. Even though *you* may consider taxes as *your* rightful resource, the IRS has other ideas. Inheritances also fall here, as do resources that come to us through other people.

To deal successfully with eighth house archetypes, we need to ask what we've outgrown, what limits us, what may be blocking us. Is it our belongings and attachments? A relationship? Our particular line of work? Whatever it is, the eighth house makes sure that the old passes out of lives so that the new may flow in.

Ninth House

In the upper reaches of the Peruvian Andes live about four hundred Indians known as the Q'ero, who are direct descendants of the Incas. Centuries ago, they made the decision to retreat from Cuzco and climb higher into the mountains so they could continue their spiritual practices without interference from the outside world.

At the end of 1996, a group of their shamans and healers visited the U.S. with an American anthropologist. It was the first time any Q'ero had come down from the mountains in more than four hundred years. They toured a number of American cities, where they shared their spiritual practices, the very heart of their reality, with American audiences. This is the nugget of the ninth house: your world view. It may be shared with people whose culture is vastly different from your own, or it may include such cultures.

Higher education, spiritual practices and beliefs, foreign cultures and foreign travel also fall in this house. Publishing is also relegated to the ninth house.

In Lucas's chart, the moon's South Node lies in the ninth house. This indicates a need to embrace larger concepts and exotic philosophies in his life, something he obviously has accomplished through his films.

Tenth House or MC

This is the apex, the highest point a planet reaches in the sky. High noon. Everything is visible, bright, apparent, *public*. This is the house of our careers, our professions. It symbolizes how we look to people who don't know us, but who need some hook to hang us on, some niche or category to slide us into. *He's a teacher. She's an accountant. He's the president.* The challenge, though, is to separate who we are from how other people see us. To do that, we have to know *who we are* beyond the work we do or the profession we practice.

Our experiences of other people also fit into this house: bosses, anyone who has authority over us, and the authoritarian parent.

Any time the sun or moon is found in the tenth or is conjunct the cusp of the tenth, the opportunity for fame is excellent. It doesn't guarantee fame, but it sure makes it easier to attain. So look at Lucas's moon, sitting up there at the top of his chart in Aquarius, the sign of the visionary.

Eleventh House

We usually network with people of like mind, who share our goals, aspirations, and interests. A bridge group. A computer group. A group of aspiring actors or writers. This group energy, this gestalt of consciousness, can be quite powerful in transforming our beliefs about ourselves. After all, if other people believe in and support us, our dreams loom that much closer. The seemingly impossible becomes possible.

The eleventh house also includes our social group, the people we hang out with, our friends. They may not be intimate friends; intimacy doesn't really enter the equation with this house. These people are a crowd that we're a part of.

To get the most out of this house, we should know

first what our dream is, what our goals are. Through that knowing, we attract the people who best reflect and support what we hope for ourselves. In return, we do the same for them.

Twelfth House

In traditional astrology, this is the house of zodiac hell, a place so negative that no soul with any wisdom at all would choose to live through it. It was known as the house of troubles, which gives you a pretty clear picture right from the start what would be included here. Even in contemporary astrology, it's often considered a weak house, for reasons that aren't quite clear. After all, the twelfth is where the sun rises just after dawn. How can dawn be weak? How can sunrise spell trouble?

But if the twelfth house symbolizes the personal unconscious, the picture makes sense. This is the place where we bury our secrets, the energies we can't or won't deal with, the power we have disowned. It may be a quality like exuberance that was squashed at a young age by a dogmatic parent. It may be a talent, a dream, an attitude. Whatever it is, this is where we bury the bones that haunt us.

Part of our challenge is to illuminate what we have buried here, to bring it out into the open. Once the hidden is exposed, it is freed and no longer terrifies us. No longer holds power over us. We're able to use the energy in positive ways.

In karmic astrology, this house is perceived as the residue of previous incarnations, our unfinished business, our "karma." The problem with this is that even if past lives can be confirmed in some way, that past matters less than *this moment*. The only thing we're sure of is now. This breath. This instant.

Quite often, any planets in the twelfth house provide us with a launching point for action simply because the energy bubbles up from inside of us and mounts until it's a force to be reckoned with.

Lucas has three planets in the twelfth house. His sun in Taurus gives him the stubborn relentlessness to dive deeply into whatever he has buried. Mercury in Taurus allows him to communicate it. Venus in Taurus tells us that part of what is buried here has to do with romance, marriage, love, and beauty.

To move through this house successfully, we need to release the ideas that have indoctrinated us. We need to find our own truth, our own beacons. At times this house can seem like F. Scott Fitzgerald's dark night of the soul. But if we remember that dawn is only a heartbeat away and trust that the answers lie on the other side of darkness, then the energy we unleash becomes an army that works on our behalf.

Aspects & Transits

We speak of "aspects" of the personality, "aspects" of the situation, and "aspects" of our emotions. To most of us, an aspect is the way something appears to us. To an astrologer, aspects are geometric angles between planets, which result from the division of the 360 degrees in the horoscope circle. Symbolically, these angles are the complex network of arteries and veins that link energies between houses and planets. Although a lengthy discussion of aspects is beyond the scope of this book, they are referred to in the sun sign sections in terms of transits.

Look at Lucas's chart again. His sun in Taurus in the twelfth house is triggered from March 1999 through early August of 2000, when Saturn in Taurus conjuncts or joins his sun. A conjunction, whether it's in the birth chart or by transit, intensifies the energy of the planets involved.

A conjunction is technically 0 degrees of separation, a sextile is 60 degrees, a square is 90 degrees, a trine is 120 degrees, and an opposition is 180. But astrologers usually allow some latitude in the orb or amount of separation. They differ, however, in how much latitude. Some astrologers prefer to work with very small orbs, maybe 1 to 3 degrees. Others work with 5- or 6-degree orbs. It often depends on the individual chart.

The aspects listed above are considered the major aspects. In Table 4, they are listed and defined. You may want to refer back to this list when you read your sun sign section.

Table 4: Aspects Defined

Conjunction* ☌, *0 degrees: Fuses and intensifies the energies of the planets that are involved. Brings power and emphasis to the house in which the conjunction occurs.

In Lucas's chart, Mercury (☿) and Venus (♀) are within a 5-degree conjunction in Taurus in the twelfth house. His moon in Aquarius conjuncts his midheaven to the degree (11 degrees).

Sextile* ⚹, *60 degrees: Represents a free flow of energy between the planets that are involved. Think ease, think lack of tension, think buffers against instability.

In Lucas's chart, look at Pluto (♇) down there in the third house. Now locate Neptune (♆) in the fifth house. Pluto is at 6 degrees, 33 minutes Leo; Neptune is 1 degree and 41 minutes Libra. It's a sextile with a 5-degree orb.

Square* □, *90 degrees: Friction, that's the long and short of it. But squares tend to galvanize us, to push us into action. They force us to grow and evolve.

In Lucas's chart, Mercury in Taurus in the twelfth house (☿06♉ 50℞) is exactly square Pluto in Leo in the third house (♇06♌ 33).

Trine* △, *120 degrees: Ease, a smooth, inner harmony. Quite often, trines indicate that opportunities come to us with little or no effort on our parts.

In Lucas's chart, his moon in Aquarius in the tenth house (☽11♒47) is trine Uranus in Gemini in the first house (♅08°♊00') at a 3-degree orb.

Opposition* ☍, *180 degrees: Forces change through conflict. Polarities are often involved in this aspect, like Gemini/Sagittarius or Taurus/Scorpio.

In Lucas's chart, one of the main oppositions is between his Aquarian moon in the tenth and his Pluto in Leo in the third house. Even though the fourth house is actually opposite the tenth, Pluto is opposed by 5 degrees and falls in the third because of the degree on the cusp of the fourth house.

Chapter 7

•

The Other Planets

Curiosities

When an astronomer gazes into the night sky, he sees one thing. When an astrologer looks into that same sky, he sees something else entirely. Yet both deal with the same set of planets, the same planetary motions, the same curiosities. The difference lies in perspective.

An astronomer sees the solar system as something external, a tidy, understandable diagram, an orderly sequence of ABC. Everything clicks right along at a more or less constant speed, along a more or less predictable path.

To an astrologer, the solar system is symbolic of inner processes and change is the only absolute. An astrologer sees the planets as personalities. Mercury is mental, very quick. The moon is emotional, moody, given to highs and lows. Mars is energetic, impatient, sometimes quarrelsome. Saturn is the schoolmarm hovering nearby with her rules, trying to teach us responsibility.

Just as our personalities are partially formed and

expressed through our environments, the personalities of the planets are influenced to a large degree by the distance of their orbits around the sun. They are classified, in fact, by these orbits.

Orbits

The planets whose orbits are closest to the sun are called "inner planets." These are the moon, Mercury, Venus, and Mars. The "outer planets" of Jupiter, Saturn, Uranus, Neptune, and Pluto are separated from the first group by a belt of asteroids. Except for Pluto, all of the outer planets are larger than the inner planets.

The inner planets orbit the sun rather quickly. The moon moves the fastest, completing a circuit of the zodiac in a little under twenty-eight days. This means it spends only a couple of days in each sign. Mercury's orbit around the sun takes eighty-eight days, but because of its retrograde motion, it takes about a hundred days to make its way around the zodiac. Venus completes its orbit around the sun in two hundred and twenty-five days. Mars takes a little over two years to make its journey around the sun, so it spends about two months in each sign.

These inner planets are known as the personal planets. They're like our neighborhood acquaintances, the personalities we deal with most closely on a daily basis. They can be raucous and mischievous, romantic and exasperating, moody and petulant, curious and impatient. They are the building blocks of our characters.

Hundreds of asteroids whiz past between the inner and outer planets. Of these, Chiron, Ceres, Pallas

Athene, Juno, and Vesta have received the most attention by astrologers. Although asteroids are beyond the scope of this book, it's worth your while to note, at the very least, where Chiron lies in your natal chart. Chiron is known as the "wounded healer." Once we heal its wound in ourselves, we can help heal similar wounds in others.

Beyond the asteroid belt lie Jupiter, Saturn, Uranus, Neptune, and Pluto. Jupiter and Saturn describe our social worlds and our connections to collectives, to social groups. Jupiter spends about a year in each sign, and Saturn spends two and a half.

The last three planets, which we've already discussed in depth, are the transcendental planets, which connect us to humanity, to the divine, to the bigger picture. They describe our attitudes toward higher levels of experience. Uranus spends about seven years in each sign and takes eighty-four years to travel the full circle of the zodiac. Neptune spends roughly fourteen years in each sign, and Pluto, more than a generation in each sign. Unless human longevity changes drastically, we aren't likely to see the complete journey of Neptune and Pluto around the zodiac in a single lifetime.

Motion

Planets do three things in terms of movement. They move direct, are stationary, and turn retrograde.

Direct movement is business as usual. The norm. A planet's energy works most smoothly when the planet is moving direct. When a planet is stationary, it means that it's about to turn direct or retrograde.

In a birth chart or during a transit, the effect on *us* is that the energy of a particular planet is intensified.

Then there's retrograde. Optical illusion, that's what's really at work with retrograde planets. They appear to go backward at certain times, but that seemingly backward motion is due to the speed of Earth relative to other planets.

Imagine that you're in a train and it's racing parallel to a car. As the train overtakes the car, the car suddenly seems to be moving backward. It isn't really moving that way, of course, but that's how our eyes and our brains interpret it. When a planet "goes retrograde," this apparent backward motion affects us according to the nature of the planet and the sign the planet is in. Only the sun and the moon never go retrograde.

Sun ☉ Rules Leo

Walk outside any morning and watch the sun rise. Light spills across the sky in brilliant colors that lend themselves to poetry. The early morning heat caresses your skin. Plants and trees seem to perk up as the light floods over them. Greens look greener, reds look brighter. Without the sun, the world as we know it wouldn't exist. It powers the universe.

In the same way, the sun in astrology symbolizes the center of our personal universe. Everything that comes in is processed, cataloged, and disseminated by the sun to other areas. It's who we are, our identity, and it is made up of our fundamental assumptions about what life is or isn't. Our sun sign is our tribal affiliation.

We share certain attributes with all the members

of our tribe. Geminis, for instance, share a general disdain for routine. They tend toward impatience, restlessness, and operate primarily in a mental realm. But the ways in which these attributes manifest from one Gemini to the next depends on their particular identities. Is the Gemini sun in the second house or the sixth? What angles (aspects) does it form to other planets? Is it strongly or weakly placed in the chart? Is it compatible with the moon?

The sun represents our ego, our conscious awareness, and the ways in which we interact with the world. It is yang, an energy that propels us to action. It symbolizes our physical strength, our stamina. When it's moving full steam ahead, it brings these qualities into our lives in a seamless manner. If the ego is fragmented, so that it lacks integration with the rest of the personality, then the sun doesn't work for us to its full capacity.

A sun that is well-placed and well-aspected in a birth chart confers a "solar" personality that tends to be outgoing, loves the limelight, and doesn't know the meaning of the word shy. This doesn't apply uniformly to every solar personality by any means, but the propensity certainly exists.

Moon ☽ Rules Cancer

Wolves howl. Tides rise. The crazies come out of the woodwork. We fall in love with love. All of these things are part and parcel of the moon's lore. In astrology, the moon symbolizes what we *feel*. It's the river of emotion that runs through our lives, the bottomless teacup of our intuition, the deepest level of our instincts.

If you're backed into an alley and surrounded by thugs, it's the energy of the moon that brings sweat streaming from your pores, that galvanizes your muscles, that hurls open the floodgates of adrenaline. It's the moon that shrieks, *Run, fast, now.* Your conscious mind, your ego, never gets a word in edgewise. The moon symbolizes our instinctive reactions.

The moon is yin, the womb, the source from which we come. It's our experience of the parent that nurtures us, the early embrace of all that makes us feel solid and secure as adults. To some extent, the moon represents our imaginations, not the celestial flights that come from Neptune, but the sort that rises from the innermost parts of ourselves.

There is something in the moon, too, that appeals to the collective mind, to that part of us that is rooted in myth. Look at Lucas's moon in Aquarius sitting right there on his midheaven. Remember that position. It doesn't guarantee success, nothing in astrology does that, but it indicates the power to influence large numbers of people by delving deeply into archetypes and myths. And what is *Star Wars* if not the very paragon of both?

Darth Vader is the archetypal bad guy, the Jungian shadow. Luke Skywalker is the archetypal hero with a quest. Han Solo is exactly as his name implies, the loner who gets sucked into someone else's drama through what appears to be chance. Skywalker's teacher is the wise man, a magician centuries old who passes on his knowledge before he finally dies. At every turn in the trilogy, there is something larger than all of us, and yet something that speaks to every one of us.

The moon is also about change. With any given month, its phases are visible to the naked eye, the shape altering every few nights from new to crescent to full, then back through the cycle, waxing and waning with maddening regularity. These cyclic changes in the moon affect us in subtle ways, through our emotions.

New moon: We experience an infusion of energy and are more impulsive and spontaneous. We meet someone new. We're eager to try new things, launch new projects, tackle old problems in new ways. We build momentum for a new cycle of growth. In practical terms, this would be a good time to launch a business.

Crescent moon: We forge ahead, seeking to fulfill our new plans and projects. Unfinished business may intrude, but spurred by promises of fulfillment, we keep going with whatever we initiated under the new moon. Under this phase, bills may come due that prevent us from expanding our inventory for the new business. But we plug on nonetheless, certain we can succeed. Even though we hit a few glitches in our new romance, we stick with it, eager to see where it may go.

First quarter: Whatever we initiated during the new moon phase is now tested. Can we continue in this new direction? Can whatever we envisioned emerge? Astrologer Dane Rudhyar refers to this phase as "crisis in action," because we have to release old habits and ways of doing things so that the new vision can succeed.

Using the same examples as before, this is the crossroad where we reevaluate the business. If we decide to continue, we may need to refine our goals, our vision. With our new romance, we find a familiar relationship pattern emerging and aren't so sure this is the right relationship.

Gibbous: The critical turn has been made, the new path is established. Now we have to live with it. If, in the first quarter, we committed to the business or the romance, then everything moves ahead. If we relinquished either or both, this is the point where we live with that decision as well.

Full moon: The cycle initiated at the new moon is now complete. Whatever we launched under the new moon has been taken as far as it can go. Now it all has to be assimilated and integrated. This is the point where we ask ourselves how the business and romance can be improved and expanded, taken to the next level. If we released either the business or the romance under the first quarter, this is the phase where we try to understand what went wrong and how we can avoid the mistakes in the future.

Disseminating moon: At this phase, we try to understand the ramifications of whatever we initiated under the new moon. In our business example, it may be apparent that we need a new computer or updated software to work at maximum efficiency. Or the romance may need fine-tuning, an honest discussion about the needs of both people involved.

Last quarter: This marks another crisis point in the cycle. Whereas the first quarter was a crisis in action, Rudhyar called this phase a "crisis in consciousness." It's under this phase that we reorient ourselves, take stock again. The business may need new employees whose visions are more in tune with our own. The romance is now perceived as it actually is rather than through the lens of hormones and chemistry.

Balsamic: This is the final phase, where the cycle is evaluated in its entirety and the new seeds are sown for the next cycle. We commit to the business, or we shut the doors; we commit to the romance or head out on our own again.

The Moon's Nodes ☊☋

These aren't planets. They're points. Specifically, they mark the spot where the plane of the moon's orbit crosses the plane of the ecliptic. Astrologically, their significance spawns debate.

In Hindu and Chinese astrology, both nodes are considered to be bad. In Western astrology, however, the North Node or Dragon's Head (☊) symbolizes the future that we should work toward, the point of our greatest opportunity to evolve. The South Node (☋) or Dragon's Tail represents things that come so easily to us that we're tempted to cling to the familiarity. Included here are old attitudes and beliefs that we need to release if we're going to evolve.

Karmic astrologers consider the nodes to be indicative of past lives. A South Node in Sagittarius in the second house, for instance, might indicate karma having to do with material resources that were used selfishly, perhaps in the pursuit of an individual truth, which was believed to be the only truth. Its opposite, the North Node in Gemini in the eighth house, would mean that in this life the individual needs to understand other people's viewpoints about money. They need to share their resources through others by communication about affairs of the eighth house—death, sexuality, metaphysics, taxes, inheritances.

The main problem with this view is that "karma" holds rather negative connotations. It implies that our problems lie in another life and essentially obliterates any power we hold in the present. But if we look at these attitudes and beliefs as security blankets that may be vestiges of other lives or vestiges of our early childhoods in this life, then in both instances they are attitudes and beliefs that *can be changed.*

In either case, Western astrology views the North Node as that which challenges our fundamental assumptions about how things work in the cosmic scheme of things. The South Node is our comfort zone, that place we struggle to retain and remember.

Mercury ☿ Rules Gemini and Virgo

Mercury buzzes along at thirty miles per second, eager to get wherever it's going, determined to get there fast. It's never more than 28 degrees from the sun, closer than any other planet.

To say that the planet represents the mind is accurate, but hardly the full picture. This is the mind as logic, reason, left brain. It's the bridge between ourselves and others, the energy that prompted prehistoric man to etch figures on the walls of his caves and the energy that brought the first spoken word into existence. Mercury symbolizes language, communication, information, the primary cultural tools to make ourselves understood. Mercury represents intelligence and ideas, as well as our ability to make abstracts concrete and practical.

Look at a map, any map will do. How do we get from city A to city D? What is the shortest route? The most scenic route? How long will the trip take?

Mercury fills in these details. In much the same way, Mercury fills in the details of our individual maps of reality and builds our perceptions piece by piece.

Gemini and Virgo manifest different aspects of Mercury's energy. Gemini, as an air sign, can be flighty, scattered, and superficial in its approach to communication and information. Virgo, as an earth sign, can be excessively picky about details. But both signs are mental and communicative, with an innate love of language.

Mercury turns retrograde every several months and stays that way for an average of three and a half weeks. In terms of human affairs, it brings about snafus in communication, travel, and anything else that Mercury rules. If you're signing a contract under a Mercury retrograde, scrutinize the small print. If you're traveling, recheck your travel plans. If you've sent a fax or e-mail that's vital to your business or personal life, check at the other end to make sure the person got it.

This isn't to say that everything decays into chaos under a Mercury retrograde. Our free will still prevails. In one instance, a family traveling under a Mercury retrograde was told that their connecting flight had been overbooked, not untypical for a Mercury retrograde. The airline made their usual offer, that anyone who gave up a seat would be given a free ticket. This resulted in a crush of people at the ticket desk and subsequent chaos as two hundred passengers jockeyed to get their names on the list.

The husband and wife, acting independently of each other, immediately seized the opportunity and got their family on the list. They figured that, at best, they would end up with one free ticket and one of them would be traveling later than the rest of the family. When the dust had settled, they had free tickets for everyone in the family and were put on a flight that got them home only an hour later.

One astrological theory contends that when we travel under a Mercury retrograde, we return to the place that we traveled within a year.

Mercury's stationary position never lasts very long, a few hours to three days. It intensifies everything having to do with travel and communication.

Venus ♀ Rules Taurus and Libra

In the evening sky, just as twilight is about to bleed away, Venus appears, a white, luminous gem close to the horizon. Its appearance somehow softens the encroaching darkness and mitigates our instinctive unease about the night. As Earth's closest neighbor, it's fitting that Venus birthed the nursery rhyme we all learned as kids: *Star light, star bright, first star I see tonight; wish I may, wish I might, have this wish I wish tonight.*

Venus symbolizes our experience of love, artistic beauty, and harmony. How do we find peace? What constitutes our individual idea of peace? Is it a particular piece of art? An ocean at sunset? Is it the place we call home?

Venus is also about relationships, specifically the relationships with our partners, whether they are lovers, significant others, spouses, siblings, coworkers, or friends. It's through such relationships that we become clearer about who we are, what we need, and what we seek to express in our lives. Through Venus, we bond, we meld with our other.

Venus's sign describes what attracts us in a partner. A Venus in Sagittarius, for example, seeks action and the exotic with a partner—sports, horses, foreign travel. A Venus in Libra seeks an appreciation of art and beauty in a partner and, above all else, needs harmony.

Venus's shadow side tends toward excess. Too much gourmet food. Flashy clothes and cars. Or even a series of relationships that play out like soap operas.

Venus spends about four weeks in a sign when it's moving direct. When it's moving retrograde, it spends about four months in a sign, with six weeks of that retrograde. This is usually a period when old issues in a relationship crop up. When retrograde in a natal chart, the individual may be shy and uncertain of himself in social situations. There may also be some doubts about self-worth.

Mars ♂ Rules Aries

In the science fiction movies from the fifties, the Martians were always the invading aliens, the marauders with rage in their hearts. They swept across our planet with their death rays, their weird technology, and changed the face of Earth forever.

Thanks to satellites and probes and the space program, our consensus reality about the solar system has changed. If life ever existed on the red planet, it was so long ago that the Martian life-forms either died off or moved on. These days, our aliens are inter-dimensional. Or they come from Sirius or the Pleides. But the fact remains that even the old science fiction movies captured the essence of Mars. Aggression. War. Energy. Courage. Action.

On a deeper level, Mars is also about individuality. Who are we separate from our families, spouses, and friends? Who are we *inside our own skins*? The slogan from the original *Star Trek* series captures this individuality in a nutshell: *to go where no one else has gone before.* This energy is what pushes us to expand the parameters of our lives even when consensus reality warns us not to. Martian energy impelled Christopher Columbus to set out on his own to prove the world wasn't flat. It sends us off to Europe at the age of eighteen on a shoestring budget.

Mars also figures into the Venus/love equation. We have to know who we are before we can merge with another, otherwise we simply merge to the point where our individuality vanishes.

When Mars's energy is blocked in our lives, it may affect our health. The block becomes a symptom of what isn't expressed. Or the block manifests as an accident. In some instances, the blockage of Mars's energy shows up in our external environment as a breakdown in something that doesn't seem to have any relation to us whatsoever. A car that goes on the fritz for no apparent reason. A dishwasher that quits. A hard-drive crash. This may seem farfetched, until you realize the connection. And recognize the pattern.

The effects of a retrograde Mars in a birth chart can mean an internalization of anger and a reluctance to assert yourself.

Jupiter ♃ Rules Sagittarius

You can see it coming on the weather map, a great, swirling blob of white with a well-defined eye that is aimed right at your corner of the world. The hurricane is massive, and all the data says it's going to hit. Then it wobbles to the west, and the forecast changes. Your neck of the woods is safe. Your relief is as large as the hurricane. Euphoria floods through you, a sense that you're protected. Your faith in life is restored.

This is Jupiter. Luck when it's not expected. A sudden buoyancy, a blessing out of nowhere.

Jupiter rules philosophy and spiritual thought, the law and the courts, higher education and the abstract mind. It symbolizes our search for truth and in this sense becomes our connection to a larger order, a greater truth. When people speak of using visualization and affirmation to attain something, it's Jupiter that shows the way.

No doubt about it: Jupiter is terrific and its placement in a natal chart confers luck. Things come to us in that area of our lives; we don't have to go looking for rainbows. We have to guard against taking that luck for granted. Even Jupiter has a shadow side, though. We may become too complacent, lazy, even arrogant. We may indulge in excesses. In some instances, we may feel we're the embodiment of a particular truth, a particular path, and may become, well, obnoxious about it.

In a birth chart, a retrograde Jupiter may indicate tremendous inner faith and a somewhat serious demeanor.

Saturn ♄ Rules Capricorn

Its traditional meaning equates it with the most dire of events and circumstances. Hell on Earth.

Satan. Destruction. All of this smacks of predetermination, destiny instead of free will. Fortunately, Saturn's meaning has transmuted over the years as astrologers have recognized that all planetary energies are multifaceted, even that old devil Saturn.

Imagine a woman of fifty. Her children are grown and she is now back in the work force as a secretary and bored out of her mind. What she really wants to be is a veterinarian, which will take her between ten and twelve years of school because she never graduated from college. With any luck, she would be out of school between the ages of sixty and sixty-two, when most people her age are counting the months to retirement. With deep reluctance, she decides her dream is totally unrealistic and sets about looking for a job that involves animals in some capacity.

This is Saturn in action, teaching us about limitations, structure, and responsibility. Yes, it's disappointing that she won't realize her dream to become a vet. On the other hand, her energy surely will find an outlet elsewhere—at a dolphin research center, at an injured bird center, at an animal shelter. And perhaps, in the long run, this path will prove more fulfilling for her.

If, as Seth says, there are many possible realities to choose from in the course of a given life, then Saturn is the planet that aids us in actualizing one possibility and shutting off others. The danger is that Saturn can also restrict us so severely that we become myopic, narrow-minded, and so rigid that we lose the ability to follow an impulse. To be spontaneous.

Since Saturn symbolizes our experience of authority, it has come to represent the father or the authoritarian parent as well. But authority can also be teachers, bosses, school, anything that teaches us the rules of the society in which we live.

When Saturn is retrograde in a birth chart, it usually indicates an unusual degree of self-sufficiency. The person is probably a loner. There may be some suppression of emotion.

Uranus, Neptune, & Pluto ♀, ♅, ♆, Rulers of Aquarius, Pisces, & Scorpio

These planets are covered in depth in the first part of the book. However, their retrograde effects in a birth chart and during transits are worth mentioning.

A retrograde Uranus in a birth chart often indicates that the individual's mind isn't restricted by consensus reality. When we watch color spread across the sky, chasing away the night, we call it sunrise. But a person with a retrograde Uranus sees it as the perfect expression of some inner collective condition, then goes on to write a best-selling book about it.

When retrograde by transit, Uranus's effect is felt most strongly in the house that it hits. Say it hits the fourth house, which represents the home and immediate environment, the mother and early childhood. This may indicate sudden and unexpected changes in the home environment. Natally or by transit, this can mean multiple moves or sudden and unexpected changes in the home.

When Neptune is retrograde natally, a person's fantasy life is quite pronounced. Psychic sensitivity is enhanced, but it may be difficult to put this to practical use without other mitigating factors. At a higher level, a retrograde Neptune may indicate the ability to tap into universal powers and knowledge.

Neptune retrograde by transit may indicate escapism through drugs or alcohol, victim type of behavior, or true mystical experiences. The house affected will tell which area of the life is impacted.

Pluto retrograde in a natal chart may inhibit an individual's expression of his personal truth. Since Pluto is always wound up with issues about power, this could indicate a feeling of personal powerlessness. On a more optimistic note, however, it can also indicate an evolving awareness about the deeper levels of consciousness and reality and the link between the two.

By transit, a retrograde Pluto brings out the issues we would rather not deal with. The deep stuff. The hidden stuff. The secrets we harbor.

Asteroids

Chiron lies between Saturn and Uranus. It has been called both an asteroid and a planetoid, although the distinction about what it is seems less important than its effect on us. Its location may hold important clues about that effect.

Its location provides a link between Saturn, the consensus reality of rules and restrictions, and Uranus, the energy that disrupts that consensus reality. In mythology, Chiron is the wounded healer who, despite his vast healing knowledge, was unable to heal himself when he was wounded in battle. Astrologically, he symbolizes our ability to look within for answers. Once we discover where we are wounded, we can get on with the business of healing ourselves, then give that knowledge to others.

Part of Fortune

This is an imaginary point in a horoscope, one of hundreds widely used in the East. Think of it as your pot of gold, the blessing that is yours without asking. It's your source of happiness, of joy, a creative power. The sign of the part of fortune describes your path of joy. The house placement describes its expressions in a particular area of your life.

Suppose your part of fortune lies in Libra, in the seventh house. This is a strong indication that relationships are of prime importance in your life, the source of your greatest joy. Your happiness is deeply affected by the state of your most intimate relationships.

Consider this section a crash course in natal astrology, your launch pad for an exploration that leads you into the next millennium.

PART TWO

Sun Signs & the Millennium

Chapter 8

•

Your Sun Sign

The Elements

In most stories about magicians and wizards, part of their power includes knowledge about how to manipulate and harness the elements for their own use. Merlin, with a flick of his wrist, caused fire to shoot from his fingertips. By manipulation of matter and air, he could vanish and appear at will.

Fire and air, earth and water. The elements. They form the basis of our consensus reality and the cornerstone of astrology. Each of the twelve signs is assigned an element that characterizes that sign and, in turn, helps define who we are.

Fire Signs: Aries, Leo, Sagittarius

With this group, think action. They're here to shatter paradigms and to venture into undiscovered countries, whether these countries are in the mind or in outer space. Their courage and brashness open new doors for the rest of us.

Air Signs: Gemini, Libra, Aquarius

This group is about intellect, the mind. Their curiosity pierces the barriers between the old and new paradigms, building intellectual bridges that ease the way for the other signs. With this group, perception is keenly developed.

Earth Signs: Taurus, Virgo, Capricorn

Grounding. Patience. Endurance. This group grounds the rest of us in practical reality. As the other two groups venture off into the unknown, the earth group calls after them: *Bring back something we can use, something practical, something tangible.* The earth signs are, above all else, resourceful.

Water Signs: Cancer, Scorpio, Pisces

Emotion is their domain. The world of feelings is as real to this group as ideas are to the air group. When they venture into unknown territory, they do it through their emotional perceptions. They nurture and protect.

While the element of our sun sign describes our fundamental approach to the world, none of us is the embodiment of just a single element. We're much too complex for that. This is especially apparent when the element of your sun sign differs from that of your moon or ascendant.

Suppose you're a Gemini (air) with a Capricorn (earth) moon and a rising in Scorpio (water). Your basic nature, then, takes you into the world of ideas and communication. But through your earth moon, your inner life is grounded and possesses a certain self-discipline and patience. Your ascendant in Scorpio compels you to feel your way through life, to pay attention to hunches and premonitions. Your watery rising works most smoothly and efficiently with your earth moon.

Most birth charts have planets in all four elements. But suppose elements are missing. Does that mean you're lacking in some area of your life? If you don't have any fire in your chart, does it mean you're passive? Unable to act on the simplest choices?

Astrologers seem somewhat divided on this issue. Some say that the absence of an element means that we've integrated the essence of that element in previous lives. Others contend that we'll be attracted to situations and people who embody that element. When free will is tossed into the argument, the issue is muddied even more. Perhaps the truth lies somewhere between the two and has more to do with how *we* handle the overall pattern of our birth chart.

The Modes

Elements are only part of the equation. The other part is called the mode.

Imagine that you wake up one night with an idea. It is barely formed at this point, a silhouette of whatever it will become, a connect-the-dot picture. But you sense it may work, grab a pen and notebook, and start to take notes. The idea seemed to come out of nowhere, rising from the soup of your unconscious with an archetypal power that forced you to take notice. Now you have to run with it and see where it leads.

In astrology, this mode or state of being is called "cardinal." It's the call of a creative wilderness, an initiation, the force that keeps change alive in the universe.

As you take notes and begin to make sketches, the idea becomes even more concrete. You're breathing shape and form into it. You're fixing it in time and space. This is the second mode, called "fixed."

Eventually, the product that you conceived is fully formed. Maybe it's a house that expresses who you really are. Or maybe it's a gadget that allows us to see the human aura. Whatever it is, it needs fine-tuning, polishing, refinement. You have to adapt it to the world. So it enters a state of flux and change. This third mode is known as "mutable." Each of the twelve signs is connected with a particular mode that further defines its nature.

Four elements, three modes. Together, these form the core of each sign.

Cardinal Signs: Aries, Cancer, Libra, Capricorn

As a group, these four initiate action, usually in a singular direction. They are composed of two pairs that fall opposite each other in the zodiac, which means their qualities can be compared and contrasted, which is known as polarity. Aries, for instance, is often blunt and brash; its opposite, Libra, flinches at the brashness and tries to soften it with tact.

Fixed Signs: Taurus, Leo, Scorpio, Aquarius

This group has staying power. They take whatever was initiated by the cardinal signs and make it real. They have enormous determination and self-reliance. Once again, polarity comes into the picture. It isn't uncommon for signs that are polar opposites to be attracted to each other. In the fixed signs, that would be Taurus and Scorpio, Leo and Aquarius.

Mutable Signs: Gemini, Virgo, Sagittarius, Pisces

This group refines what the first group initiates. They are as adaptable as mutating viruses, capable of changing in the blink of an eye to fit corresponding changes in their environment.

The Tribes

Whatever our sun sign, all of us reflect bits and pieces of every element, every mode. It isn't enough to say that every Virgo is picky about details or that every Leo is a boastful show-off. There are plenty of Virgos who could care less about details and Leos who remain behind the scenes.

A transit of Pluto in Sagittarius (fire) may spur Virgo to action in uncovering her own truth and verbalizing that truth. A transit of Neptune in Aquarius (air) may kick Leo into claiming his own power. But again and always, the stars are merely signposts, broad patterns of possibilities. We create our destinies. We write the scripts.

The Aquarian Age Begins . . .

. . . When? Not on January 1, 2000. According to some astrologers, the age of Aquarius has already begun. Others believe it will begin in several centuries. The most commonly held opinion among astrologers is that it begins in 2001. This opinion is also held by the U.S. Naval Observatory. The ideals that represent the Aquarian age—humanitarianism, idealism, unprecedented innovations, newfound freedoms, and the cultivation of a higher consciousness—stretches from 2100 to 3200. But the path toward that time is already in place.

Using the Sun Sign Section

In the section that follows on sun signs in the millennium, only the first ten to twelve years are covered. The opportunities each of us will have to effect change in our own lives during that time are pegged into the following:

1) Energizer: solar eclipse on August 11, 1999. This eclipse, often called "the eclipse of the century," occurs in 18 degrees, 21 minutes in Leo, a fixed fire sign. It's part of a grand cross configuration, which means there is at least one planet in all four of the fixed signs: the sun in Leo, Mars in Scorpio, Saturn in Taurus, and Uranus in Aquarius. Some astrologers refer to this eclipse as a "crisis." But a crisis can also be something that galvanizes us in a new direction. A solar eclipse affects our conscious attitudes.

The eclipse shadow passes over the southern end of Great Britain, northern France, southern Germany, Austria, Hungary, Romania, Turkey, Iran, Pakistan, and India. These areas will be the ones most affected by the eclipse.

The fixed signs as well as planets in fixed signs that fall between 17 and 19 degrees will be the most heavily influenced by the eclipse. In your birth chart, look for the house with Leo on the cusp. This house (and any planets it contains) is the one the eclipse impacts. Generally, something that has been hidden or concealed in the affairs of that house will come to light. You'll have to confront it and deal with it, which will galvanize you in a new direction. The effects of the eclipse can be felt for several months on either side of the actual eclipse.

2) ***Catalyst:*** the grand alignment with seven planets in Taurus, May 3, 2000. This alignment obviously affects Taurus, but also affects Scorpio, its polar opposite. Also, individuals with a lot of fixed planets in their charts will feel it. The lineup applies pressure to the house and planets where it occurs.

Jupiter and Saturn are part of this conjunction, which happens every twenty years. The conjunction on May 3 begins a new Jupiter/Saturn cycle. U.S. presidents who have been elected under this conjunction, always in years ending in zero, have died in office: Harrison (1840), Lincoln (1860), Garfield (1880), McKinley (1900), Harding (1920), Roosevelt (1940), and Kennedy (1960). Reagan, elected in 1980, may have broken the pattern, even though he was nearly killed in an assassination attempt.

3) ***Transformation:*** Pluto in Sagittarius, 1995–2008

4) ***Innovation:*** Uranus in Aquarius, 1996–2003

5) ***New Paradigms:*** Uranus/Neptune in Aquarius until 2003

6) ***Truth Within:*** Uranus in Pisces, 2003–2010

7) ***Spiritual Expansion:*** Neptune in Aquarius, 1998–2012

What you can expect in the millennium is also described in ten different areas of your life:

1) Self: anything that affects you personally

2) Finances: how you earn and spend money, your attitudes toward your material resources, and what you value

3) Communication: how and what you communicate

4) Your home: your immediate environment

5) Creative potential: ideas, innovative techniques, your creative expression, your kids

6) Health and work: your general health in the first decade of the millennium and your work environment

7) Partnerships: intimate and business relationships

8) Spirituality: your world view, your religious and philosophical beliefs

9) Career and profession: what you do for a living, your "public" persona

10) Personal unconscious: the power you've disowned

At the end of each sun sign is a section called "Tapping the Source" that deals with synchronicities and our inner oracle. Most of us have experienced coincidences. We're thinking of someone we haven't seen for a while, then that person calls. Or we hear an unusual new word, then suddenly hear that word a dozen times in two hours. There are many levels of these coincidences or synchronicities, some more startling than others. All of them are intended to seize our attention and turn it toward a particular pattern that is emerging or which is already prevalent in our lives.

In this section you'll find tips for you sun sign on how to cultivate an awareness of synchronicities, which increases their frequency in your life.

Chapter 9

Aries, the Ram

March 21–April 19
Cardinal, Fire
Ruled by Mars

Aries Man

You're new in town and your neighbor has invited you to a party. The moment he opens the door, his smile vanquishes your unease and he welcomes you as if he's known you all his life. He introduces you to his circle of friends, chattering away the entire time about this or that. Never mind that you don't get in a word edgewise. You've just met an Aries, and this is how it's going to be.

Never forget that Aries is a pioneer, and this holds true whether he's pioneering his backyard or the outer reaches of the solar system. He ventures where others are afraid to go. His courage and brashness are legendary. His bluntness can be irritating, but at least he's honest about who and what he is. And that's really the bottom line with this sign: what you see is what you get. Nothing hidden. No secret agenda.

He does hope, however, that you like him. He

wants to be liked. Needs to be liked. He may even ask you if you like him. And if you don't answer yes immediately, his expression may cave in briefly, but that's all you'll see of how crushed he is. Showing weakness is anathema to his personality. In any situation, in fact, his bravado can be overpowering and, well, somewhat annoying at times, too.

As a Mars-ruled sign, Aries is physically strong. But his brashness usually results in his taking chances that another person would deem insane. See that sheer rock cliff over there? No problem. Aries climbs it because it's there and he knows he can do it. Like the ram that symbolizes this sign, he is sure-footed, certain of himself, and utterly fearless. His physical stamina makes him a great lover of and participator in sports—the more raucous the better. At least once in the life of an Aries, though, he probably suffers an injury to his face or his head. He may run high fevers when he's ill, or he may be accident prone. Burns are a possibility with this sign.

Due to the aggression and temper evident in Aries, he may be prone to type A ailments—high blood pressure, stroke, heart attack. But it's unlikely that Aries is afflicted with depression or gloom, unless he's got a water sign moon. He simply doesn't slow down enough for that to happen. This isn't to say that all Aries will inevitably suffer or not suffer from these kinds of ailments. It simply means that certain patterns exist for the sign.

Aries is no paragon of patience. Long lines drive him crazy. He's not a couch potato. He would rather be out there involved in the action, moving around, doing whatever needs to be done. Give him a specific goal, one that isn't too distant, and if it interests him, he gets it done in half the time it would take another person.

He's a good one to have around if a hurricane is on the way. He puts up the shutters, lays in supplies, battens down the hatches. But you don't want to ride out a hurricane with Aries. He'll be bored to death within the first hour of the storm and out of his mind when the hurricane moves on. All that sitting around. All that waiting.

Aries rarely holds a grudge. Once he blows his top, that it's for him, he's purged, he may not even remember what made him angry. But then he doesn't understand why the other person isn't as quick to forget it and move on.

Aries is happiest when he's with people who share his views and interests. When he has to defend what he believes, he does it with considerable passion and zeal—unless he loses interest. Then he just walks away without a second thought. Although he's terrific at getting things off the ground, finishing them may be another matter altogether. The secret is to keep him interested.

In romance, that's also the secret with this guy. If he loses interest, he's gone in a flash. But if his passion is ignited, he courts you the way you dream of being courted, as if the sun rises and sets in your eyes. Once he's in love, he isn't likely to stray, unless you lose interest in what interests him. In his heart he's looking for the ideal romance, the ideal marriage, the great career, all the best in life.

In business he's astute, he knows what he wants and isn't afraid to go for it. Even though his strength lies in launching projects, he's smart enough to delegate the responsibility to someone else for completing what he starts. As a father, the Aries man plays touch football with his sons and goes fly-fishing with his daughter. He's there for his kids and pity the fool who ever hurts one of them.

Aries Woman

Yes, she's forward. She's brash. She tells you exactly what she thinks and may not choose the most tactful way to say it. She doesn't wait around for a man to make the first move. If she's interested, she gets your number and *she* calls *you*. If it offends you, then hit the road. This lady isn't your type.

The Aries woman is just as brave and reckless as her male counterpart. She's probably into sports, but more for the competition than for the exercise. Her idea of a vacation is to bike through Europe, a competition of endurance with herself.

She's certainly capable of living alone and liking it. That is to say, she can put up her own hurricane shutters. And yet she still needs romance in her life, the candlelight, the drama, the pining, the highs. She wants all that. If you make it too easy for her, though, if you pour out your heart before she's sure about her deeper feelings for you, then you risk losing her. As much as she wants romance, she can't abide boredom. Like her male counterpart, she's a passionate lover and she enjoys feeling wanted and needed and made to feel special. Just don't overdo it. But don't be too detached, either. In romance, you initially walk a fine line with this woman.

As far as careers go, the Aries woman is as good at what she does as the Aries man. Both are probably better off working for themselves, at something that flames their passion. If they work for other people, they'll be content only when they are the bosses. They set their sights on the seat of control.

As a parent, this woman isn't particularly nurturing. She's not a big hugger. But what she lacks in that department is compensated for in her urge to protect and provide for. She stands up for her kids with all the passion she holds for her own ideals. She'll forgive you if you hurt her. But she'll never forgive you for hurting her offspring.

She's got her quirks. When something piques her interest, she leaps into it and rolls around in it until it permeates her life. For that matter, so does the Aries man. She is rarely shy about anything, but she may keep things to herself in the beginning; particularly if the idea, project, relationship, or whatever is new to her. Once it has seized her, she spills the beans to whoever will listen. Yet she exercises circumspection with other people's secrets. Contradictions. Dichotomies. Go figure. She doesn't think about it, she's not introspective in that way. To her, it's just business as usual.

This is just how she is. Take it or leave it. She's not going to change. She has never been and will never be subtle.

This isn't always a quality to admire. One young Aries woman wasn't much of a cook. Every evening when she got home from work, she boiled a chicken for dinner. That was it. Just a chicken. No potatoes, no vegetables, no soup or bread, just the chicken. Within an hour the stench filled her apartment, apparent to anyone who walked through the front door. But she was oblivious, too busy racking up $300 phone bills with her friends in other states. When her roommate mentioned it to her, she got angry, blew up, apologized, and promised it wouldn't happen again. But the next night, the chicken went into the pot of boiling water again.

The Aries woman means well, but she's adhering to her schedule, not yours.

She's bossy at times and gets incredibly irritable when you don't get it right the first time. To her it's so obvious, so utterly clear, she doesn't understand why it isn't that way for you. She lacks the insight to see her own flaws with any perspective. If you call her on it, expect a scene. She won't be criticized. She won't be demeaned. She won't be used.

When it suits her, she's all charm and grace, as congenial as they come in a room filled with strangers. So is the male Aries. Their approaches differ, but the end point is the same. Both want you to like them and to find them as interesting as they find themselves.

Aries in the Millennium

The good news, Aries, is that anything new suits you. And what can be newer than a brand-new millennium? You'll enjoy the freedom, the innovations, the individuality. You'll love this new frontier. The bad news is that you may go through periods when you don't feel like you're in control. Everything seems chaotic, fragmented, broken, like light in a swinging prism of glass.

As a loner, you may have trouble learning to see things from someone else's perspective. But see you must. The process can be easy or difficult, depending on how you handle it.

Energizer: The eclipse in Leo on August 11, 1999, affects your fifth house. Something that has been hidden or concealed concerning your creativity, your pleasures, or your children comes to light. You may already suspect whatever this is, so it doesn't come as a complete shock. The difference is that now you have to deal with it. You feel the influence of this eclipse for several months before and after August 11 and must honestly evaluate your relationship with your kids, your lover, or your creative partnership with yourself.

Catalyst: The alignment in Taurus in May 2000 may make you feel like you're on a Tilt-A-Whirl, with all the gravity weighing down your side of the world. Even though the seven planets don't line up in *your* sign, they line up right next to your sun. And when that happens sometime after high noon on May 3, there won't be a single planet in your sign. This alignment is a *catalyst* for you, Aries, the cosmic kick in the butt that prompts you to look at the imbalances in your own life.

Are your relationships demanding too much of your time? Is your job dragging you down? Do you wish you were in another career altogether? The pressure subsides a bit at a time as the faster planets move into Gemini, which is more compatible with Aries. By the end of August of 2000, you should have a much clearer picture of how to balance your needs with those of the people around you. If you skirt the issue, it may come around to haunt you again by mid-October, when Saturn slides into Taurus once more and stays there through mid-April of 2001.

In the early part of 2000, however, Jupiter will be in Aries, which gives you some support before the catalyst point in May. You may be traveling quite a bit during the first four months, which may actually trigger the process you'll be going through after May 3.

Transformation: During the catalyst stage, only Pluto is in brother fire sign Sagittarius, so that despite your sense of imbalance, you can still speak your truth. You may, in fact, be speaking it louder and more stridently than ever before. You didn't have much fun when Pluto was in Scorpio because events prompted you to look within, to clean out all those shadowed nooks and crannies in your life. You would much rather act than be introspective, so Pluto in Sagittarius is certainly more compatible with your basic nature.

And yet, as you speak your truths, you may already be questioning whether they really are *your* truths. That endless loop that often plays in your head is just surface noise, the vestiges of years of acculturation. If you can still the loop and listen to the music that plays beneath it, you discover the truths that you actually hold.

Pluto in Sagittarius rubs up against any pockets of resistance you have and keeps rubbing until you pay attention. You're better off paying attention early in the game because it will make your passage through Pluto in Sagittarius much easier. Don't forget: Sagittarius sees the big picture and, like you, Aries, is always on the prowl for new experiences. So go with it, don't resist.

Innovation: The first several years of the millennium may try your patience time and again. Uranus in Aquarius asks that we participate in community and group activities and efforts. As a loner, Aries, this can chafe at your need to strike out alone. You'll have to cultivate patience, which is going to strain your nerves.

However, in attempting to cultivate such qualities within yourself, you'll discover that certain things can be accomplished more quickly in a group than with any individual acting alone. There are many ways of doing something, and even though those ways might not be your way, they work. As you see this for yourself, you gradually realize you're not always right and that your way isn't the only way. In short, Aries, you become more tolerant.

As a result, you begin to experiment with new ways of thinking and living and consistently surprise yourself. You plant the seeds for this experimentation through 2003, gradually building a lifestyle and belief structure that are more in line with who you really are rather than who you thought you were. In this context you uncover innovative solutions and answers to problems and questions that stumped you in the past.

New Paradigms: Your new paradigm, Aries, is brought about by your new tolerance toward other people's perspectives. Your intuitive and psychic skills increase in direct proportion to that tolerance, almost as if the cosmos is rewarding you for your breakthrough. You now listen to that inner voice when it speaks. You're more aware of synchronicities and are able to decipher their meaning within the context of your immediate life. You listen to the oracle within and act on that higher wisdom.

The more closely you listen to and act upon this inner oracle, the clearer your particular path becomes. From this vantage place you begin to understand how vital your beliefs are in the creation of your reality.

Truth within: Initially, you're wary of Uranus in Pisces. Your basic nature revolves around the beginning of cycles, not their completion, as Pisces symbolizes. However, a lot of what will happen during this cycle will seem familiar to you simply because Pisces is the sign immediately preceding your own. And by this time you understand completely that one cycle has to end before another can begin.

You're more aware of subtleties by now, so you feel fluctuations in energy as they move through the groups you work and live with. You begin to see that what affects one affects all and understand how this immutable law extends well beyond your personal life.

Spiritual expansion: For you, Aries, this period ushers in a period of tremendous growth. Once you get past the seemingly blurred boundaries between fiction and reality that are part and parcel of Neptune in any sign, you realize, for perhaps the first time in your life, that spirituality has little connection to organized religion. You see it as a state of mind and a way of life. You won't feel a need to be in control, at least not like before. Your resistance in various areas has dissolved, and you're more in touch with the higher wisdom that guides your life.

Self: As the millennium starts, you begin to reach out for newer experiences, but aren't quite sure what you're looking for. Excitement? Romance? Just good old adventure? Between February and March of 2000, your temper and patience may run a bit short, with Mars in your sun sign. Learn to think before you speak, to bite your tongue before you blurt out what's on your mind.

Between 2000 and 2003, you may feel the urge to move. This could be a physical move from one city or state to another. But it may also be a metamorphic move, from one set of beliefs to another. During the transition period, learn to trust the hidden order that runs just beneath the surface of chaos.

In late 2006, your spiritual quest is bolstered when the sun conjuncts Jupiter in Sagittarius, the sign it rules. The sun joins Pluto in the same sign, and this infusion of energy is just what you need to further clarify where you're going.

When Pluto goes into Capricorn in 2008, the inner work you've done for the first eight years of the millennium begins to pay off in a big way. You're able to structure your life around your newfound beliefs. Those around you who cling to the old paradigm—some of whom may hold authority over you—aren't going to like what you're doing. They may challenge you on it. There may be power struggles. Just remember what you've been learning and know that when Uranus goes into your sign in late 2010, you're ready to defend who you've become. And you do it with brilliance.

Finances: The millennium starts off with the alignment in your house of money. You're feeling security conscious, maybe for the first time in your life. You may find yourself window-shopping but not buying, saving instead of splurging. If you play the stock market, stick to what you know. Don't take unnecessary risks at this time.

You may join some sort of investment or financial group somewhere between the start of the millennium and 2003. This group, in fact, may be your first foray into any kind of group. At first, you resist the communal spirit or you get in there and want to lead the group. Just chill out, Aries. Get into the group spirit, and see what happens. The results could surprise you. By late summer of 2002, Jupiter in fiery Leo hits your house of creativity, and you're burning up with new financial ideas.

Between 2004 and 2005, you may enter some sort of financial partnership with another person or a group of people. A new business, perhaps. Whatever it is, it reflects your changing views and beliefs, and puzzles those who are closest to you.

Financially, you seem to be working toward something, but you're not quite sure what that something is except that it's different than what you've done before. Money for the sake of money may not be as important to you now. You come to view money as energy.

Uranus in Pisces, sitting in your twelfth house of the personal unconscious, is doing a tune on you, changing around all your concepts about finances—and everything else in your life. If you get confused at any point, just sit quietly for a few minutes, Aries. Sit even though you hate sitting. Sit and shut your eyes, turn your attention inside, and ask if you're on the right path.

Listen to that inner oracle even in financial matters.

Communication: Your inner oracle won't be the only thing you're listening to, Aries. With the eclipse in August 1999, you realize that one of the imbalances in your life has to do with listening to what other people say. Really listening. You learn to listen with your heart. Once you master that, you're able to listen to what isn't said, to read between the lines.

This gets easier to do in mid-2001, when Jupiter and Saturn in Gemini hit your third house and Jupiter forms a beneficial angle (trine) to Uranus in Aquarius. Jupiter expands your skills and Saturn provides a structure through which you can express them. You may have to practice those skills with a brother or sister who may not see things the way you do.

These communication and listening skills may be augmented and enhanced through any groups you join. The collective energy of the group could actually speed up the progress. By 2003, when Uranus goes into Pisces, you're well-prepared to navigate the formerly unfamiliar waters of your own psyche and to communicate whatever truths you find there.

Neptune in Aquarius through 2012 can initially make you feel uncertain of yourself. Boundaries may blur. But as you become more familiar with this uncharted country you've entered, you get into the spirit of the adventure and find your own rhythm.

Your home: During the summer of 2000, you may do renovations to your home, expanding it. Or you may have new additions to your family—a child, an elderly parent, even a friend in need. Between 2003 and 2005, when Saturn is in Cancer, unresolved childhood issues may surface. If you don't deal with the issues now, they keep cropping up until you do.

You may begin working more out of your home, trying to establish your own business. At this time, if you play your cards right and listen to your inner oracle, an avocation may become a vocation.

When Pluto goes into Capricorn in January 2008,

you could experience conflicts between your home life and your career. If you've done your inner work to this point, it shouldn't be a major obstacle. You'll be aware if you've laid the groundwork, because in June 2008, Pluto slips back into Sagittarius until late November and old issues may crop up again.

Around 2010, you're feeling rebellious about everything. Uranus is in your sun sign then and you revolt against any strictures on your personal freedom. If any of those strictures involve your home life, this could be a trouble spot. But forewarned is forearmed.

Creative potential: Your creativity and your children are highlighted for about a year, beginning in August 2002. For part of this year, Jupiter and Pluto form a trine to each other, an aspect that denotes ease. This creativity shouldn't be used strictly for yourself, because it may not work to your advantage. By using it to benefit others, perhaps a group with whom you're associated, it works flawlessly. This may also be a time when you find favor with someone in power who is attracted to your high ideals.

Opportunities seem to come out of nowhere, with everything flowing in exactly the direction you want. Your creative endeavors may be publicly recognized at this time and prove to be quite successful.

Your relationship with your children is likely to flourish during this time as well. If you don't have kids, you may be considering it.

In the latter part of 2006, your creative endeavors have you working hard and furiously. You're looking for some sort of structure for your creative ideas and projects. You're also going to feel some inner conflicts, however, over the structure of your life. At times you have difficulty distinguishing what is real from what is imagined.

Keep in mind that nothing is as bad as it might seem. Maintain your equilibrium, keep in sight of your goals, and keep listening to that inner oracle. You may uncover "ghosts from your past," residue of old issues that you need to confront—and put behind you. Once you do that, the pressure eases.

Health and work: Aries rules the face and head. Any health problems you encounter during the first decade of the millennium are likely to show up first as headaches, migraines, or even sinus problems. Instead of grabbing for a quick fix of Tylenol or running off to the doctor for a prescription, first try to understand what the real issue is. Are you avoiding a confrontation with another person? With part of yourself? What are you resisting in your life? Be honest. Then delve inside to look for the answer.

This doesn't mean you should avoid medical attention altogether. It simply means that it behooves you to treat the problem as an opportunity to find the real issue. Don't be afraid to try alternative treatments—homeopathic remedies, acupuncture, hypnosis, herbs. This area is part of your new personal paradigm, Aries. Explore it with the same sense of adventure that you bring to every other area of your life.

Partnerships: This area is a big one for you in the millennium, the place where much of your transformation occurs. As the millennium opens, it may be business as usual for you, Aries. But that doesn't last long. Early on, your relationships undergo change, with some people dropping out of your life and others moving in. In each case, the exit and the arrival mark important junctures in your changing beliefs.

You always enjoy romance, and that won't change. But you may find yourself in relationships that are more egalitarian, especially as you begin to listen with an open heart to other people. You begin to see that your way isn't always the best and only way; that the other person has legitimate ideas as well. As your relationships change, so does your perception about the connection between all living things.

From 2003 to 2005, relationships are particularly important for you. During this time, you learn to balance your needs with those of your significant other, and your group involvements may have a lot to do with this lesson. By the time Uranus enters your sign in 2010, you're well on your way toward living the equality you've been learning.

Spirituality: Regardless of your religious affiliations up to this point, the millennium offers you the opportunity to honor the sacred in every facet of your life. Spirituality won't be confined to one day a week at the church or synagogue of your choice. It won't be separate from the rest of your life.

Neptune in Aquarius is going to blur some of the fine lines in religious beliefs for you, but this allows you to delve into areas where you may not have ventured before. You might dabble for a while, borrowing a little of this, a little of that, pasting a picture together. Then, suddenly, the whole becomes clear to you. Whatever the ultimate belief is, once you find it, you apply it to your life in general.

In practical terms, this may mean that you invest in earth-friendly companies. Or that when you take a vacation, you seek out mythical places or spiritual power spots. The point is that you not only understand the connection among all living things, you start living it. You begin to integrate it into who you are and what you hope to become.

Career and profession: For about the first eight years of the millennium, you're working toward an evolving vision of what your true passion is. Since you're experimental and adventurous by nature, this is the time when you begin to acknowledge your imagination as a force in its own right. Some of your wackier ideas suddenly don't seem so strange or impractical. By listening to your inner oracle, your intuition expands tremendously, and you learn to rely on it when making professional decisions. As your confidence grows, so do your professional victories.

At times old patterns and habits return to haunt you. Maybe you feel like telling off your boss. Or you start to argue with the powers that be. Try to remember to bite your tongue, Aries, no matter how hard it is, so that you don't become the vehicle of your own undoing.

Personal unconscious: Neptune plays a major role in this area of your life. As you navigate the millennium, reinventing yourself and your life so that you can fulfill your potential, the stuff of your dreams will change. The REM Dreams.

Your own dreams, in fact, may become one of the places you explore most deeply. First, you learn how to request a dream to answer questions and find solutions to problems. Then you have to train yourself to remember them and remind yourself to record them. The interpretations may seem awkward and strange at first. What does a racehorse mean? Why were you wandering around in the musty cellar of a scary Gothic mansion? What did the old crone say to you?

As you study your own dreams, symbols reappear. A new language. A personal language. A language that comes from the deepest part of you, Aries. This is the key. Neptune in Aquarius is rather like a gate between dimensions, and once you walk through it, nothing is ever quite the same again. Here you can learn how to accelerate your own healing and to ferret out the unresolved issues that may be blocking you. This place is where your journey into the millennium really begins.

Tapping the Source

Synchronicities & Your Inner Oracle

In the new millennium, synchronicity will become increasingly important to you, Aries. By cultivating an openness to this type of message, you increase the frequency with which it occurs. Since you're always pressed for time, here are some things you can do to nurture these kinds of experiences. It won't take you more than five minutes a day.

1) As you're falling asleep at night, give yourself the suggestion that you're open and receptive to synchronicities happening in your life. Do the same thing before you're fully awake in the morning. Both times, think of something about which you would like guidance or information. Request an answer.
2) At least once during the day, write your request in a notebook that you use expressly for this purpose. State your receptivity and your request out loud. Then release it.

3) Repeat this procedure until it produces results. If you're sincere in your request, it shouldn't take long to see the results. Maybe five minutes, maybe a day.
4) When the synchronicity happens, record it in your notebook. Tell friends about it. The telling reinforces your receptivity and encourages a repetition of the experience. Once the universe knows you're aware and listening, it goes out of its way to give you what you ask for.

Creating Your Future

The future lies in *your* hands: that's the challenge and the message for every sign in the millennium. You, Aries, are already aware of this. You've been a lone wolf for so long that it is absolutely obvious to you that you're at least a participant in the creation of your future. And yet, when it comes right down to it, right down to the practical everyday stuff, you aren't sure how it's done. The actual process eludes you.

You read books on visualization and affirmations. You surf the Web in search of specific techniques, some magic bullet that will bring the future into the now with a snap of your fingers. Then at some point you get frustrated and bored with the whole thing. Action is so much easier. You go out and seize what you want and make things happen: that's how you have always created your world.

But if you're willing to invest another few minutes each day in pursuit of your ideal, here's what you do. It's simple.

1) Create a small ritual that marks the boundary between ordinary life and these few moments of conscious creation. Light a candle. Burn a stick of incense. Go to a particular spot in your home or office where you won't be disturbed.
2) Plop down in a comfortable chair, kick off your shoes, and close your eyes. For the next sixty seconds, imagine yourself in a situation or a place that embodies whatever it is that you desire. Maybe you want to start your own business. Fine, imagine yourself in your new office, as your own boss. Make it vivid. How does the air smell? What does the view from the window look like? What decorates your walls? Is the coffeepot on? Is there a vase of fresh flowers in sight? What kind of flowers? Add detail, color texture.
3) Hold this image as long as you can—then release it. Really release it. Don't worry and fret about how it's going to come about, just trust that it will. Trust that you will attract the people, circumstances, and opportunities that bring your vision into the present.
4) If this sounds to easy, if it sounds like New Age pabulum for the bereaved and the lost, release that, too. This stuff works. All you have to do is believe.

Chapter 10

•

Taurus, the Bull

April 20–May 20
Fixed, Earth
Ruled by Venus

Taurus Man

Remember Ferdinand the bull in the children's story? What Ferdinand enjoyed most was being left alone to graze contentedly on his hill, in the warm sunlight. His mother worried about him because he wasn't like the other bulls; he didn't have any desire at all to go to Madrid and fight in the ring.

Then one day Ferdinand sat down in the wrong spot and got stung by a bee. He went ballistic, bellowing, snorting, racing around. The spectacle was witnessed by men from Madrid who were looking for bulls for the rings, and believing he was fierce, they hauled him off to Madrid. But when he was put in the ring, Ferdinand refused to fight. He wasn't making a statement of any sort. He simply wasn't interested. And nothing would change his mind.

Welcome to the world of the Taurus male, the strong, silent type who minds his own business, the most stubborn man in the zodiac. Once he has made up his mind about something, he digs in his heels, hunches his shoulders so that his thick, sturdy neck nearly vanishes in his collar, and that's it. He won't budge. You can threaten him, beg, plead, or shriek, but it all falls on deaf ears.

And yet one day out of the blue, someone pushes too hard, says exactly the wrong thing in the wrong way, and all that poise and control explode wide open, and he charges. This is the bull's rush, the legendary Taurean temper, a rage that mows down anyone and anything in its path. Pity the fool who figures it's just for show. This is a blind rage, an archetypal rage that sweeps across his path with a primal power that screams, *Get outta my way.*

You'd better do just that. It would be wise, too, to stay away until the dust settles.

Like the bull he's named after, the Taurus man is healthy, strong, as stolid as they come. The women are physically strong as well, and both genders can eat virtually anything without a trace of indigestion. Add a Virgo moon or ascendant, though, and the picture changes radically. Then they may be picky eaters, with a heavy emphasis on health foods and diet consciousness.

Their necks often take the brunt of stress or accident. A Taurus who sits for long hours at a computer may develop a chronic soreness in the neck that eventually extends into the muscles of the shoulders and arms. Massage, chiropractic treatments, and acupuncture can help mitigate discomfort. Both men and women of the sign benefit from regular exercise, whether it's a workout in the gym, yoga, or long, brisk walks. Taureans generally enjoy gardening, hiking, canoeing, anything that takes them into the outdoors. Their love of nature feeds their solitary souls and invigorates them, renews their spirits.

The Taurus man enjoys women, hardly a surprise since he's Venus ruled. But he isn't the type, like Aries, to pursue a woman to the ends of the earth, courting her with flowers and gifts and late-night phone calls in which he proclaims his undying passion. His methods are more subtle, dilatory, thoughtful. A prolonged look across a crowded room. A call that sets your heart on fire. He won't bring you roses, but he may bring you a lush bird of paradise for Valentine's Day. Or he may bring you a bouquet of wildflowers from his garden. Don't expect a typical date with this guy. He's more likely to ask you to go canoeing or camping with him. Or he may invite you over to his place for a gourmet meal that he prepares from scratch. He won't sweep you off your feet like a Leo, but when he plays, he plays for keeps.

There are few men in the zodiac who are more patient than Taurus. He can outwait anyone or anything, especially if he wants what he's waiting for badly enough. If he is a double Taurus, with a moon or ascendant in the sign, then double the patience—and the stubbornness. He lives at his own speed, and if it doesn't match the speed at which other people live, well, so what. That's their problem, not his.

He's a warm, patient father with a generous heart. Whether his child is a male or female makes no difference to him. He can take a daughter canoeing and camping just as easily as he can a son. He gets involved, too, driving for field trips or outings, welcoming his children's friends as he would his own.

If he's sports-minded, the sports are usually of the solo variety—jogging, windsurfing, yoga, the gym. This rubs off on his kids and so does his love of books, which he enjoys as readily as he does good food and harmony.

He's astute and creative with money, part of his need for financial security. He builds his empire slowly, thoughtfully, and always outlasts the competition to succeed against whatever odds are tossed his way.

Taurus Woman

She can't abide a phony and it doesn't matter whether it's the President of the United States or a neighbor down the street. She herself is as genuine as they come, and this is evident in the people in her life. All of them, from the most intimate to the most casual, from the weirdest to the culturally extreme, are real people with real concerns, who don't have a phony bone in their bodies.

She's as resilient as her male counterpart, able to shoulder whatever extremes and hardships come her way. She's often just as still and silent, too, and won't be pushed to do what she doesn't want to do. Cajole her, scream at her, try to prod her, and she simply looks at you with those ancient eyes and stays put. Once her mind is made up, that's it. Sound familiar? She and the Taurus male obviously have many traits in common, but the traits are often expressed quite differently.

Take the bull's rush, for instance. Where a Taurus man might take umbrage to some idiot on the highway who cuts him off and goes after the guy like they're on the autobahn, the Taurus woman would lean on her horn, then forget it. But try to pull the wool over her eyes about something that is personally important to her, and her temper erupts. You don't want to be around when that happens.

Her sense of touch is as finely developed as that of the Taurus man. All her senses, in fact, are acute and sharp. The scent of a particular flower or of cookies baking in a kitchen, trigger memories for her, vivid, detailed memories. The feel of soft silk against her body is paradise. Sensual, that's what she is, and she makes no bones about it when she's smitten. She's a sensual lover, just like the Taurus male, and there are times when sex and passion become transcendental for them both, a vehicle through which they escape the gravity of Earth.

She's a good mother, a nurturer who always goes the extra mile for her kids. She's a sucker for infants and toddlers and as her own children mature, she treats them fairly. Both she and the Taurus male, however, aren't fond of clutter. Remember: home is their castle.

She isn't a complainer. Then again, neither is the Taurus male. Both of them can endure more physical discomfort than almost any other sign. They're the types who can camp under primitive conditions that would send a Scorpio or a Capricorn fleeing for the nearest Holiday Inn.

There's something of the mystic in this woman. It may take a lot to bring it out, particularly if her ideas run counter to the possibility that what you see isn't all there is. But under the surface, beneath the ego defenses and the acculturation, lies ancient knowledge that may become conscious rather quickly during the early part of the millennium. A fascination with herbs and alternative healing may manifest. She may begin delving into reincarnation, oracles, magic. Or she may simply awaken to her own power as a

Taurus. However the change comes about, she won't be quite the same person that she was in the 1990s.

She, like the Taurus male, has the ability to use her dreams to answer questions she has, to solve problems, to tap into higher wisdom. When she sleeps, her fixed and stubborn ideas about how things work, her ego's hold on reality, loosen enough for such information to come through. By consciously trying to recall her dreams and working with them to understand the symbols of her own unconscious, she can become an accomplished lucid dreamer.

There are many layers to this woman, and some of them are unknown even to her. As she enters the millennium, however, the thread of her own mysteries begins to unravel. If she's smart, she seizes that thread and follows it with the same relentless determination and grace that have brought her this far.

Taurus in the Millennium

You're already primed in many ways for the new millennium. Pluto in Scorpio prepared you through confrontations with hidden parts of yourself and taught you to release situations and people that no longer fit into your life. Now the pace picks up somewhat. You become more of who you already are, activating areas of potential in yourself that have lain dormant too long.

Your fixed ideas about things are going to change. They may change rather rapidly, which won't be to your liking at first. But as you loosen up and uncover hidden reservoirs in yourself, you get into the spirit of the change. It's like stepping into a swift, bone-chilling river. Your feet have to get used to it first.

Then your calves and thighs. When you finally dive into the river, it's because you have *chosen* to do so. That's vital to you. The choice. In the millennium, you will face a number of choices.

Energizer: As a fixed sign, the solar eclipse in Leo in August 1999 affects you more strongly than it does mutable or cardinal signs. It hits your fourth house, which represents your immediate environment, your home. Something that's concealed or hidden in this area comes to light, which you will have to confront and deal with. A pregnancy or birth of a child may be involved, or a parent who comes to stay or live with you. This event triggers your first challenge in the millennium. In some ways it might become one of the themes of your transformation.

This energizes you in new directions and you may feel the influence for several months before or after the actual event. The eclipse creates a grand cross in fixed signs and one of the planets involved is Saturn in Taurus, which is going to somehow restrict you or provide a structure or discipline that you need in your immediate environment.

Take a look at Lucas's chart. The eclipse hits his fourth house.

Catalyst: The grand alignment of seven planets in Taurus on May 3, 2000, is certainly a catalyst for you, Taurus. Not only are these seven planets in your sun sign, but they square both Neptune and Uranus in Aquarius. You're challenged to honestly evaluate your deepest attitudes and beliefs. Which beliefs no longer work? How can you expand your existing beliefs into a structure that more truly reflects who you are and who you are becoming?

The Jupiter/Saturn part of this grand alignment of

planets may trigger unexpected changes in your career, allowing for new opportunities. Don't burn any bridges during this career change, but stay clear about your goals.

During the 1993 Uranus and Neptune conjunction in Capricorn, a fellow earth sign, you were able to change or not change—the pressure was minimal. But now the heat is turned way up. Whatever seeds you planted during the 1990s, whatever changes you initiated, now become visible. Do you like what you see? Does your life, in general, reflect how you see yourself? If you could change things in your life, what would you change? This alignment prompts you to ask yourself some rather hard questions with profound ramifications.

The initial process goes on just beneath the surface for you, Taurus, in those still waters of your inner life. During the early part of the millennium, pay close attention to your dreams; they hold vital clues about where you're headed.

Transformation: Pluto in Scorpio wasn't much fun for you. Situations surfaced that you didn't want to deal with and you were urged to make some significant changes in your life. In Sagittarius, Pluto is moving through the metaphysical part of your life, prompting you to find your own truths, speak those truths, and live them even if everyone else around you disagrees or is completely perplexed by what you're saying and doing.

During this process, you're going to encounter parts of yourself that may have gotten the short end of your attention in the past. Your roles in relationships could be affected—as a spouse, a parent, a coworker. Things that you've kept to yourself won't be private anymore. But this is your choice, the result of your discoveries.

If you have your birth chart, find the house with Sagittarius on the cusp. Note the degree on that cusp. Between January 1, 2000, and November 27, 2008, the degrees of Pluto range from 11 to 29 degrees in Sagittarius. Unless your Sagittarius house begins at one degree, Pluto will be traveling through at least two houses in your birth chart. These houses represent the areas where Pluto will bring about your greatest transformation.

Innovation: For seven years, from 1996 to 2003, Uranus in Aquarius gives you the opportunity to make brilliant strides in your career. Whatever seeds you sow, changes you make, or innovations you put forth during these years bring terrific dividends for the next fifteen to twenty years.

By the beginning of the millennium, Uranus has already been in its home sign for four years, so you've already seen evidence of what it can do. Your intuitive skills undoubtedly have deepened and continue to do so through the early part of the millennium, until they are completely integrated into who you are.

Your intuition is like a beam of light that travels out into this new millennium several steps ahead of you, Taurus, testing the waters, sampling probabilities. Trust its voice. Listen to it. That voice is bolstered by Neptune in Aquarius, and is going to get a lot louder as you move through the millennium.

At the end of 2006, your entire belief system expands to embrace things that a decade earlier were unimaginable to you. You may look back to the person you were in 1996 and wonder who he or she was. Your ideals are now firmly in place.

New paradigms: In July 2005, when Saturn goes into Leo, squaring your natal sun, you feel pressured by whatever you perceive as authority—a domineering parent, teacher, mentor, boss, even the larger society of rules and regulations. You also feel more confident and better able to assert your individuality.

Guard against the bull's rush at this time. If you feel the urge to tell off someone who has power over you, take a couple of deep breaths and walk away. Then go out into a field or into your room and scream or beat a pillow or take a five-mile run. Do something to vent your anger. This is part of your new paradigm, Taurus, to direct the bull's rush elsewhere. Don't just bite your tongue and internalize it, because that could impact your health. Get rid of it in a way that doesn't involve anyone else.

Another component of your new belief system is to nurture your belief in yourself. Your tremendous willpower can bring about change in any area of your life. All you have to do is apply it, believe in it, then trust the process. In some ways, this is something you've been working up to for most of your life.

Truth within: Your idealism and newfound beliefs are fairly well integrated by the time Uranus is midway through Pisces. In late 2005, Jupiter in Scorpio opposes your natal sun, a positive time for tremendous growth in all areas of your life. Everything comes more easily now and you'll be tempted to pursue everything you want in the material sense. Nothing is wrong with that, but you also need to maintain an inner awareness of what you're doing.

In the fall of 2006, someone in power supports your idealism and newfound beliefs. If you've handled the Jupiter transit well, this could be a time for culmination for you.

Uranus in Pisces from 2003 through 2010 is a time when friends may provide the impetus and opportunities you need in some area of your life. The personal truth that you've been nurturing finds new expression, perhaps through the very groups that offer you new opportunities. The visualizations, meditations, and inner work that you've been doing now pay off in tangible ways. You seek to bring your knowledge into a wider sphere so that it will affect the larger world.

Spiritual expansion: Initially, you feel uncomfortable with Neptune in Aquarius. You're an earth sign, Aquarius is air. And yet you're able to utilize the blurring that occurs between reality and illusion. By living consciously, you're able to delve into what is mystical and hidden in you and use it to expand your spiritual awareness.

This can happen in odd, unexpected ways—reconnecting with friends you haven't seen in years, a visit to the town where you grew up, or discovering some new place that touches that mystical part of you. On an inner level, you may experience out-of-body experiences and vividly detailed dreams that address some concern that you have in waking life. Somehow, the internal and the external come together for a period of time. They merge, they blend, they change you at profound levels.

By the time Neptune moves into Pisces from 2012 to early 2025, you're on your path, Taurus, a conscious, self-realized individual.

Self: Back to Ferdinand. You're in that field, just minding your own business, enjoying the beauty of the day. Those scents. The light. The softness of the grass under your feet. Then along comes that grand alignment in your sun sign, the equivalent of the bee that stung the bull. The actual event doesn't last long; Mars moves into Gemini the next day, joined a day after that by the moon, and nine days later by Mercury.

But the repercussions of that sting are likely to be felt for quite a while. Look what the bee sting did to Ferdinand's life, turned it inside out, upside down, and he still ended up exactly where he was supposed to be. And so will you.

During the early part of the millennium, all of us are being pushed away from what is familiar and understood. The uncertainty of what lies ahead may drive us half crazy and, at times, seems to send our lives straight into chaos. But when we come out on the other side, we are better and improved versions of what we were. Even Ferdinand didn't go back to business as usual in that field after his trip to Madrid. Now he looked behind him before he sat down. Now he lived *consciously*. And so will you.

If you were born between 1940 and 1957, then your natal Pluto is in Leo and is opposed by Neptune in Aquarius. Part of what this opposition brings is an upheaval of the power structure, similar to what this generation did in the sixties. By the same token, it softens the power the 1940–1957 generation has had for so long and urges them not to resist whatever is coming. On a personal level, this means surrender and go with the flow.

You feel pretty good when a planet is in an element that's compatible with earthy Taurus. So you're going to do just fine with Uranus in Pisces from 2003 through 2010. Pisces takes you deep, but not with the same intensity that Scorpio does. You have more time to get accustomed to it. You come through the passage with a new understanding of your own power.

Finances: No two ways about it. That grand alignment in May 2000 leaves you *security conscious.* You need, you want, you desire, you have, you wish, you seize, you fail, you triumph. Within a week, you feel a little more comfortable with your financial situation and already have new ideas about earning and investing money. By July 2000, real estate looms as a viable possibility.

In the summer of 2002, your self-restraint is tested. Usually, you're the very paragon of self-restraint, but while Jupiter in Leo is square to your natal sun, pride can get the best of you. By the same token, this represents a time of incredible opportunity for you. The deep confidence you feel urges you to be adventurous, to sample new financial opportunities.

In the summer of 2005, you feel more balanced about everything, and this is reflected in your financial situation. Between then and the fall of 2006, you may have legal details to attend to, but as long as you keep your cool, it's nothing to worry about.

In fact, not worrying and obsessing about money is part of what you learn in the millennium. You finally understand that money is energy, nothing more, nothing less. If you can create debt in your life, then you can also create wealth. If you can create wealth, then you can create joy. And if you can create joy, then you can create virtually anything.

Communication: The ways in which you communicate change dramatically during the first decade of the millennium. You don't become more verbose, Taurus. But you're (smartly) no longer hesitant to communicate what you're thinking or feeling. That private mulling you've been doing until now just won't work anymore in your interactions with others. You can't assume that others divine what you think or feel. You can't assume anything.

If you've had a rocky relationship with a sibling in the past and are still locked into the old negative patterns, now is the time to break those patterns by saying what you think or feel. Do it gently but firmly.

When Jupiter goes into Capricorn at the end of 2007, you find the structure that allows you to communicate your truths to a larger audience. Maybe you write and publish a book that encompasses these truths. You might transmit these truths to your children or your spouse or your employers. You might find that you're telepathic. Or perhaps you sense what your family pets are feeling. However this plays out, you begin to live your truths in the most conscious way possible.

When success and financial abundance flow into your life, you're ready for it in the elevated sense of the word.

Your home: Children play a prominent part in your life during the early part of the millennium. They might be your own children. But they may also be children that you teach, children of friends, or children that you reach through your creative work.

Midsummer of 2005, when Saturn goes into Leo, squaring your natal sun, issues in and around your home require your attention. In late 2006, Jupiter joins Pluto in Sagittarius and conjuncts it in late 2007.

During this period your ideals expand and spill over somehow into your home life.

If you work out of your home, this expansion of ideals may translate into renovations on your house. You may change the color scheme, buy new furniture, or add an addition to the house. Neptune in Aquarius attracts people into your home for group activities that may include past-life regressions or group work with meditation or yoga.

Creative potential: As you begin to change, your goals and creative interests expand. Uranus in Pisces from 2003 until late May of 2010 brings about heightened intuition and the ability to delve deeply into the unconscious for inspiration. During this period your dreams are a source of ideas, so pay attention to them. Work to understand them. Decipher the symbols of your personal unconscious.

In the summer of 2005, when Saturn goes into Leo, squaring your natal sun, you may go through periods of discouragement. Authority figures seem to be working against you, restricting your freedom. Your best response is to work patiently and calmly, with your sights always on your goals. Focus on your creative projects that are successful and realize that ideas or projects that fall away from your life are inconsequential, even if you can't see that now. Through your perseverance, this period becomes merely a trial that helps to clarify your goals.

By fall of 2007, the pressure has eased considerably. You probably have more work than you can handle and love every minute of it. In December, Jupiter goes into Capricorn, which boosts your professional life. Your creativity literally hums along. Just go with the flow, Taurus. Follow your creative impulses and don't listen to that left-brain censure that whispers, *Prove it to me.* Flexibility is required of you now, not just in your external life, but within yourself. Your very *consciousness* needs to become more flexible if you're going to keep your creativity running at full steam.

Health & work: Your neck is the strongest part of your body. In fact, most Taureans have thick, sturdy necks. If you have a moon or rising in Taurus, your neck may be noticeable in some way, too. As your body's "shock absorber," your neck takes the brunt of your tension. Usually it can take quite a lot of abuse, but there are times when those muscles ache so much, even the bull can't stand it and seeks relief.

Massage and chiropractic treatment help. So does yoga. But in the millennium, Taurus, part of what you have to learn is to communicate with your body. What condition, event, or relationship in your life is "a pain in the neck"? Look at physical problems as symptoms of some inner condition. Look at them as oracles. What's the message? What is the pain trying to tell you?

Being as strong as a bull—literally—stems from your relentless determination and stubbornness. You're able to endure physical discomfort that would drive the rest of the zodiac crazy or to the nearest emergency room. But when you're worn down—which neck pain usually indicates—and don't stop, then swollen glands, sore throats, and thyroid problems may be the end result. So stop and enter into a dialogue with your body.

How do you do that? One Taurus did it through a dream.

The man was stung in the heel by a stingray while

he was out windsurfing. Although the pain was excruciating, he endured it in typical Taurean fashion and didn't seek medical help. The pain began to subside within several hours. By the next day, the site of the sting had become infected. He treated it with the usual over-the-counter remedies.

Within two weeks the sting hadn't healed completely. He felt the stinger might be inside, so he probed around with a needle, which infected it again. Then he went windsurfing one afternoon and was stung by a bee in the same heel, within three yards of where the stingray had gotten him. With this glaring "coincidence," he realized he'd better figure out what the stings were really about.

He asked for a dream that would throw some light on the real meaning behind the stings. The dream, too lengthy to recount, made him realize what should have been obvious: *that he should watch where he stepped, or he would get stung where he was most vulnerable* (*Achilles' heel*). At the time he was involved in a writing project with another man. The novel had movie interest, and his percentages weren't spelled out. He felt vulnerable and took steps to rectify it.

Within several days the sting site had healed completely.

Partnerships: Venus-ruled, you're the perennial lover, a man or woman who enjoys everything that comes with romance. That won't change in the millennium. The changes have to do with letting go.

This doesn't mean severing ties with your significant others. It simply means allowing people you love the freedom to express themselves. Even if your business partner eats Twinkies and drinks diet Coke for breakfast and you, as a vegetarian, eat healthy foods and jog six miles a day, your partnership shouldn't be affected.

Maybe your significant other is a clutter freak, one of those people whose work area is strewn with papers and books, and your work area is pristine, ordered. Does that give you the right to stroll into his or her work area and make caustic remarks about the clutter? Granted, some order could help this person thrive. Yet this clutter is self-expression, just as your pristine work area expresses who you are.

These are petty details, but you get the point, Taurus. As you learn to give others the space to express themselves, you find that they give you the same freedom. In the end, you realize that what really matters in any relationship, whether business or personal, is that each person feels comfortable to be who they are. Only then do you know for sure the real person you love!

Spirituality: Your religious affiliation, if you have one, matters less in the millennium than your questions and feelings concerning the cosmic issues. The biggies. What happens when you die? Where do you come from? What is God? *Is* there a God? And how do you fit into the overall picture?

If you've followed an organized religion throughout your life, you may find that it no longer answers questions to your satisfaction. Everything may begin to sound the same to you, fear-based and shortsighted. If you have never known what you believed, then you're going to find out during the first decade of the millennium. And if you left the religion you were raised with and now believe in a little of this and a little of that, then you're going to be redefining the fine points.

In the end, spiritual thought in the millennium may boil down to two factions. On the one side will be those who believe that God is an external force that rules each of our lives, while others will believe that God is beyond anything we can imagine, a force or power that endowed us with free will to write the scripts of our lives.

If you fall on the side of fear, Taurus, then you will be called upon to confront those fears. If you fall on the side of free will, then you will be called upon to confront your will and all its ramifications. It doesn't get any simpler or more complex than that.

Career & profession: This area improves dramatically during the millennium. Again, though, it requires risk on your part. It requires that leap into the void that Carlos Castaneda wrote about with such eloquence. It requires a leap of faith, Taurus. And you, better than anyone, understand what such a leap could entail.

You may decide to start your own business, which would require a leap of faith in your own abilities. Any earth-oriented business would be beneficial for you as would anything dealing with finances. In the summer of 2005, Jupiter in Libra brings you luck through other people in work matters. You make the right connections and are in the right place at the right time.

While Jupiter is going through Libra, Saturn goes into Leo, squaring your natal sun. This tests your career goals because you may encounter obstacles from people who have authority over you. But if you think of it as a weeding process that removes the inessential from your life, you should get through this two-year transit intact.

Personal unconscious: As you enter the millennium, it all begins for you *within.* The contents of your own being become more obvious as you work consciously with your beliefs and bring your enormous willpower to any endeavor that you undertake. You perceive the intimate link between your beliefs and your experience. As a result, your consciousness becomes more flexible, allowing you to experiment with altered states through meditation, yoga, and similar venues.

The millennium awakens the mystic in you.

Tapping the Source

Synchronicities & Your Inner Oracle

A synchronicity can occur about virtually anything, at any time. You tend to be more aware of synchronicities that many people, perhaps because you're in less of a hurry than your air and fire cousins. But unless you pay attention, they're of no use to you.

In the story about the Taurus man who was stung twice, the second sting was the synchronicity—same heel, at nearly the same location as the first sting, within two weeks of the first sting, and also while windsurfing. The second sting reinforced the need to understand what the stings symbolized. If the man had figured it out after the first sting, perhaps the second sting wouldn't have happened because the same *need to know* wouldn't have been there.

You won't lack for synchronicities in the new millennium, Taurus, but you should try to decipher the experience as soon as it happens. Here are some tips to make that easier:

1) Write down the experience as soon as you can after it happens. Include details like the time of day it happened, the particulars involved, and how the synchronicity made you feel. Also include what you were doing when it happened.
2) Note the key words in what you've written. In the sting example, key words might be sting, heel, stingray/bee, sudden pain.
3) Did the synchronicity revolve around a name? Numbers? A part of the body? A date or a particular time? What type of activity were you doing? Attempt to see the underlying theme. Sometimes, in order to understand a synchronicity, you have to go to other sources.

   In the example of the woman for whom 33 was a recurring number while traveling, she had to go to the *I Ching* before she began to understand what the synchronicity meant.
4) Interpret the synchronicity as though it were a dream. Who are the major players? What are they doing? What happens in the dream?
5) Keep a notebook or open a computer file for recording these experiences. Over a period of time, you'll notice recurring themes and symbols. This is your own unconscious speaking to you. Pay attention.

Creating Your Future

You're especially good at conscious creation through the use of your body. When your physical self is involved in something, you quite often tune in on other realms and dimensions. Yoga, hikes, canoeing, windsurfing, swimming, workouts at the gym: any of these activities engage your physical self and free up inner energy that can be used to create your future. The physical activities can be augmented with five minutes of meditation at some point in your day to help you focus on what you're trying to create.

Since touch is such an important sense to you, you may want to find a stone or an animal figure that embodies your personal power. As you meditate, touch the object, rub it, become aware of its texture and how it feels in your hand. Imagine that the object links you with the future you want to create.

In your journey through the millennium, you're sure to find other methods that work for you. But the most important thing to remember, Taurus, is that *your point of power lies in the present.*

Chapter 11

Gemini, the Twins

May 21–June 21
Mutable, Air
Ruled by Mercury

Gemini Man

Imagine two men in a single body. One is witty, inquisitive, with a voracious appetite for words and language. He has so much restless, nervous energy that he's usually ten feet ahead of you when you're walking. He's into everything—books, movies, art, theater, music, and he can talk about all these things in the space of a single breath. His way with words is so slick, so utterly seamless, that you're convinced he's an Einstein in disguise. He knows exactly what he believes—but only right now, in this moment. By tomorrow, it may be have changed.

Then there's the other man, the darker twin, the one who can be moody and petulant, critical and impatient. His words are sharp, capable of cutting you to nothing in seconds flat. He breaks dates and appointments with complete indifference to the inconvenience this may create for other people. He's here today and literally gone tomorrow without so much as a call, a note, or an explanation.

Welcome to the Gemini world, a place where just about everything you see may be totally changed five minutes from now. Geminis of both genders are hard to pin down for the long run. They're social butterflies, ephemeral, whimsical, and difficult to know because they usually don't allow you to see their deepest hearts. Quite often this is because they aren't sure what lies in their hearts. The terrain changes too often.

Gemini is a mental sign, and it's in this arena that they shine. They excel as writers and editors, in public relations and advertising, in publicity and in sales. They're so adaptable that they've been called chameleons, able to blend and change in the blink of an eye to fit whatever situation they're in. This adaptability is one of their survival mechanisms.

The Gemini man, like his female counterpart, is so quick with words that you're better off not arguing with him. He'll talk circles around you. He'll literally make you dizzy with his arguments and counter arguments, taking opposing sides with such ease that by the end of the debate you're not sure what side he's on.

He's flirtatious. This holds true whether he's seriously committed or not and shouldn't be something that offends you if you're involved with him. Most of the time it doesn't mean anything other than the fact that he enjoys the woman he's talking with.

Many people assume that Geminis are prone to marrying at least twice, but there's no hard-and-fast rule. What *is* true is that Geminis are capable of doing more than one thing at a time. Your Gemini man, for instance, might be flirting with a woman on the other side of a room, rewriting a chapter of his book in his head, and listening to the radio or TV. His energy isn't scattered; it's simply engaged to its fullest.

For Gemini men and women, things come in twos. It's not uncommon to find them holding down two jobs to pay for two houses and two cars. Or they may have two primary passions in life—one that's expressed through their work and another that's expressed in their free time.

The Gemini man usually makes a good father. He isn't particularly structured in his approach to his children, which the kids love even if his wife doesn't (unless she's a Gemini, too). He's the dad who buys books for his kids, encourages their verbal expression, and makes sure they're offered a vast panoply of experiences—dance, soccer, horseback riding, baseball, camp, swimming, and books books books.

Most Geminis are slender, with widely set eyes. This can be mitigated somewhat by the sign of the ascendant and moon. If you meet a Gemini with a soft round face and body to match, then Cancer or Pisces may be prevalent in his chart. Both men and women of the sign need a lot of rest to even out the pace at which they live. But they generally aren't sound sleepers, and all that nervous energy allows them to get by with much less sleep than they need.

If you're intent on involvement with a Gemini man, then always remember there are two of him and one of you. No matter how you do the math, it comes up with three is a crowd. You won't change that, so either accept it or move on.

Gemini Woman

Remember that movie *The Three Faces of Eve*? Well, loving or living with a Gemini woman can be a bit like that. You're never sure which twin you'll wake up next to in the morning. Will it be the charmer with the quick wit and the explosive laugh? Or will it be the petulant twin who has her own agenda this morning, an agenda that may not include you?

This woman always has a lot going on in her life. Some of it may be frivolous by your standards, but that won't stop her from indulging. After all, she lives according to her own standards, not yours, not anyone else's. She makes this known in a pleasant way, unless you keep bugging her about it, then she simply gets fed up and, well, a bit cold. But she keeps doing things her own way.

If Uranus is conjunct a Gemini sun, then it's quite likely she needs her freedom the way an Aries, for instance, needs romance. You can't pin her down unless she chooses to be pinned down. She may not be marriage material with this configuration, but then again, that depends on your definition of "marriage material." If you're looking for mental stimulation and excitement, for variety and a certain touch of enigma, then she fits the ticket.

Your best route to a Gemini woman's heart is through her intellect. Unless the intellectual camaraderie is there, the romance won't last. Although great cooks are fine, food is never going to be the focus of her life. And if you're into sports, she'll join you in the sorts she likes. Even though the sexual chemistry between you is important, you must romance her mind. Be as passionate about her intellectual interests as she is, and she's yours for life.

In business, she's quick to learn and eager to put her knowledge to work. What she doesn't know probably won't hold her back because her glib facility with language and her easy way with people covers the gaps. If she has a moon or a rising in an earth sign, then she probably is going to be happiest working for herself in some capacity. If she has a moon or a rising in a water sign, she may be quite intuitive.

Like her Gemini brother, she has strengths and weaknesses as a parent. She isn't much of a nurturer in the traditional sense, not like a Cancer mother. She won't enjoy playing dolls with her daughters or rolling around on the floor in foot combat with her sons. But she loves talking to and listening to her children. The flow of communication is open and bilateral. Yes, she gets distracted by a million other things, but when her children need her, she's there. She brings books, she nurtures their artistic and intellectual interests, she stirs up their passions, and through all the talking, she communicates that it's fine for them to express who they are.

She's a good friend to other people, compassionate when compassion is called for, helpful when they need help. But she can't abide people who take up her time with what she considers petty concerns and problems. Don't call her daily just to gossip or gripe or bitch about things. Be direct, be honest, state your case, then sign off.

Gemini rules the parts of the body that come in pairs: lungs, arms, shoulders, hands, and the nervous system in general. When they're ill, it usually shows up in one of those areas. Even though they rarely look their age and feel younger than they are, they benefit through sensible diets, regular exercise, and all the things the experts say promote longevity. But Geminis, naturally, have their own ideas about health and have to discover it for themselves.

Gemini in the Millennium

You're so adaptable that the rapid changes coming about during the millennium should stimulate you and satisfy your urge for the new, the experiential. You'll have opportunities to communicate to a wider audience, but should develop an acute awareness about *what* you communicate. This process actually began in late 1995, when Pluto went into Sagittarius, which may have resulted in dramatic changes in your personal and professional life.

During the first decade of the millennium, Gemini, you're going to find that when you change just for the sake of change, it leaves you empty. There must be purpose now to any changes you make in your environment. As you hone and polish your goals, it's easier for you to stay focused on what you want and where you're going.

Energizer: The solar eclipse in Leo in 1999 hits your third house of communication. Since this house also deals with siblings, neighbors, and your fundamental thinking process, something that has been concealed or hidden in that area comes to light.

Maybe you've had an unsatisfying relationship with a brother or sister. The eclipse brings the reasons for that into your conscious awareness and you can now confront and deal with it. If you have enemies in your neighborhood, you now find out who they are. Perhaps you're writing a book and have gotten stuck; now you identify whatever is blocking you, deal with it, and move ahead. There are numerous and varied ways the eclipse can work.

For several months on either side of the eclipse, you feel the change as an internal process. You know something is going on, but may not be sure *what* it is. Whatever comes to light becomes one of your "themes" for the millennium.

Catalyst: The grand alignment of planets in Taurus on May 3, 2000, which squares Neptune and Uranus in Aquarius, is going to make you feel unbalanced for a while. The alignment hits your twelfth house of the personal unconscious, so probably a lot of *stuff* will surface that you have to deal with. The Jupiter/Saturn conjunction in Taurus during this alignment expands your understanding of the issues you have to ideal with and provides a structure in which you can do it.

During the conjunction of Uranus and Neptune in Capricorn in 1993, certain things you took for granted in your life began to break down and fall away. This was a necessary step that allowed you to expand your communication skills. A relationship with a brother, sister, or neighbor may have begun to change or break up at this time. Whatever the events and the changes, you had to adapt and move on.

Transformation: By the time Pluto moved into Sagittarius in 1995, your transformation was well underway and it continues through 2008. You're called upon to communicate your truth now, Gemini, and are given ample opportunities to do exactly that. First, of course, you have to know what your truth is.

If, by the beginning of the millennium, you are still uncertain about the nature of your particular truth, then you'd better get busy and find out. The old ways of communicating don't work as well anymore, Gemini, and this is as true in your relationships as it is in your professional life. Sagittarius, after all, is your polar opposite, and if nothing else, it demands that you be truthful with yourself. If you are, then you can understand your feelings about where you want to go from here.

Look at your birth chart and find the house with Sagittarius on the cusp. What degree is it? Between January 1, 2000, and November 27, 2008, the degrees of Pluto in Sagittarius range from 11 to 29 degrees. Unless the house with Sagittarius on the cusp is at one degree, Pluto travels through at least two of the houses in your birth chart. These houses represent the areas where Pluto will bring about the deepest changes in your life.

For one Gemini, Pluto in Sagittarius affected his second house of finances and opposed his natal sun in the eighth. His career bottomed out and he went into debt. He was forced to find new ways to bring in income and turned to his deepest interests to do that. In his birth chart, Pluto sits in his tenth house of profession and careers, so this is the area—natally—where he experiences his deepest transformations.

By early 1997, when Pluto's impact in his second house had begun to stabilize, he was earning income doing what he loved best and his entire professional life opened up again. This is how Pluto operates.

Check out the house positions for your North and South Nodes in your birth chart. The sign and house placement of your South Node holds clues about the truths you're leaving behind and the North Node offers a direction in which you can go.

In the spring of 2004, Mars goes into Gemini for several months, which should infuse you with renewed energy. For five months in 2007, Pluto turns retrograde, so you may find old issues cropping up again. This won't be a problem if you've done the inner work this transit requires.

Innovation: For seven years, from 1996 to 2003, Uranus in Aquarius gives you the opportunity to renovate your entire belief system and the ways in which you live those beliefs. During this period it's important that you set aside times for yourself when you can chill out, answer to no one, and do whatever your heart desires. Read. Watch movies. Browse at bookstores. Do Gemini things. You need these periods to absorb and assimilate the changes going on in your life so that you're better equipped to apply them practically.

In the summer of 2002, Jupiter goes into Leo, which holsters your communication skills. During the next year, you experiment with your beliefs by using visualization and affirmations. Geminis usually aren't very big on meditation, perhaps because they don't like sitting still too long, but if you try it for a few minutes a day, it speeds up the manifestation process.

During this time, you join groups that share your interests and beliefs and discover the power of collective energy. Group activities, even if they're something you attend just once a month, help to clarify your goals and personal vision. Since you don't like to be held down to any particular time schedule, don't sign up with any group for the long haul until you're sure you want to be a part of it. The idea here, Gemini, is to be a part of a group as much for what it offers you as for what you bring to it. Experiment with collective energy, be innovative, and then bring what you learn to your communication skills.

New paradigms: At some point in 1998, things may have gotten a little fuzzy for you in some area of your life. The clue lies in your birth chart, in the house with Aquarius on the cusp. This house represents an area where something began to dissolve for you when Neptune went into Aquarius. Boundaries began to erode. The structure started to decay.

Say that Aquarius rules the fourth house in your birth chart. With Neptune in Aquarius transitting, your home life began to undergo some sort of change. This change was probably subtle at first, with fissures appearing in the structure that holds your home life together. Perhaps one of your parents got ill. Maybe your spouse or significant other began to drift away from you. Or maybe you started writing the great American novel. This transit doesn't have to be bad; it's simply that the boundaries and structures that hold this most personal of houses together start to dissolve.

As the millennium opens, you probably have a much clearer picture about what's eroding. You may not understand all the ramifications yet, but you won't be as confused as you were in 1998. In fact, the new beliefs that you've been nurturing should help you make the most of this transit.

Neptune's job, especially in Aquarius, is to make you question the beliefs that you hold to be immutable. Perhaps you have identified so closely with your profession that you have *become* the work you do. In that case, Neptune teaches you otherwise, and yet its eye is always on the big picture. And it's this big picture that becomes your new paradigm.

When you toss Uranus into the Aquarian pot with Neptune, things get very strange indeed, even for you, Gemini. You suddenly discover that all this erosion and dissolving that's been going on allows you to uncover levels of awareness in yourself that you never knew existed. You might experience startling synchronicities, prophetic dreams, and may turn to some kind of oracle as a tool for self-knowledge. The tarot. The *I Ching*. Runes. Maybe you even take up the study of astrology.

You, the most mental of sun signs, learn just how powerful your thoughts are, especially when combined with intent, desire, and vivid imagination. Once you integrate this lesson into who you are, you begin to meet people who reflect your emerging paradigm of beliefs.

This whole process becomes much easier for you in the summer of 2005, when Saturn goes into Leo, sextiling your natal sun. This is an opening for personal and professional advancement, a time of opportunity. You, however, will have to recognize the opportunities, seize them, and then fulfill whatever is required of you. During this period your hard work and any goals you make should take you exactly where you want to go. At some point during the two and a half years of this transit, you may be publicly recognized for your efforts and achievements.

By the autumn of 2007, the groundwork you did for the last two and a half years may be challenged in some way by your employers, your boss, a parent, whoever you perceive as authority. Don't give in to discouragement. Trust the process and the inner work you've been doing, and let the pattern unfold. Defend your own work, but avoid open confrontations.

Truth within: Isn't this what you've been working toward, Gemini? Knowing who you are at the deepest levels of your being? Your opinions should last longer now than a New York minute. Uranus in

Pisces, in fact, gives you the perfect venue for expressing who you are; Pisces is a mutable sign, just like Gemini. Even though the water element isn't particularly compatible with air, the pair of fish get along well with your twins.

Your intuition is at an all-time high and you use it to its fullest in both your personal and professional lives. Your ideals now begin to connect in a personally meaningful way with your work. Groups that you're a part of or which you join during this time are loose enough to contain your energy without making you feel imprisoned.

In December 2006, Jupiter joins Pluto in Sagittarius, your polar opposite, and opposes your sun. This should be a time of expansion and luck in every area of your life. You literally reap what you've sown.

Spiritual expansion: The years that Neptune is an Aquarius are actually good ones for you, Gemini, once you understand the rules of the game. Aquarius isn't just an air sign; it's one with which you feel very compatible.

Through this period it becomes increasingly obvious to you that your individuality isn't being swallowed by group energy. You're able to perceive the connections among all people, all living things. If you have a special bond with animals, this is the period when that bond flourishes and deepens.

Neptune enters Pisces, the sign that it rules, in 2012 and stays there until early 2025. This is when you feel as if you're living inside a hologram, when the whole is greater than the sum of its parts and the parts contain the whole. In ordinary life, this translates as a sense of being connected to something greater than yourself, and yet you contain that greater something as well.

Self: Maybe, in the back of your mind, you've got this secret dread about the millennium because some of the millennial fever has rubbed off on you. *Who, me?* you're saying, as you stash away food and supplies. *No way.*

It's time to empower yourself, Gemini, and that's what the first decade of the millennium is about for you. To a stranger, of course, it would seem that you're already empowered, that you don't have a care in the world. This popular misconception of Gemini can be as irritating to you as someone who thinks Geminis are flakes or schizophrenics.

By the summer of 2000, you've found the right rhythm, at least for the moment, and feel an urge to broaden your perspective on life. You may decide to go back to school, travel abroad, or do something that takes you out of restrictive circumstances. Your optimism carries you forward, your excellent health makes you feel invincible. Just be careful that you don't go overboard in whatever you decide to do. Don't blow every penny you have.

At this time you're also going to be working hard at whatever you do. Be careful about taking on too many responsibilities at once. Instead, complete the things you're working on to the best of your ability.

By the summer of 2004, with Uranus in Pisces square your natal sun, you may feel friction about what you're doing. For some Geminis it could go deeper than mere friction; it might be one of those crises where you start questioning everything you're doing. You're feeling rebellious, restless, on edge. Every disruption seems to deepen the crisis. But if you persevere in your path, whatever it is, and deal with each crisis as it arises, instead of trying to suppress it or ignore it in the hopes it'll go away, then you'll be ready to reap the benefits through the latter half of the decade.

Finances: At the rate you move, who has time to pay bills? To reconcile bank statements? To invest? Most of the time, you can barely remember where you put your car keys or if you've fed the hamster or watered the plants.

The pace is going to pick up considerably in the millennium, so none of the above will get any easier. The secret to successfully navigating this part of your life is to take a few deep breaths and slow down. It's not enough to just slow down physically; you have to do it *consciously.*

One Gemini woman learned what this meant when slowing down was thrust on her. While she was out running errands one day, a link on her car's manual stick shift broke. The only gear that worked was first, so she had to putt across town at about fifteen miles an hour. At first it annoyed her, *wasting all that time.* She fumed, she ranted and raged to herself. Then, gradually, she began to look around and saw how bright and colorful everything looked. And where had that new shopping center come from? And that new housing development? And where did that beautiful shaded side street lead to?

For months she'd been racing through this very neighborhood and had never really *seen* it. Suddenly her neighborhood became something entirely new and mysterious to her, a place worthy of her exploration.

What does this story have to do with your finances

in the new millennium? *Everything.* Pay attention to the money you earn, Gemini, and how you put it to work for you. Money is energy. It symbolizes the manifestation of your beliefs. If you lack for money, then take a deep and honest look at your beliefs about money. Listen to what you say about money in casual conversations. *Oh, she's filthy rich.* Why "filthy"?

Quite often our deepest beliefs about money are reflected in casual conversations. If you catch yourself saying something like this, then explore your feelings about money and work to change your beliefs.

Look at your birth chart and find the sign on the cusp of the second house. If it's Taurus, then you can expect the alignment on May 3, 2000 to affect your financial situation. If it's Aquarius, then both Uranus and Neptune are going to be transitting that house. Your financial affairs are influenced according to the nature of the transitting planets.

Communication: This is an important area for you in the millennium and not just in the way that you communicate personally. This era will see unprecedented booms in the telecommunication industry and with your quick intellect and varied skills, you're a natural for taking advantage of the innovations. Communication is what you're about, Gemini, and the sky is really the limit here. Remain alert for opportunities, pay attention to any synchronicities that surface, and look for your niche in the boom.

Uranus is considered the higher octave of Mercury, the planet that rules Gemini, so with Uranus in Aquarius until the end of 2003, serendipitous opportunities come your way. In early June of 2004, some opportunity in the communication field opens up for you in a big way.

In January and February of 2008, you have enormous energy and are able to implement and carry out your goals. These two months, however, can be an explosive time as well, so watch your temper. Keep that Gemini humor and charm working for you.

Your home: For you, home isn't the castle that it is for a Taurus or a Cancer. But in the millennium, it may become your base of operation, your hub, the place where your mind literally hums along, planning and analyzing.

In August of 2003, Jupiter transits your fourth house. This expands your home and immediate environment in some way. You may build an addition to your house, your family expands in some way, or you may even move. You might even buy real estate. At this time Jupiter is also squaring your natal sun, which boosts your confidence in general and may cause you to overextend yourself. Use the transit wisely and don't squander the resources you have.

In your birth chart, look for the sign on the cusp of the fourth house. If it's in Sagittarius or Aquarius, then the first few years of the millennium are going to mean significant changes in and around your home and in your home life. If the sign on that cusp is Pisces, the major changes a coming after the spring of 2003.

Creative potential: Your intuition is greatly enhanced with both Uranus and Neptune in Aquarius. You may experience sudden flashes of insight and genius that your restless mind then seeks to channel in a practical way. As you learn to integrate your beliefs and goals, you find that you have more energy and drive to act on creative ideas.

In June 2007, Mars, Jupiter, Saturn, and Pluto are all in fire signs, so your energy is plentiful and focused. With Jupiter and Pluto both opposing your natal sun, this is a culmination period, and your chances for success are great. The Pluto opposition gives you enormous power, but be careful that you don't alienate those who have power over you.

Health & work: Geminis can be notorious procrastinators, and when they procrastinate about their health, the consequences can be serious. If you don't already have some sort of exercise program, then start one. The program doesn't have to be anything complicated, no personal trainers, no gym, no aerobics classes. Go walking. Ride your bike. Get a workout video. Keep it fun and do it regularly. This mitigates stress and increases your vitality.

Geminis are prone to upper respiratory problems—bronchitis, laryngitis, general congestion. When this happens, look for blocks in communication that happened several days prior to the illness or ask yourself what it is you're avoiding. Try herbal and alternative therapies before rushing off to the doctor for a quick antibiotic fix.

Your work conditions should improve considerably in the millennium. But if you find that you're getting sick more frequently, then try changing your work area. Sometimes all it takes is a rearrangement of furniture to "unblock" energy in the room or adding green plants and fresh flowers. Feng Shui has excellent suggestions in this area.

Partnerships: As you learn to communicate in new and better ways during the millennium, your relationships and partnerships should improve vastly. Part of the problem with you and your significant others is that one of the twins take a single event or conversation and picks it to death. The other twin, meanwhile, sits aside, twiddling his or her thumbs, waiting impatiently for things to move forward again. You need to learn to integrate these two sides of your personality.

Spirituality: Like most signs in the millennium, your spiritual beliefs are likely to be transformed. Until now, religion may have been an intellectual thing for you, a set of aphorisms you learned as a child and carried into adulthood.

Perhaps you still belong to the church in which you were raised. Perhaps you left organized religion a long time ago. The point is that whatever spiritual path you follow is something that you must *feel*. You have to *feel* its rightness for *you* and ignore what the people around you think about what you believe. Intellectual games in this arena don't cut it anymore, Gemini. But as you get more in touch with *who* you are, this spiritual transformation unfolds on its own.

Career & profession: The major challenge in this area is that you set goals that are in keeping with your deepest beliefs and incorporate them into the totality of your life. In a nutshell, Gemini, this means that job-hopping is pointless. Find what you love. Find what you feel passionate about it. And then go after it, using your considerable intuitive skills to feel your way through the dark.

At the end of June 2000, Jupiter in your sun sign brings luck and success in just about everything you touch. This transit lasts for about a year and makes you feel that you can do virtually anything. While this may certainly be true, don't yield to the temptation to take on everything. Saturn is also in your sun sign and that spells responsibility. A lot of it. Finish what you've started before moving on to new projects.

Personal unconscious: You already know how to tap your unconscious for the answers you need. The problem is that you probably don't take the time to do it. The reality is that it doesn't take much time. With Neptune in Aquarius, in fact, you can tap your unconscious with greater ease and less time than it might take otherwise.

Start by working consciously with your dreams. Look at it as a mental exercise. Buy a book on dreams and follow the instructions on suggestions for dreams, recalling and recording them. As you get into the rhythm of dream recall, you probably will begin to have synchronicities related to whatever issues you're working on. You may also have prophetic dreams. Use all of it, Gemini. This information comes from the deepest part of you—and who can you trust more than yourself?

Tapping the Source

Synchronicities & Your Inner Oracle

Synchronicities often happen in clusters, with several in one day, then none for a period of time, then another slew of them. Keep track of them. Even though you probably think this will be too time-consuming, especially if you're also keeping a dream notebook, it's to your advantage to do so. After all, synchronicities are messages from your inner circle.

Synchronicities, like dreams, have common themes and archetypal messages; and yet they reflect the individuality of the person who experiences them. Once you are familiar with the themes around which your synchronicities revolve, you may want to stop writing them down and simply recognize them and decipher them as they happen. Sometimes, though, the message can be complex, as in the case of the woman for whom the number 33 recurred. Then you may have to dig a little deeper, using other oracles to interpret the experience.

For some people, animals may be involved in synchronicities. One Gemini woman had a particular affinity for tree frogs. Every time a baby tree frog appeared in her house, seeming to materialize out of thin air, she knew it meant that good news was on the way. Pretty soon her husband and daughter were also on the lookout for frogs.

In one instance she and her husband and daughter returned home from a trip to find a dead frog in the family room. There was also a broken ceramic frog on the floor, apparently knocked off a shelf by one of the cats. The woman's daughter immediately remarked that bad news was on the way. She knew it involved someone in the family because the frogs were in the family room.

Two days later they received word that the woman's father-in-law had died.

Creating Your Future

Just as Taurus is particularly good at conscious creation by using his or her body as a vehicle, you're good at doing it intellectually. You may read a book or see a movie that transforms you. Another sign might have to go through years of therapy or intense inner work to make that leap.

Books are often your venue for self-discovery. If you're unfamiliar with books in this area, begin with two of the best: *Creative Visualization* by Shakti Gawain, now considered a classic in the field, and *The Nature of Personal Reality* by Jane Roberts.

Chapter 12

Cancer, the Crab

June 22–July 22
Cardinal, Water
Ruled by the Moon

Cancer Man

If you ever have any doubt about the nature of the Cancer male, just walk outside on a moonlit night and gaze upward. He's the embodiment of the celestial body that governs the sign, luminous with reflected light. Now look along the beach for a crab. Study its habits, the way it moves, how it stands utterly still or retreats into its shell when it feels threatened. Explore these two images if you really want to know a Cancer man—or a Cancer woman.

Just as Gemini relates to the larger world primarily through the mind, Cancer relates through emotions. He's kind and affectionate, moody and changeable, psychic and nurturing. But when he doesn't want to be bothered or he's hurt or doesn't want to talk about what he's feeling, he moves like the crab, sideways, evasive. Quite often he's an enigma even to himself.

When he's in a good mood, this man is filled with life. He's fun, imaginative, caring. You feel as if you can tell him anything and probably do. Even if you haven't known him long, there's something about him that urges you to spill your secrets. Don't expect him to respond by telling you *his* secrets, though. You will never touch, never know a part of this man. He's not intentionally secretive or malign about it. This is simply how he is.

And yet, you won't find the male of any other sign as generous as a Cancer. Despite his shell, he's a sucker for a sob story. He bleeds for anyone in need. But he may not be the first out of his car at the scene of the accident. Even though he makes the call to 911 from his cell phone, he holds back in the hopes that someone else will go over to the wrecked car first. This tendency toward self-preservation causes others to believe he's selfish, but it's really not that at all. In his heart he believes that his energy is finite and that he only has so much of it to go around.

In the matters of the heart, he's hard to figure. Sometimes he's so romantic you may feel you're living inside a fairy tale. Other times he's as remote as the next solar system, and nothing you say or do will change that when he's in his retreat mode. Solitude and remoteness is how he replenishes his energy, especially if you've hurt him. Even when you make up—and you will, a dozen times—he doesn't forget the slight. Twenty years may pass and someday, out of the blue, he tosses it out in vivid detail, blow by blow, and you can't even recall the incident.

His feelings about his home run deeper than that of a Taurus. Cancer's roots are forever. Even if he has moved from his place of birth, a part of him remains stuck back there, remembering how the air smelled and how soft the summer grass felt against his bare feet. Memory. He is made of memories. And on the rare occasion when he can't remember, his imagination fills in the details.

As a father, he's tops, although maybe a bit overprotective. He gives freely of his time, his love, his wisdom. His love for his family reads like a political campaign ad. No matter how much money he has stashed away for his family or himself, it's never enough. "Security" isn't in his vocabulary. He is forever hedging his bets against the future—with money, food, supplies, emotions.

The men, like the women, usually enjoy the water. They may not be into water sports per se, but the water itself is a source of pleasure, peace, and perhaps spiritual satisfaction. They like looking at it, basking beside it, swimming in it, and watching the sun rise out of and sink into it. Hardly surprising for a water sign.

Cancer Woman

Never make the mistake that you know her, really know her. You'll only be deluding yourself. She shares certain characteristics in that sense with Scorpio women, although she's not nearly as intense and is rarely vindictive. She's not an open book, and any attempts on your part to ferret out her secrets before she's ready to let you into her private world will fail.

Never lie to her. She'll eventually see through it and will cut you off cold—perhaps as quickly as you're telling the lie. Her psychic antennae hone in on you whenever you confide in her. Make no mistake, her intuition is like an X ray, powerful but subtle. A flick of the switch, a hum that lasts seconds, and presto, your heart is visible to her.

To say this woman is kind and nurturing, compassionate and maternal is a cliché. She is, of course, but there's more. She's an astute businesswoman, good at handling money, as well as an excellent psychic who may also have psychic healing ability. Like the Cancer man, she's saving against the future, against inflation, another Great Depression, against disaster and acts of God.

She isn't *domestic* in the old-fashioned sense of the word, but she can be. She's not necessarily a good cook, she enjoys consuming good food. And she's not the type who oohhs and aahhs over every infant she sees, unless the infants are hers.

Of all the signs, a Cancer sun is the easiest to spot in a crowd. That rounded face, those soulful eyes, that smooth complexion. Her body may also be rounded, but that isn't a given. Never assume anything about a Cancer. Like our notion of the moon, these people are complex, layers and layers of self that you have to peel away to find the core. And even the core may be difficult to know, to find, to scrutinize.

But know this. Don't criticize her, her children, or her home. If you aren't nuts about her decor, keep your mouth shut. If you don't like the outfit she's wearing, then find something in her attire that you admire, and compliment her on it. Like Cancer males, she shines when you appreciate her. Oh, and by the way, she isn't adverse to the limelight. True, she doesn't go after publicity like a Leo, but if fame comes her way, she'll accept it. Anne Morrow Lindbergh, Meryl Streep, Linda Ronstadt, Helen Keller: get the picture?

For both men and women, MOM is an archetypal

theme. How could it be otherwise with the moon as ruler? But we aren't just talking about mom as an abstract; we're talking about *her* mother. The woman is royalty, she's wisdom, she's the best. If you see her mother as a witch in suburban clothing, keep it to yourself.

Now: fair warning. We also associate the moon with lunacy. And, yes, she has plenty of that. So does the Cancer male. The moon governs their moods. It governs the tides of their blood. We are ninety-eight percent water, isn't that what they say? Well, just imagine what the moon does with all that H_2O. So if she gets a bit weird, blame the moon. Never, never, blame her.

Cancer in the Millennium

Forget the hordes of food you're stashing away for the earth changes in the millennium. Forget the silver and gold tucked away in your attic. Forget all that, Cancer. Pause right where you are and look around slowly. Notice the paint on your walls, the floor under your feet, the wonderful and familiar clutter of your personal life. Listen to the laughter of your children from the other room, hear the soft footfalls of your significant other on the stairs. Quite a bit of security surrounds you, don't you think?

During the millennium, you're going to redefine your attachments to all of your security blankets. This may seem disorienting at first, even a bit frightening. But ultimately, the process frees up more of your energy and allows you to create a paradigm that is more in keeping with who you are.

Energizer: The solar eclipse in Leo in August 1999 has been called "the eclipse of the century." This solar eclipse affects Cancer's money house. Something in this area that has been concealed or hidden now comes to light. It may concern your attitude about money—how you earn, spend, save, and invest. It may concern your values, which are connected to what makes you feel secure.

To find out how your personal chart is affected by the eclipse, look to the house with Leo on the cusp. The eclipse point is 18 degrees in Leo. That is the sensitive point for you. Also note where Mars, Saturn, and Uranus lie in your chart. Those are the other three points in the grand cross or grand square created by the eclipse. All the points are in fixed signs. Notice which houses all four planets occupy. These will be the areas of your life that are energized.

Look at Lucas's chart again. The eclipse point (☉18♌) hits his fourth house. It's conjunct (in the same sign and degree) his natal Jupiter (♃). For several months on either side of the eclipse, he's going to feel its impact in anything having to do with his home. Something will be brought to a head in that area, energizing him in a new direction. The conjunction with his natal Jupiter puts that planet into a higher energy state, which he'll feel when another planet transits the eclipse point.

Catalyst: The millennium ushers in new principles and beliefs that you share with like-minded individuals. For June and July of 2000, you may host these gatherings in your own home, but that may change in early August. All the planets lined up in Taurus create an imbalance between your need for friends and your need to be with your family, specifically with your children.

In July 2000, with Jupiter going into Gemini for a year, your fundamental beliefs begin to expand. You're intuition deepens, and you're able to draw on your considerable prophetic abilities to stay ahead of the changes that are unfolding around you. When Jupiter conjuncts your sun in July of 2001, your optimism blossoms, and suddenly everything and anything seems possible.

And yet, in between these moments of optimism, you feel restless and uneasy. Thank Saturn in Gemini for that. You now acknowledge that your old ways of handling people and situations don't work very well. An old cycle is ending, but the new cycle hasn't begun yet.

Transformation: This process actually started for you in late 1995, when Pluto went into Sagittarius. It probably hasn't been a very pleasant time for you because you've had to confront issues from the past, things you've buried inside yourself.

But Pluto is like a psychic plunger, thrusting into the deepest recesses of your personality to dredge up the old muck. The sooner you deal with the muck, the sooner you reap the considerable rewards of doing so. Through handling whatever Pluto tosses your way, you free up energy that can be used to create the kind of reality you want *now*. Yes, it upsets your routine, your peace of mind, even your sense of security. Even more to the point, it disturbs your memories.

The past is one of your most important reference points. You're the person who hasn't forgotten anything since the day you were born. You find comfort in these memories, get lost in them at times, feel an inordinate amount of nostalgia for *what used to be.* You're as attached to these memories as you are to your roots and your home. But these deep attachments to memories holds you back in the present.

Pluto's job is to dredge up the hurts and injuries associated with these old memories and heal them so you don't keep reexperiencing them. This enables you to build new reference points and experiences. To do this, of course, requires change, something you definitely aren't fond of, particularly when it's deep change.

The crab, after all, always scurries to the side when frightened or threatened, and that is likely to be your first reaction. Evade, then burrow into the sand to hide. With Pluto in Sagittarius, it becomes increasingly difficult to do that. If you resist, then you continue to attract situations and people who represent whatever it is you don't want to confront or deal with.

By the time the millennium opens, Pluto is 11 degrees into Sagittarius. By your birthday in late June or July, it has turned retrograde and is in 10 degrees. By your next birthday, Pluto fluctuates between 12 and 13 degrees In other words, Pluto is far enough into Sagittarius so that the hard work should be behind you and you should be enjoying its benefits. If you aren't, then you're still resisting.

In the summer of 2003, Saturn goes into your sun sign and tests what you've learned so far. In the summer of 2006, you get a financial boost and may find a creative outlet that really suits you. As Pluto travels closer to Capricorn, a cardinal earth sign that is more compatible with Cancer, you have learned a new way of thinking and feeling about yourself and your life.

Innovation: Your new perceptions and feelings urge you to be innovative, to try new things, to venture out of the areas where you have felt secure for most of your life. Uranus in Aquarius encourages you to reach out to other people in ways that were impossible for you a decade ago or even five years ago.

When you glance back toward the place you've come from, you barely recognize the person you were. It's as if you have *changed probabilities.* With your incredible memory for details, you can probably even pinpoint the juncture points where you followed one path instead of another. Now and then, you may feel a certain nostalgia for the road not taken, but these moments don't last long. You realize you couldn't have remained where you were.

You find that your psychic ability allows you to communicate with others in ways that were impossible five years ago. And these "others" may not just be people. You might look into the face of a dolphin and see not only intelligence, but sentience, compassion, and wisdom. The dolphin, in turn, responds to you as a kindred soul. These are the kinds of experience that the innovation phase makes possible for you in the millennium. The interconnection of all living things becomes a reality, not merely a buzzword.

New paradigms: Right about now, you're saying: *New paradigms? Fine, give me some examples.* So let's get specific. Up until now, Cancer, your paradigms have centered around the belief that abundance is finite, so you must hold on to what you have at all costs.

The new paradigm is this: abundance is infinite, and you live in a safe universe.

Oh, sure, you reply. *What planet are you living on, anyway? Just tune into the evening news and tell me that's a safe universe. How is abundance infinite when a third of the world's economies are collapsing?*

Forget newspapers, forget the evening news, forget fear mongers. Listen to your own heart. Heed the voice of your intuition. And turn your powerful memory toward times when it seemed that everything around you was threatened, that the lives of your friends were falling apart, and yet *you were not harmed.* Nurture the feeling you had then until the emotion is fully conscious. Then seek to integrate it completely into who you are. That's how new paradigms are born and how your personal new belief system comes into being.

Uranus in Aquarius disrupts your old way of thinking and being, and blows everything you took for granted to smithereens. Then Neptune steps in with the big idealistic picture. Suddenly you begin to piece together a new world view and find the next step in the millennial process—the truth within.

Truth within: Uranus in Pisces is an astrological oxymoron, something that looks, on the surface, like a contradiction. How can electrical and disruptive Uranus express itself in a water sign? Through intuition and the unconscious.

If you've done your inner work, Cancer, this should be a productive time for you. Uranus in Pisces trines your sun, which makes change easier for you. You feel excited about things going on in your life and are eager to try out new ideas. As you open up, new relationships, friendships, and romances flow into your life.

At some point during Uranus's transit through

Pisces, you may decide to go through therapy or you begin to study some sort of spiritual discipline that helps you understand who you are. This type of reaching out empowers you and fits seamlessly into your daily life.

This is an excellent time to establish new routines. You may join a gym, take up running, become more interested in nutrition and health. Now is a good time to quit smoking or give up other habits that may be detrimental to your health. Be cautious, however, that you don't fall back into old insecurities and patterns of thinking that can undermine all the inner work you've done.

Spiritual expansion: The foundation of this process began in 1998, when Uranus and Neptune both entered Aquarius. In 2003, Uranus goes into Pisces, but Neptune remains in Aquarius until 2012. This is the period when all your inner work should reach fruition.

You'll be fine-tuning at this time, and group involvement may be your vehicle for doing this. If you're interested in alternative healing techniques, for instance, then you may attend workshops, seminars, and retreats on various techniques. Whatever your interests now, other people play a vital role in your spiritual growth.

During this period stay away from negative people. You're like a psychic sponge now and don't need to absorb someone else's problems. Also avoid people who take advantage of your compassion by dumping their problems in your lap or who seek your friendship just to waste your time.

By navigating these fourteen years with conscious awareness, you are well prepared to confront just about anything that comes your way.

Self: Back in the mid-nineties, your intuition probably tipped you off that you were in for some dramatic changes. You undoubtedly got a taste of these changes when Pluto went into Sagittarius in 1995 and then again in 1996, when Uranus went into Aquarius. All these transitions marked turning points in your life. If you embraced the changes and sought to understand them, then by the time your birthday rolls around in the summer of 2000, you should be primed for the millennium.

In late June of 2000, Jupiter enters Gemini, which indicates an expansion in your knowledge of yourself. You may take up some sort of metaphysical study or discipline that allows you to perceive yourself in a dispassionate light. Even though your compassion for others is running at an all-time high, you're able to spot the phonies much more easily now, thus saving yourself time and aggravation.

When Jupiter conjuncts your sun in the summer of 2001, you're feeling lucky and enormously optimistic. It seems like nothing can go wrong. However, at precisely this time you shouldn't just kick back and think that everything will come to you with little effort on your part. Take advantage of how flawlessly things work for you, so that in another year you have tangible results to show for this transit.

In July of 2002, as Saturn trines Uranus, you become more comfortable with any changes you've made in your life. You seem to have a lot more patience now. This is an excellent time to work on any long-term projects—finishing your college degree, learning astrology or some other metaphysical discipline, or even building your dream home. Whatever you undertake at this time should be something that allows you to grow.

Finances: In late summer of 2002, financial opportunities come your way. Take advantage of them without going overboard, but don't horde for the future. Remember: abundance is infinite.

You may want to invest in your own home at this time, either by refurbishing it or perhaps adding onto it. You may spend money on your children's education, too, perhaps through some sort of college saving plan.

In the summer of 2003, Saturn is in Cancer and Uranus is in Pisces. With both these planets in water signs, your intuitive sense of money and finances is apt to be much stronger than usual. Saturn conjuncting your natal sun spells hard work and urges you to complete any financial projects you're involved in before taking on anything new.

The Uranus in Pisces trine to your sun lasts through the end of 2011. The effects are stronger or weaker depending on the exact degree of your natal sun—and on your willingness to develop yourself. Every time you feel flutters of panic about security and money, take a few deep breaths and repeat: *I live in a safe universe that is infinitely abundant.* In fact, it would be to your advantage to say this at night as you're falling asleep and before you're fully awake in the morning. Eventually, you're unconscious mind will believe it. Allow your money to work for you, to *flow* in the same way that water flows, filling empty spaces, never pausing.

When Pluto goes into Capricorn in early 2008, you should have a structure in place that provides you with a sense of security that won't leave you feeling obsessed.

Communication: One change that comes about for you in the millennium is the way in which you communicate with yourself, which in turn affects how you communicate with others.

The first three years are important because you learn to spend more time by yourself rather than sacrificing your time for others. During these periods of solitude and reflection, you recharge your emotional batteries and communicate with parts of yourself that you may not have realized existed until now. *I don't have time for that,* you're saying to yourself. But that's just an excuse. The bottom line is that unless you make time for yourself, then events may force you in some way to make the time.

As you learn to seek these periods of reflection, you feel less threatened generally and are able to communicate more openly and honestly with others. You may find that you don't hold back as much now. It's easier to confide in other people. You aren't as evasive as you used to be when it comes to confronting certain issues. In the past you worried about every little detail. As you begin to communicate more honestly with yourself and others, however, you discover that you worry less. Your fundamental thinking process is changing.

By the summer of 2008, the communication skills you began to develop four or five years ago now begin to pay off. So stick to your course and trust the process.

Your home: This is one of the millennial biggies for you, Cancer, and is all tied up with your most intimate and personal relationships, your family and significant other. For a number of years now, you have been the anchor for everyone else, the one who nurtures and comforts everyone else, the rock who everyone turns to in a crisis. And for a long time that role suited you. But lately you've been chafing at the bit, playing the *what if* game with yourself, and finding that you need and want more time for yourself.

So now you're going to take that time.

There are certain types of crabs that change shells the way the rest of us change clothes. In the span of a single day, they may have four or five shells they call home. Sometimes a shell might be home for as long as a few days. If the tide goes out, if a child picks up the shell they're using as home, if some other crab happens along and wants that shell, then they vacate and simply find another empty shell and settle in. They are the ocean's nomads, these crabs, and in some ways, Cancer, that's how the first several years of the millennium is for you.

In ordinary life this may translate as a complete reversal in the way you've been living. Perhaps, if your kids are grown and out on their own, you and your spouse buy a camper and take off across country. Or perhaps you buy a second home, someplace near water, where your soul can breathe more easily. Maybe you get divorced or married. Maybe you move from one state to another. However this reversal manifests for you, one thing is certain: five or ten years into the millennium, you will not be living as you are living now.

Relax and enjoy the journey.

Creative potential: In the latter part of 2005, a new creative opportunity opens up for you. Perhaps you sell a novel or a screenplay or a painting. Maybe you change professions or land a job that answers your creative urges. Maybe you have a child. Whatever the opportunity, your first impulse may be to do your usual sidestepping routine, evading it in the hopes it will go away. If you surrender to that impulse, then the road ahead only gets more difficult, more challenging, and deepens the old tapes that you play with such sublime predictability. Instead of evading the opportunity, embrace it. Be adventurous. See where it leads you. And repeat your mantra: *I live in a safe and infinitely abundant universe.*

Health & work: In the movie *As Good As It Gets,* the character Jack Nicholson played had a particular routine that defined his life. He ate lunch at a certain restaurant every day, at the same table, in the same chair. He washed his hands a dozen times a day and wouldn't step on a sidewalk crack. The routine not only defined his life, it became his life. In many ways, that's you, Cancer.

The external factors that broke Nicholson out of his mold were a dog and a woman. For you, the millennium itself is the external factor.

If you don't change willingly, then your resistance may show up as problems in your stomach or digestive tract or through difficulties in your work environment. In both instances, you must be aware of your emotional limits and boundaries. As a water sign, you benefit from proximity to water—the ocean, rivers, lakes, even a pond will do—and through drinking water, the purer the better. Seafood is beneficial to you, especially during stressful periods. This holds true if you have a moon or ascendant in Cancer or if the sign is prominent somehow in your natal chart.

One Cancer woman, for instance, lives on an island off the coast of Georgia, surrounded by water. She also makes an annual pilgrimage to a center in the

Florida keys where she swims with and interacts one on one with dolphins. These aspects of her life are not only intrinsic to who she is, they are also vital to her health and spiritual well-being.

Partnerships: As your understanding of yourself changes, so do your needs. And as your needs change, your intimate relationships change. From the fall of 2004 to autumn of 2005, you may be feeling overconfident, arrogant, and rather full of yourself and the strides you've made. And that's fine. These feelings have their rightful place in the scheme of things. But during this time, keep these feelings to yourself. Pat yourself on the back in private. Otherwise you're going to antagonize the people who are closest to you.

When Pluto enters Capricorn in late January 2008, your relationships with others is tested because of power struggles of one kind or another. This may involve your trying to make someone else understand that you or your path is correct and their path is wrong. If you're aware of what's going on, however, the conflict can be mitigated.

This period also tests the work you've done for the first eight years of the millennium. The inner work. The work with yourself. The work of understanding who you are and what you want and where you would like to go. By following your impulses and intuition in the first eight years, Pluto's transit through Capricorn will serve you well.

Spirituality: As the millennium opens, you are already questioning religious and spiritual beliefs you've held most of your life. Perhaps they no longer answer the questions you have. Or you may feel some deep dissatisfaction but aren't sure why. The bottom line is that you can't cling to a particular religious or spiritual belief just because you've always believed that way. It's not enough anymore.

As you begin to explore what *you* believe, rather than what you've been taught to believe, your intuition strengthens and you attract people and experiences that somehow clarify your search. Once you learn to trust the process that's unfolding in your life, you surrender to it and go with the flow.

Career & profession: Your professional goals seem to change with startling rapidity during the first decade of the millennium. Instead of applying the brakes, try to go with it, to get into the spirit of change. If you resist, you may have difficulties when Saturn moves into your sign in the summer of 2003.

During this two-year period, you're going to be working very hard to finish up projects that you started before the millennium opened. If you go with whatever changes are happening, you may decide to switch jobs, change careers, or completely alter your working conditions. You might, for instance, work out of your home or condense your working hours into three or four days a week so you have more time for yourself and your family.

When Uranus trines your sun from 2003 through late May of 2010, you're ready to make the needed changes in your career. You're hungry for it.

Personal unconscious: This is an important area for you in the millennium. Everything you need to work with and to change begins inside, in those deep recesses where your memories lie. By developing your intuition, you're able to delve into those areas and illuminate them.

There are many ways to do this. Dream work, therapy, writing, art, drama, charity or volunteer work, oracles: go with whatever feels right to you. Whatever venue you select, start paying attention to the contents of your conscious mind. What you think. What you think about. Your reaction to people and events. What do these things tell you about your deepest beliefs and needs? If someone close to you irritates you, ask why. Look deeper. What part of you is that individual reflecting?

Once you get into the rhythm of living *consciously*, everything opens up for you.

Tapping the Source

Synchronicities & Your Inner Oracle

One way to initiate synchronicities in your life is to actively seek them. The best way to start the process is by finding and using some type of oracle with which you feel comfortable. These days there are numerous oracular systems from which to choose.

You may want to start with a birth chart, so that you become aware of the broad patterns that are inherent in your life. Then march off to your nearest bookstore and browse through the many types of oracular systems that are available. Some of the best are the *I Ching*, tarot, medicine cards, and runes.

You may even want to combine several oracular systems. Certain questions are better for the metamorphic language and deep insight of the *I Ching*, and others are perfect for the free-flowing intuitive interpretations of the tarot. The idea is to play around with various systems until you find several that work for you. Initially, you may want to keep a record of your questions and the answers you get so that you prove the system's accuracy to your own satisfaction.

By working with oracles, you're sending a clear message to your unconscious that you're ready for deeper knowledge and new experiences. This, in turn, attracts people and situations that are in line with your desires and makes it easier for you to recognize synchronicities when they happen. Ideally, you won't need any oracular system because you're able to interpret experiences through your own intuition.

Creating Your Future

Your emotions are your best vehicle for conscious creation. By learning to direct intense emotion toward an ideal image of what you want, you set energy in motion that seeks to make the imagined real.

When you imagine what you want your future to be like, fill in as many emotional details as you can. Imagine yourself as happy, fulfilled, and buoyant in this new situation or environment. If you aren't sure how to do this, then read Richard Matheson's book *What Dreams May Come* or see the movie.

The character played by Robin Williams has died in a car accident and comes to in the afterlife, in a place called Summerland. He discovers that in this place, his thoughts are instantly manifested. If he wants to go to a particular place, he has only to think of that place and he's there. If he wants to dress differently, he thinks of how he would like to dress, and voilà, it's done. Instantaneous transformation. This should give you some idea of how to work with your emotions to create the future you want.

Your most powerful and enduring experiences, Cancer, hit you viscerally, smack in the gut. Your emotions then shoot out from that point, transforming your world.

Chapter 13

Leo, the Lion

July 23–August 22
Fixed, Fire
Ruled by the Sun

Leo Man

He loves the spotlight, plays to it, flirts with it. Center stage is where he's most comfortable, and he doesn't like to share it with anyone. He's the king, after all, and don't you ever forget it. Like any king, he prowls around his kingdom, surveying it with both benevolence and arrogance, a curious mixture of ego and heart.

But beneath that kingly demeanor lies a much softer core. This is the guy who melts beneath a loving touch, enjoys the laughter of children, and feels deep compassion for others. He needs to know that he's loved and appreciated, too, and if you give him reason to doubt your feelings for him, he's profoundly hurt.

The Leo man has a dramatic flair about everything he says and does. He can be a flashy dresser, may drive a flashy car, may live in a flashy home, and have a flashy significant other on his arm. However his flamboyance shows itself, he's always got an audience in mind. For this reason, many Leo men are drawn to politics, the entertainment industry, any kind of work that brings them before the public.

At his worst, the Leo man is arrogant without apology. This type thinks you and everyone else should see things as he does. When you don't, he's the first to be hurt by it. At his best, his charisma dazzles and mesmerizes. Bill Clinton is a good example of both types of Leo men.

Physically, Leo men and women have unusual hair. It may be straight or curly, dark or light, but it's nearly always thick and luxurious, shiny and enviable. This trait is especially prevalent for people with a Leo ascendant and less frequently for Leo moons. On a hot day, a Leo is easy to spot because his cheeks are usually flushed. Most Leos, men and women, also have a rather regal bearing, a certain dignity about them. Robert DeNiro and Michael Douglas both have it, and they project it in every part they play. Leo men also move gracefully, deliberately, perhaps aware that they're being watched. They tend to speak carefully and slowly, with an awareness of how their language affects others.

This man is a true romantic, passionate and dramatic in all affairs of the heart. Once he's committed, he tends to be loyal as long as he knows that you're as deeply committed as he is. If your attention lapses, if you neglect those ego strokes, his feelings get hurt and he goes off to sulk and lick his wounds.

Leos of both genders enjoy children and make excellent parents. The Leo father is the type who gets up in the middle of the night when the baby cries, who drives for field trips and out-of-town soccer games. His heart is as huge as the outdoors, and yes, that can translate as extravagant spending at Toys "R" Us. But so what. He's there for his kids. They may resent his arrogance at times and get fed up with his pontificating, yet they brag about him to their friends. And whenever Dad walks in the door, there are squeals and hugs and shouts that he's home.

Leo rules the heart, back, and spinal column. These areas are also the most vulnerable parts of the body for people of this sign. When they're stressed, they may feel tension through the back or along the spinal cord. Their hearts may race or skip beats. They need some sort of physical outlet for tension, preferably some type of sport they don't have to do solo: tennis, swimming, soccer, baseball. Even a workout at a gym with a trainer would allow them to blow off steam.

The Leo man has an enormous amount of energy, and when that energy gets blocked for some reason, it shows up in his body. Therefore, he should pay attention to physical symptoms and try to interpret what they're actually saying about his life.

The Leo man is often portrayed as a gigantic ego that needs constant stroking as well as reassurance that he's lovable. While those traits apply to Leos in general, there's far more to this man than that. He's layered and complex, generous and gregarious, and often compassionate to a fault. You won't ever be bored with this man, but you may have trouble keeping up with him.

Leo Woman

In appearance, the quintessential Leo woman of the television age was Jacqueline Kennedy Onassis.

All the Leo adjectives fit her: regal, beautiful, dignified, and, yes, even her hair was pure Leo. The dramas in her life were so profound they became part of American history. Even though she never sought the limelight, it followed her. To escape public scrutiny and to protect her children from it, she ran off to the Greek Isles with one of the richest men in the world, a very Leo thing to do.

The Leo archetype ran like water through her life.

The Leo woman is usually direct about what she feels and about what she thinks. There's no secret agenda with this woman. If she's got her sights set on the CEO position, she's the first to tell you that's where she's headed. She'll probably get there, too. Leos in general don't enjoy working under other people and strive diligently to advance themselves. Once they get where they're going, they excel at what they do.

The Leo woman, like the man, is a social creature whose sphere of friends includes powerful and influential people. She enjoys doing things, going places, participating in all the activities that interest her. She is apt to have a number of hobbies and passions, which may not have anything to do with her professional life. She enjoys spending money on her various pleasures and often spends when she can't afford to.

The Leo woman certainly has her vanities. She probably spends a small fortune on her hair, dresses well, and enjoys buying things for her home. Even if she's strapped for cash, her home undoubtedly has something unique and eye-catching about it. Huge potted plants. A great patio. A room with a skylight. Feng Shui symmetry. A Steinway piano that she doesn't even play.

In romance, she seeks the unusual, the dramatic, the passionate. Like the Leo man, she needs to be the focus of your attention, the sun around which the rest of your life revolves. She also needs to be needed and has to know that your feelings run as deeply as hers. This trait also applies to a woman with a Leo moon, but it affects her emotionally. For a woman with a Leo ascendant, the face she presents to others is likely to be quite flashy.

Quite often she won't commit to you until you commit to her first. Even then, the commitment itself sometimes won't be enough. She wants gestures, tokens of your commitment. Seasonal tickets to the theater or a surprise trip to Hawaii would be a fine place to start. If that strains your budget, then five dozen roses delivered to her office, where everyone else can see them, would also qualify as a token of your commitment. Remember: make it dramatic, make it sweeping, make it a *statement*.

When she marries, it's usually for keeps, unless you give her reason to stray. The operative word here is *reason*. Maybe you've neglected her on weekends. Maybe you've been spending too much time with the guys. Maybe she feels all your attention is going to the kids. You never know what constitutes a *reason* for the Leo woman unless you ask her. But if you ask, be prepared to hear exactly what's on her mind.

As a mother, she's warm and loving and protective. But she doesn't smother her kids or hover over them, anxiously biting her nails about every sniffle, every skinned knee. She encourages their independence and helps them find their own interests and passions. She's generous with her kids. They probably get twice the allowance that their friends do and have more privileges. In return, the Leo mother demands their respect.

Leos have tempers and it's not a pretty sight when they blow. Although the degree of the explosion isn't anything like the Taurus "bull's rush," you clear the decks fast. But once they blow, that's it. They usually don't hold grudges, the air is cleared. If you remind them about that little blowout two days ago, they barely remember it.

The Leo woman is competitive and can certainly hold her own in any male-dominated field. She's as organized as the Leo male, as driven, as relentless. As a business partner, she's not the silent type. Let her work the room at any professional function. She turns up the charm and remembers every face and the name that goes with it. Never criticize or demean her, even in jest, and never, never do any of the above in public, because that's a transgression she won't ever forget.

Leo in the Millennium

As a fixed sign, you dislike having change thrust on you, but that's exactly what's going to happen in the first decade of the millennium. Blame Aquarius, your polar opposite, a sign that's concerned with group consciousness and the betterment of the whole. Your primary focus is on the individual conflicts with the Aquarian vision, so you work on integrating group consciousness into who you are.

Actually, this isn't as difficult as it sounds because you probably began experiencing some of this when Uranus went into Aquarius in 1996. Some integral part of your life probably was disrupted then, forcing you to find new venues for self-expression. And that wasn't all that bad, was it, Leo?

Energizer: The solar eclipse in your sign in August 1999 brings to light something that has been concealed or hidden in your personal life. Perhaps people who have authority over you are involved, or it could pertain to your health and vitality or to the self that you present to others.

In your birth chart, look at the houses with Scorpio, Aquarius, and Taurus on the cusps. Any planets in those houses will also be affected because of the grand cross formed by the sun in Leo, Mars in Scorpio, Saturn in Taurus, and Uranus in Aquarius.

In general this eclipse and grand cross challenge and energize you to find new means of self-expression that are more in line with who you are. You feel pressured to incorporate new ideals into your work. The old methods don't seem to work as well now and as the millennium progresses, the old way begins to break down altogether. By honestly appraising the things in your life that no longer work, you're able to release them with a minimum of discomfort and move forward with all that leonine energy. If you have a moon in Leo, the above applies to your emotions, to your inner life. With an ascendant, it applies with your public persona.

Take a look at George Lucas's natal chart (page 67). Leo is on the cusp of his fourth house, with natal Jupiter at 18 degrees and 31 minutes (♃18♌31). The degree of the eclipse is 18 degrees in Leo, which means that it conjuncts his Jupiter. Directly opposite the fourth house is the tenth in Aquarius. The other part of the cross hits his Taurus intercepted (contained) in the twelfth house and Scorpio intercepted in the sixth. So the affected houses are the fourth, sixth, tenth, and twelfth. All except the sixth are angular houses, which makes the impact more dramatic and important.

For Lucas, the eclipse triggers a new creative phase that could result in films and technological advances far beyond anything he has done. The ideals reflected in artistic projects in this new phase are both deeply personal and almost mythic in scope. The birth of this creative phase may not be the easiest thing in the world, because unconscious or early childhood issues are likely to be involved in the process. But if he sticks to his course, the results may surprise even Lucas.

Catalyst: The grand alignment of planets in Taurus all fall in your tenth house, highlighting your career. The alignment squares your natal sun, which creates friction and some resistance to change.

The Jupiter/Saturn conjunction bodes well for professional successes. At times, though, you feel like a piece of taffy, pulled in opposite directions. While Jupiter urges you to expand, Saturn imposes restrictions and limitations. The two energies seem to work against each other until you realize that during this period of expansion, Saturn reins in your urge toward excess. It whispers, *Don't be overly confident, don't overspend, read the fine print, don't dissipate your resources.*

Think of Saturn as the schoolmarm strolling through the aisles in your head, slapping that ruler against the palm of her hand; that ruler can just as easily slam against your knuckles.

The pressure eases somewhat in late summer of 2000, when both Jupiter and Saturn go into Gemini, sextile your natal sun. Things flow more smoothly now, and your optimism literally carries you forward. Your goals and your ideals seem to be within reach. Opportunities drop into your life out of nowhere, and you're recognized in some way by people who have authority over you. If you take advantage of the opportunities that come your way during this period, you can make enormous strides in all areas of your life.

Transformation: The good news, Leo, is that when the millennium opens, Pluto has been in Sagittarius for five years and you already have some idea what that means. You've done some soul-searching about your relationship with power—the power you hold over others and the power others hold over you. You may not have arrived at any hard-and-fast conclusions yet, but you're on your way.

This period is easier for you than other signs because Pluto is in a fellow fire sign and trines your natal sun. You can make significant strides now in every area of your life. People who have power over you recognize you as someone who gets things done, so you advance professionally. Your entire life seems to transform for the better during this period.

This isn't to say that everything works so smoothly on every level that you can just kick back and do nothing. Uranus and Neptune, after all, are still in Aquarius, your polar opposite, which puts some stress on your joint finances and resources. But overall, if you stay focused, you come out way ahead of the game.

Innovation: When Uranus went into Aquarius in 1996, it probably didn't feel innovative to you. It felt uncomfortable. It felt as if you were buried under a dozen itchy blankets in a room where the temperature hovered around ninety degrees. But as the millennium opens, you've had four years to get used to this energy, and by now you're revved up, tackling new creative projects with all your usual energy.

Uranus in its home sign brings vision and originality; Leo is about creativity and creative expression. This winning combination puts you at the forefront as an innovative pioneer. Before Uranus leaves Aquarius in the spring of 2003, Jupiter in Leo helps you to expand and idealize your projects, and Saturn in Gemini provides the mental structure through which you do this.

You may feel at times that your plate is way too full to accomplish everything you want, but your abundant energy and drive take you the distance.

New paradigms: As the millennium gets under way, you turn your energy inward, seeking to connect your spiritual beliefs or world view with your self-expression. Instead of seeking the limelight just because you like the applause and enjoy the recognition, you create the kind of life that embodies who you are when you're not playing to an audience.

This may entail significant changes in your close personal relationships that start with some very simple questions about your needs versus the needs of the people you love. Once you begin to develop your inner resources, you realize you don't need such constant ego validation from other people. The limelight still interests you, but not in the way it did before, perhaps because you're doing what *you* want rather than what you think your audience expects.

Truth within: Uranus in Pisces affects your eighth house, the one that reads like a Woody Allen script—

death, sex, taxes. It's also the house of rebirth, resurrection, and metaphysics. With Uranus here, your individual truth doesn't evolve; it comes to you in sharp, brilliant flashes of insight. These truths may disrupt your present belief system and play havoc with your joint finances, which also fall under the rule of the eighth house. But by working honestly with these new truths and attempting to integrate them into who you are becoming, you can successfully navigate Uranus's passage through Pisces until the spring of 2011.

One of the areas of disruption has to do with authority. You may be challenged by anyone who has authority over you—a boss, parent, employer, significant other, the government. Possibly others may infringe on your time. Instead of telling them no, you take on their problems out of guilt or compassion and then resent them later. You need to develop discernment about who really needs your help and who is just leeching your energy.

Spiritual expansion: Since Neptune in Aquarius blurs the boundary between what is real and what is imagined, you may go through periods where you feel quite confused about what you feel and think. Instead of struggling to clarify your confusion, simply be as direct as possible in your dealings with others. The clarity comes once Neptune has been in the sign for a while and you're more accustomed to its energy.

As the millennium opens, Neptune is still in the early stage of Aquarius, at a little more than 3 degrees. By now, you know what it feels like and are learning how to work with it. You may be involved with a new group of friends or coworkers whose ideals are more in line with your own. If so, then you may be learning it's okay to be part of a group where you aren't top dog and people aren't groveling for your attention or constantly stroking your ego. You're aware that your needs are changing and are willing to participate in the group's collective energy to further the cause or ideal that unites you.

Your humanitarian ideals become increasingly important while Neptune opposes your natal sun. Everything you learn during this period prepares you for Neptune's passage into Pisces, the sign it rules, in 2012.

Self: You've never been short on self-confidence, at least not on the surface. But while Saturn is in Cancer from 2003 to mid-2005, hitting your twelfth house, you begin to explore who you really are, the self separate from the person others see. For part of this time, you've got help from Jupiter in your sign, which urges you to expand your worldview as well as your understanding of yourself.

From 2005 to the fall of 2007, you're in a completion phase. Tie up loose ends and finish what's on your plate before taking on anything new that's apt to be long-range. In September 2006, Jupiter goes into Sagittarius for a year, forming a trine to your sun. This gives you a much needed boost in creative energy and helps you reach out beyond your usual environment. Your self-confidence runs high and strong, making you feel that you can take on anything and succeed.

Pluto is also trining your sun during this period and provides another, deeper layer of confidence and vigor. Other people are likely to see you as a powerful and dependable person who gets the job done.

This can all go to your head, feeding that familiar need and desire for limelight and applause, so remain grounded through your inner work.

Finances: As you embrace new ideals in the millennium, your attitudes toward money change accordingly. You may want to invest in Earth-friendly companies or in those that somehow reflect your emerging ideals and worldview.

When Jupiter goes into Virgo in August 2003, impacting your solar second house of finances, you scrutinize your personal values and resources. What do you value most? Possessions? Land? Money? Spiritual ideals? Whatever it is, you get more of it during this period. Even though the abundance and prosperity you experience during this period seems endless, be cautious about wasting what you have.

One of the things that may benefit you financially is an affirmation, Leo. Repeat: *I have more money than I will ever need.* Suzie Orman, author of *9 Steps to Financial Freedom,* recommends this affirmation, and hey, it worked for her, so why can't it work for you? Even though money for the sake of money isn't your thing, you enjoy money because it makes you feel powerful.

Communication: Okay, Leo, this one may be difficult for you because you need to change the way in which you communicate who you are. This requires *conscious* awareness of what you say to others and how you act and treat others. It can be simpler than it sounds if you observe yourself dispassionately and really listen to what you say.

When you express an opinion, for instance, is it really *your* opinion or are you merely paying lip service to the other person to win them over? If you commit to something but don't feel the commitment, then what are your true motives for committing?

To some extent, this type of internal scrutiny is the work of Pluto in Sagittarius. *Speak your truth and mean what you say.* Practice it until you get it perfect.

By 2005, when Jupiter goes into Libra and Uranus has left Aquarius, you breathe more easily. Jupiter in your solar third house of communication brings you opportunities to expand your communication skills, perhaps in ways that haven't occurred to you before. You try your hand at a novel or a screenplay. You work up a comedy routine. You start keeping a journal.

During this time, you pay more attention to how you actually think. Your perception about your thought patterns changes in some intrinsic way so that you release familiar, habitual ways of thinking and seek new connections and images for your "mental database." And this is really the level where your new and improved way of communicating begins.

Your home: In the early part of the millennium, you may experience sudden and unexpected changes that affect your home and personal environment. This could be a blowup with a boss, an employer, a supervisor, or in a personal relationship. A major blowup. Maybe you're fired from your job or your significant other heads for greener pastures. Maybe your company is involved in a reorganization. Or maybe none of these events happen, but other, similar events and situations unfold.

However this disruption plays out in your life, the events release tension. They're volcanic. All the dreams you sacrificed, the ideals you shoved aside, the innocence that you buried in the course of living your life has created this tension. External events now force the inner tectonic plates to shift, to rearrange themselves, and the tension billows and hisses into the atmosphere. Once it does, the disruptions cease being disruptions. They are powerless. You've pulled their plug.

Creative potential: This is where you shine in the millennium *if* you've been following your hunches, your impulses, your urges to understand what's happening to you. It has always been easy for you to place blame elsewhere for the challenges you've faced. Psychologists call it projection.

Let's say you land your dream job. Great salary and benefits, terrific coworkers, marvelous creative potential. But your immediate supervisor turns out to be hell on wheels, an opinionated and frustrated creative type who nitpicks about everything you do or don't do. Instead of telling him off or quitting on the spot, ask what aspects of yourself he might be reflecting.

This is the emotional bedlam that leads to deeper insights into yourself and your world, which in turn results in greater creativity. These are the kinds of experiences that Saturn in Leo may toss into your life from mid-July of 2005 to early autumn of 2007. If you go with the flow, experimenting with your emotions, intuitions, and creative self, then ultimately you claim your own power, Leo. And how can that be such a bad thing for the king?

Health & work: As a fixed sign, you have hard-and-fast opinions about health in general and your health in particular. In the first decade of the millennium, those ideas are likely to change as you begin to explore various lifestyle alternatives. If you don't have any regular exercise routine, then now is the time to start one.

When Saturn goes into your sun sign from 2003 to 2005, it's likely that any health problems you experience are related to work. Be careful at this time that you don't take on more than you can handle. Since your heart and spine are the most vulnerable parts of your body, aerobic and stretching exercises are important. Walking, jogging, swimming, or yoga would fit the ticket. Any of these activities also would allow you to vent when you're stressed out. Even more vital to your continued health, however, is to learn your body's language. Look at symptoms in terms of metaphors. If you've got indigestion, what in your life aren't you "digesting" or understanding?

There are numerous books on illness as metaphor. Louise Hay's *How You Can Heal Your Life* provides a list of illnesses and diseases, their probable emotional origins, and affirmations to help correct the problem. *Anatomy of the Spirit,* by Carolyn Myss, explores illness in terms of the body's chakras or energy centers. *Awakening Intuition,* by physician Mona Lisa Schultz, and Andrew Weil's *Spontaneous Healing* also provide insightful information about the body's metamorphic language.

In early 2008, with both Jupiter and Pluto in Capricorn affecting your solar sixth house of health, your interest in these facets of health may deepen. But the bottom line is not to take your abundant vitality for granted. Nurture it just as you do the parts of yourself.

In terms of your work, 2008 to 2010 brings you opportunities for advancement and changes in your work environment as long as you maintain your self-control and carefully evaluate what you're being offered.

Partnerships: While your humanitarian ideals expand, you may experience confusion about your personal relationships. Thank Neptune in Aquarius for that. Sometimes this spells the end of an important relationship, but it doesn't have to if you and your significant other are committed to expressing your mutual and individual needs and being honest about them.

While Neptune brings about confusion concerning your personal relationships, Saturn in your sign from 2003 to 2005 tests them. During this period you may be doing some soul-searching about your needs versus those of the people you love. Is it really so important if your significant other doesn't see everything the way you do? Why do you need such constant attention and ego-stroking? Discernment, Leo, that's what this period is about. Weed out the nonessentials and stick to what really matters.

By the time Jupiter enters Aquarius in 2009, you should have all the relationship details worked out. If you do, then the next year bodes well for all kinds of partnerships, particularly marriage. You may be involved with someone from another country or meet someone special while traveling in another country. Any relationships you have during this time somehow expand your perceptions and consciousness.

Spirituality: Whatever your spiritual and religious beliefs are when the millennium opens, they won't be the same by the end of the first decade. You open up to humanitarian ideals that permeate your spiritual beliefs, and as a result, spiritual beliefs are no longer something you practice or recognize just one day a week or strictly within a church or synagogue.

Part of this process may happen for you through a group of individuals who share your ideals and think along the same lines that you do. Like you, they are spiritual seekers.

Career & profession: The millennium starts with a focus on your career. That's the Jupiter/Saturn conjunction in Taurus, which highlights your tenth house. Your creativity runs high at this time, and you're able to tap your intuition to come up with new ways of doing things. Some of this may happen within a group setting, your first millennial taste of group energy and cooperation.

With Saturn in Leo from 2005 to 2007, your energy becomes quite concentrated and focused and your workload increases. As long as you maintain your course and don't assume new responsibilities, unless they're connected to what you're doing, then your potential for reward and success is great.

During this period it would be wise for you to reassess what you value. This may prompt you to start some sort of savings plan, if you haven't already, and to rein in your free spending.

Personal unconscious: What issues from your earlier life have you buried? With Saturn in Cancer from June 2003 to early July of 2005, hitting your twelfth house of the personal unconscious, you're sure to stumble across the issues and feelings you've disowned over the years. They may surface in dreams or in your encounters with other people.

Quite often, when other people mirror the disowned parts of themselves, we don't like what we see. This is precisely when we need to view these people as teachers, and glean what we can from the experience. During this time you're going to get into situations that also mirror some disowned part of yourself. Once you recognize what's happening and tackle it, you're able to integrate what you've learned.

Tapping the Source

Synchronicities & Your Inner Oracle

Think of the last time you had one of those *aha*! experiences. How did it feel? How did *you* feel at the time? Recall as many details as you can about the experience and jot them down. Include the issues that were involved, the approximate time of the day, the weather, what was going on in your life at the time. Vivid details add clarity to the memory.

Even though an *aha*! moment usually concerns a deep and immediate understanding of something, it doesn't necessarily involve a synchronicity—but it can. This moment may feel very much like a synchronicity, with the same feeling tones and recognition that something important is going on. If you can remember the overall tone of an *aha*! moment, you can cultivate it in your daily life, which creates a fertile atmosphere for synchronicities to unfold.

What happens during a synchronicity? For one Leo woman the synchronicity involved a name. Her husband was waiting to hear from a potential client, whose last name was Gale, about whether his bid for a project had been accepted. The woman was on her way home from running errands and was wondering if her husband had gotten the call yet. Just then, a white truck pulled up in the lane beside her. Across the side of it, written in bright red letters, was the word Gale. She felt sure this was her answer, and the moment she walked into the house, her husband said the client had called and accepted the bid.

Our inner oracles work with whatever is available to answer our questions and provide us with the information we need. All we have to do is ask—and then listen.

Creating Your Future

Conscious creation is actually easier for you than for other signs, Leo. Your enormous energy and vitality, combined with your passionate nature, provides the basic fuel for manifesting what you desire. The secret for you is to be consistent about what you're trying to create.

One Leo woman made a list of the attributes she was looking for in a man. These traits were very specific and included things like kindness to animals and a fondness for pets, a love of books, someone who was grounded through regular employment and who owned his own place. Several months after she made this list, which she continued to refine, she met the man. He had most of the attributes she'd listed, except for one thing she'd overlooked. He didn't share her interest in metaphysics.

Be careful what you ask for because you just might get it. Isn't that how the adage goes? To this, add another, Leo. Be specific about what you want.

Chapter 14

Virgo, the Virgin

August 23–September 22
Mutable, Earth
Ruled by Mercury

Virgo Man

His mind moves like lightning, making luminal connections among scattered bits of information stored in his memory. But for all his mental quickness, he remains the quiet, reserved type, the guy who stands at the edge of the group, observing, watching, alert.

He may look worried or preoccupied, his brow slightly furrowed, giving the distinct impression that he's gnawing at some problem or concern, trying to solve it. And he probably is. Virgo men and women are the natural worriers of the zodiac. They worry about things that happened in the past, about things that are happening now, about things that may happen in the future. But their worrying is of a specific sort, not worry for the sake of worry, but worry as a quest toward perfection.

Physically, the Virgo man is apt to be short, sometimes muscular, but not always. Stephen King is a notable exception; he's tall. Many of them are worriers, so they tend to be slender. Those that aren't, usually internalize their worry and often have stomach problems—colic as infants, ulcers as adults. Virgo, after all, rules the intestines and abdomen, so "nervous stomachs" are pretty much business as usual for Virgos.

In romance, this man isn't the candlelight dinner type. Don't expect romantic walks on the beach at twilight or high-flying adventures to exotic ports on nothing more than a wing and a prayer. He's too conservative for that. What's more likely is that he shows up on your doorstep one afternoon and says he knows of this great little bookstore with a great café down by the river. The bookstore turns out to be a hole-in-the-wall jammed with out-of-print gems and esoteric tomes, and the café serves the best coffee outside of Colombia. He prefers spots like this to crowds and social gatherings.

The Virgo man, like the woman, is a tireless worker. Again, look at Stephen King. He's been writing professionally since the early seventies, when his first published novel, *Carrie*, became a best-seller and a movie. Since then, he has produced at least one best-seller a year in addition to screenplays, novellas, and short story collections. Tireless? Definitely. Driven? Most certainly. And money seems to have little to do with his output. The man simply loves what he does.

Walk into a Virgo man's office at any hour of the day or night, and his desk is probably tidy to a fault. Letters here. Memos there. Pencils in that holder, pens in this holder. His computer keyboard won't have a fleck of dust on it. There won't be any dust bunnies under his chair. He knows exactly what he has to do today, tomorrow, and next week. His organizational skills send Gemini, his fellow mutable sign, running for the hills. But there's also the Virgo guy who doesn't mind clutter and mess, as long as his mind is sharp and uncluttered.

He may not have a flamboyant style, but he usually dresses neatly and practically. Pragmatism, in fact, is one of the priorities in his life. If something isn't practical, he could care less about it. He can be quite practical about money, too, stashing dollars away in several accounts, watching them accrue interest with a kind of satisfied glee. When it suits him, though, he can also be a big spender.

Virgo men and women are health conscious, even if they don't always follow their own advice. They are nitpicky, too, about health details. The Virgo man, for instance, probably likes to have his own bathroom, with his own sink, and the items he places in his refrigerator must always be where he puts them. If he has an exercise routine, then he likes to do it at the same time every day. They can be the worst hypochondriacs in the zodiac, but sometimes a health complaint is just an excuse to get out of doing something they don't want to do.

And yet, when a friend is in need, the Virgo man, like the female, is the first to help. If you're stuck downtown in the middle of a snowstorm with a dead battery and no way to get home, the Virgo man comes to your rescue with his toolbox, his battery cables, maybe even a tow truck. And he does this without any thought of recompense. He's pleased that you called him.

Virgo Woman

On the surface, she may seem easy to know, uncomplicated, rather easygoing, with a certain shy sweetness that makes you want to protect her. And while all of this may be true about her, it's a long way from the full story.

This lady is often as complex as a Rubik's Cube. Just when you think you've figured out what she's about, you discover that one of the pieces doesn't fit. So you have to take the whole thing apart and start all over again. Don't forget she's a mutable sign, infinitely adaptable. While she may not be the total chameleon that her mutable Gemini sister is, she can adapt so fast to new situations that she leaves the other earth signs way back there at the starting line.

There are some things, however, that you can count on with this woman. She's bright and possesses a dry wit that comes out at the oddest moments. Like the Virgo man, she's a relentless worker, but only as long as her work interests her. When it doesn't, a sense of obligation may carry her a little farther, but then even that dries up and nothing can entice her to continue.

In romance, she's as practical as the Virgo male. But within her exists an ideal of what love can be and of what she's looking for in a mate. Intellect is high up there on the list and so are wit, curiosity, common interests, and a genuine appreciation of who and what she is. Her ideal is something that she perfects, just as she does with everything that's important to her. A perfectionist, yes, she's certainly that, but for every Virgo this tendency shows up in a unique way. One Virgo woman may need perfection within her home, the bed made just so, the furniture arranged in a special way, no clutter. But another Virgo woman may not mind clutter; her thing is perfect alignment of pillows on the couch or absolute perfection in her detailed line artwork.

The Virgo woman enjoys feeling needed, but not in the same way as a Cancer woman. For Virgo, she must feel that she's contributing something, that she's helping in some way. She's often artistic or involved in the arts, perhaps because it provides her with an outlet for her own emotions. With practice and diligence, she may become quite accomplished at her art, and if she finds that she loves it, she does everything she can to make a living at it.

Virgos are meticulous parents. They don't cling to their kids as a Cancer is apt to do, and they don't smother or overprotect them. But they take parenting seriously and are available to their children through every step of their growth. They're good at counseling and giving advice in a way that fits what the child needs to hear at that age. Virgo mothers also sense instinctively how to be fully in the moment with their kids so that their time together is fun and memorable. They balance the various facets of their lives with admirable poise.

The Virgo woman is honest. Ask her a question, and she answers it to the best of her ability. But she's sensitive to other people's feelings and won't be blunt, like a Sagittarian, for instance, if she thinks she might hurt your feelings. She can't abide hypocrites or liars, and if she finds out that you are either, she cuts you off cold and that's it.

The Virgo woman is usually deeply intuitive, even if she doesn't call it that and even if she's not aware of it. Quite often she acts on her gut instinct about things and people and doesn't give it a second thought. It's simply a part of who she is and how she lives her life. Then there's the other kind of Virgo woman, the one who diligently studies esoteric disciplines in a search for understanding. With both types, though, the thread is the same. They are seeking some ideal of perfection.

Virgo in the Millennium

Hold on to your seat, Virgo, because the first decade of the millennium is going to be a roller-coaster ride for you. The acceleration at which things are changing initially strains your meticulous, detailed mind.

You like to change at your own pace so that you have time to incorporate what you learn. But you may not have that luxury in the early part of the millennium. Your idea of "perfection," that ever present theme in your life, undergoes radical change unless you were preparing yourself during the nineties with intense inner work. Despite all the change that occurs in your life during this time, you're eminently adapatable when you have to be and should come out just fine.

Energizer: The solar eclipse in Leo (at 18 degrees) on August 11, 1999, affects your solar twelfth house of the personal unconsciousness. Something that has been hidden or concealed in your unconscious may surface now and demand your attention. Childhood issues, power that you've disowned, even experiences from past lives may be involved. The fixed grand cross in this eclipse affects Mars (your energy) in Scorpio, Saturn (your limitations and karmic lessons) in Taurus, and Uranus (your individuality and freedom) in Aquarius. If you have planets in any of those signs, in the middle degrees, then the eclipse affects you.

In practical terms, this means that for several months on either side of the eclipse, you may feel odd, not quite in synch with the world around you. You sense an internal shift, but aren't quite able to pinpoint what it is or what it means. This could be reflected in your outer world as a period when everything is a bit off. You're late for appointments. Or the area of your life where you've been concerned with perfection now slides into disarray. Instead of fretting about it, you let it go. You have better things to do right now.

Back to your birth chart. If Leo sits on the cusp of any of your angular houses (first, fourth, seventh, or tenth) or you have planets in those houses in the middle degrees of Leo (within a tight orb of 1 to 3 degrees), then the affairs of that house will be intensified, highlighted, as if a 1200 watt bulb is burning in the center of it. You will have to deal with whatever issues are endemic to that house.

But by confronting the issues, you prepare yourself for the catalyst stage.

Catalyst: The lineup of planets in Taurus on May 3, 2003, hits you in the solar ninth house, your worldview, your spiritual beliefs. The Jupiter/Saturn part of this conjunction brings opportunities for travel and teaching and may involve foreign cultures or foreign people. You're able to expand your spiritual and philosophical views through everything new that you encounter. You're exposed to so many new experiences during this time that you can no longer cling to your old beliefs.

With Saturn tossed into the equation, you have to integrate these new experiences so that you can put them to work for you. This process may unfold more quickly than you like. After all, there are so *many* experiences, and you're not quite sure how everything fits yet. Don't fret about it, that's part of the secret. Just let the whole journey unfold and trust the process. As your worldview begins to stabilize and you understand your spiritual beliefs, your ideas about yourself also become much clearer. This boosts your self-confidence and may take the edge off your quest for perfection. The themes that come into play during this lineup are the dominant themes of your foray into the first decade of the millennium.

Transformation: In late 1995, you began to feel some deep discomfort in your life, Virgo. All of a sudden, it seemed you had all this *emotion* to contend with. Emotion is fine, in its place. But when it spills over into too many areas of your life, you have to pay attention. And that's what happened when Pluto went into Sagittarius, squaring your natal sun. And it's going to be there until 2008.

How can earth and fire possibly be compatible? They can't. But they can certainly coexist, and more to the point, both Virgo and Sagittarius are mutable signs. They're adaptable. And perhaps that's the secret for your successful navigation of Pluto through Sagittarius. *Adapt to the energy.* Try to work with it.

For one Virgo woman, Pluto's passage into Sagittarius coincided with the breakup of her marriage to a man nearly thirty years her senior. Yes, it was painful and terrifying, and her life went through momentous upheaval. But instead of blocking her emotions, she tried to move with them and pursued the things that interested her. She became a massage therapist and studied alternative medicine and body energy work, very Virgo stuff. She also fell in and out of love and gradually established a life for her and her daughter. She *grew.* She *evolved.*

For another Virgo, a writer, Pluto's entrance into Sagittarius (which rules his second house of money) rearranged his finances. He went into debt, wrestled with writer's block for a while, and his financial situation worsened. Then he began to study the *I Ching* and to work with his dreams. By tapping his intuitive resources, he began to understand the patterns that had led to his debt crisis, and he began to write again. Things started to change. Once he understood the pattern, his situation improved.

Pluto in Sagittarius insists that we deal with issues we have buried and creates circumstances and situations that compel us to do exactly that. Once we do, then the transformation process begins.

Innovation: When the millennium opens, Uranus has been in Aquarius for four years, long enough for you, with your exacting mind, to have a clear idea what it means. Its energy may feel more innovative to you now than it did in 1996, but you still aren't entirely comfortable with it.

At times you aren't sure what to do with the intuitive flashes that you get. But if you train yourself to work with these nuggets of brilliance, whatever they are, then you're better able to incorporate them into a solid framework that works for you.

Don't be afraid to express any innovative ideas you have now. The time is ripe for being recognized for your ideas and achievements. By late August of 2001, you get a boost from Jupiter in Cancer, a compatible water sign. You're more sensitive to emotional nuances and may find that a lot of your ideas come to you through dreams and relaxation periods, when your left brain isn't standing guard at the gate to other worlds.

In early September of 2003, Jupiter goes into your sign, Virgo, and the foundations you laid two to three years ago start paying off big time. The innovative ideas you have now broaden your perspective on life in general. This is a good time to go back to school or to delve into topics that expand your awareness and spiritual ideals.

Your health is excellent with Jupiter in Virgo and you're able to utilize some of your new ideas for the maintenance of your good health. This could include herbs, acupuncture, body energy work, hypnosis, and other alternative health treatments.

Overall, the first three years of the millennium are good to you and also important to your spiritual and emotional growth. But you have to listen to inner cues that help you adjust to the rapid changes and which urge you in particular directions. Your main challenge, Virgo, is to turn down the analytical part of your brain so that your intuitive brain can do its work.

New paradigms: When Neptune went into Aquarius in 1998, you may have felt befuddled for a while, Virgo, as though you were looking at everything through a piece of gauze. That feeling diminishes as you journey into the first three years of the millennium, when Neptune shares the Aquarian spot with Uranus, affecting your solar sixth house of health and work.

During this period, your health and working conditions change in ways that aren't always easy to define. In the health area, the cause of symptoms may be elusive. This is when it's important that you know how to carry on a dialogue with your body and to interpret the symptoms in terms of what they're trying to say. Metaphor, Virgo. Look for the metaphor.

You may experience misunderstandings with the people you work for, which are usually due to you or others not saying exactly what they mean. With Uranus tossed into the picture, you may want to blurt things out. Instead, follow your mother's advice: think before you speak. Then strive to say what you feel and think as clearly as possible.

If you have your birth chart handy, look at the house with Aquarius on the cusp. This is where Uranus and Neptune are making themselves felt. Suppose Aquarius is on the cusp of your twelfth house. In terms of your ordinary, daily life, Uranus and Neptune here could mean that you're involved with institutions of some kind—hospitals, jails, prisons, nursing homes, and psychiatric and Alzheimer's units. It doesn't necessarily mean you're going to end up in one of these places, only that you have experiences connected to them. It could just as easily represent doing something behind the scenes—ghostwriting, for instance, or charity work. However the experience manifests, your compassion is awakened and you experience your connection to the divine.

In this way, service in the highest sense becomes a part of your new paradigm.

Truth within: Remember polarity? Uranus goes into Pisces at the tail end of 2003 until the end of 2010, opposite your sun sign. You feel a tremendous urge now to break free of anything that restricts you, whether it's a relationship, a job, money, kids, or your family. Sudden changes occur in the area where you are the most rigid and inflexible.

Much of this process occurs on an intuitive level. You may suddenly have feelings, hunches, and precognitive experiences that you can't ignore. Also, since the mutable water sign Pisces is compatible with Virgo, a mutable earth sign, the process itself isn't as disruptive for you as it is for other signs. In fact, with Saturn in your sun sign from 2007 through mid-July of 2010, you find the structure you need to integrate these experiences.

Saturn in Virgo may bring some heavy responsibilities during this time, but the blossoming of your intuition helps you through whatever challenges you encounter. By the time Pluto has gone into Capricorn in late 2008, your inner truth is as apparent to you as the clothing you wear.

Spiritual expansion: For you, talking about spiritual expansion is sort of like talking about the outer reaches of the solar system. How can the rational, analytical mind even embrace such vast distances? Such incomprehensible spaces? By the same token, how can the analytical mind grasp the notion of expansion in an area that is basically invisible, intangible, and maybe even nonexistent?

The answer is that it can't. Forget your rational mind when it comes to this area, Virgo. Listen to your intuition, follow the promptings of your heart, and act on your impulses, which seek to push you in new spiritual directions. Above all, especially from 2003 to 2012, while Neptune is in Aquarius, trust that things in your life are unfolding as they should.

Self: In the early part of the millennium, you may be feeling somewhat overwhelmed by the changes that are taking place around you and within your own life. But the Jupiter/Saturn conjunction in Taurus helps to ground you and to expand your worldview. Once you get into the rhythm of this expansion, you begin to feel quite prosperous and seek to nurture this feeling in all areas of your life.

From the beginning of the millennium to mid-January of 2008, you feel as if you're being tested. And you are. Pluto is square your natal sun, and that creates friction at deep levels in your psyche. The better you know yourself by this time, the better off you are. Power issues are likely to surface regardless, but if you know who you are and what you want to accomplish, you're able to deal with these issues with a minimum of harm to yourself. Outright confrontation and total passivity won't get you very far with these issues. Your best defense is a middle ground, some blend of the two.

Finances: If you have done your inner work, then the fall of 2003 to the fall of 2004 is likely to be a good financial year for you if only because you feel so self-confident. In 2004, from the end of September to mid-November, Mars in Libra affects your solar second house of finances. This is a good time to evaluate and assess your financial situation, to balance the books. A lot of your energy goes into money matters.

The next year, Jupiter goes into Libra, which affects your solar second house of money, so that any financial decisions you made or projects you started in 2003 really begin to blossom. You feel optimistic about life in general, and this spills over into the financial decisions and choices you make. During this time it's wise to be prudent, however. Don't allow yourself to go overboard because you feel so invincible. Build on and expand what already exists rather than spreading yourself too thinly. You can expect strokes of luck, success, and serendipitous experiences related to finances.

Communication: One of the gifts the millennium brings you, Virgo, is other people, specifically groups of like-minded individuals who share your ideals or interests. You have to be open to working cooperatively with a group, however. It's not going to work if you approach it as just another duty or obligation.

Uranus and Neptune in Aquarius prompt you to experiment with groups as a way of clarifying your particular vision and understanding how that vision can service large numbers of people.

If that sounds vague, there's reason for it. Neptune. Not everyone responds to Neptune in Aquarius in the same way. For you, this group urge could mean therapy, group hypnotic regression, working with some sort of service organization, or joining a group of artistic people. It could also mean that you work with an animal rights group or join an equestrian club. The group itself isn't as important as what you learn.

Your home: With Pluto in Sagittarius until the end of November 2008, hitting your solar fourth house of the home, these years spell fundamental changes in that area. This could mean that you move or that your home life goes through a profound change. An elderly parent may move in with you or move out. One of your children may move back into the house. Divorces and deaths may happen within your family. One thing is for sure, though. Childhood issues surface now and may come to you in the guise of your mother, a partner, or anyone within your immediate environment who mirrors these issues.

You should know where Pluto in Sagittarius affects your birth chart, so look for the house with Sagittarius on the cusp. Let's say it's the tenth house, the midheaven or MC, but you have a late degree on that cusp. That means it travels through both the ninth and tenth houses during its time in Sagittarius and transforms both your worldview and your career. The specifics of how that transformation unfolds depends on your choices, of course, and your free will.

Creative potential: Uranus goes into Pisces in March 2003 and opposes your sun until March 2011. This pressures you to find your true creative voice and to break free of anything and anyone that restricts the expression of that creative voice. That means that a relationship, job, college major, or even a profession may bite the dust *if* it has prevented you from expressing who you are.

The secret to this transit, Virgo, is not to resist the changes. Whatever you have to release are actually things and people that you don't need, even if you think you do. If you can go with the flow, your creative expression takes off as never before.

From late August of 2003 to late September of 2004, Jupiter is in your sun sign, urging you to broaden your worldview and your personal horizons. This primes you for the Uranus opposition by bringing opportunities to expand your creative abilities. This expansion could happen through foreign cultures and people from foreign countries and through the study of law or mataphysics.

You should be aware of synchronicities that may

happen during this period of your life, Virgo. Quiet your analytical mind and allow your intuitive self greater freedom. Find an oracle that feels right and start working with it—the *I Ching*, tarot, runes, whatever speaks to the inner you.

If you're not into that sort of thing, then set aside time each day when you do something that is strictly *for yourself.* Work internally with your questions and be alert for answers that may come to you through unconventional means. The whole point is to develop openness and awareness of your inner oracle.

Health & work: Virgo is the natural ruler of the sixth house of health and work. That means that you come by your health concerns naturally, and your innate awareness is more telling than any other sign. Quite often, your body acts like a receiver, picking up cues from your environment or absorbing energy from the people around you.

A particular symptom—sinus problems, for instance—could be indicative of minor irritations in your immediate life that should be addressed. A sudden depression when you have no apparent reason for being depressed could be negative energy that you've absorbed from someone around you. A blockage of creative energy may show up as a cold or the flu. In other words, Virgo, it's important that you learn your body's language and decipher symptoms for their deeper meaning.

In the new millennium, it's vital that your diet be as healthful as possible. This becomes especially necessary during the Uranus opposition, when creative blocks may manifest more easily in your body. Even more important than diet, though, is the awareness of the block itself. Once you learn to listen to your body and to act on what it tells you, your immune system is greatly strengthened. You may want to read some of the classics in the field of mind/body medicine: *You Can Heal Your Life* by Louise Hay; *Anatomy of the Spirit* by Carolyn Myss; *Awakening Intuition* by Mona Lisa Schultz, M.D.; *Spontaneous Healing* by Andrew Weil, M.D.; and *Quantum Healing* by Deepak Chopra.

During Uranus's transit through Pisces, opposing your sun, health problems may arise *if* you haven't been paying attention to your body's language. Such problems could involve your circulatory system, heart, and feet. Another time for caution is when Saturn is in Gemini, squaring your natal sun, from April 2001 to June 2003.

Again, these are only broad *possible* patterns. Illness is merely one way that some people choose to evolve; there are certainly easier ways!

Partnerships: If your partnerships, both business and personal, allow you the full range of your creative expression, then Uranus's journey through Pisces won't hold any nasty surprises in the relationship arena.

Your intuition plays a major role in any relationships you develop during this period and provides vital clues about people you meet. If, for instance, the hairs on the back of your neck rise when you meet someone or you feel suddenly and inexplicably nauseated, then head for the hills immediately.

Your intuition can be valuable in interpreting external events, too. Say you're engaged to someone, but one fiasco after another messes up the wedding plans. What are these fiascos trying to tell you? Interpret them as you might a dream, and look for common themes. You may end up rethinking your commitment.

There are two periods in particular when problems may develop in your relationships. The first period is when Saturn goes into Gemini in 2001 and stays until the summer of 2003. The second period happens when Saturn is in your sun sign from September 2007 to October 2009. During both these periods, relationships that are holding you back end of their own volition. These relationships, either business or professional, scatter your energy or distract you from what you should be doing.

Spirituality: Your spiritual development in the first decade of the millennium is deepened and speeded up through your participation in groups who share your interests and goals. These groups are instrumental in showing you how to balance your fine analytical mind with your natural intuitive and psychic abilities.

If you have Pisces rising or a Pisces moon, then Uranus's passage through Pisces works through your dreams, which may become quite prophetic and clairvoyant, and through sudden flashes of insight and inspiration. Your proximity to water is important during this time because it deepens your psychic abilities and calms your analytical brain.

Career & profession: You're the workaholic of the zodiac, Virgo, and this probably won't change in the millennium. What *does* change, however, is the thrust and focus of your work. You find new venues for your creative expression that involve cooperative efforts with large groups of people. Your service orientation expands tremendously and encompasses areas that seemed beyond your scope five or ten years ago.

With Jupiter in Virgo from the fall of 2003 to the fall of 2004, your career really takes off, expanding into new areas where your gift for analysis and your innate intuition blend seamlessly. The trick in maintaining the momentum of success is to stop worrying about every little detail. Don't spin your mental wheels trying to connect the dots; focus on the big picture and trust the universe to take care of the small stuff.

In September 2007, Saturn goes into your sign for roughly two years. This brings increased responsibility in your work and an inner need to tie up loose ends. If you're willing to put in the long hours and assume the burdens, the potential for reward can be considerable. The focus during this period, however, is to finish what you've started. Don't flit from one new thing to another, because you will burn out.

Personal unconscious: In August of 2002, Jupiter goes into Leo and affects your solar twelfth house. This spells a one-year period in which you embrace many new concepts that ultimately expand your unconscious mind. Any foreign travel that you do at this time broadens your perspective and benefits you in some way. During these travels you may feel ancient stirrings in your blood, the call of distant places that could be related to past lives. Synchronicities often happen when you're away from home, so be alert for them.

From March 2003 to March of 2011, Uranus in Pisces is passing through your solar twelfth house, where it acts as a kind of psychic plunger that frees stuff you've stashed away, power you've disowned, and issues you don't want to confront. This period isn't as bad as it sounds as long as you're making a sincere effort to make your "invisible" or core beliefs conscious.

Tapping the Source

Synchronicities & Your Inner Oracle

Remember how the world felt when you were very young? It was as if magic breathed in every moment, and everything seemed possible, even the things that your parents told you were impossible. In some ways a synchronicity is a glimmer of that childhood world, evidence that magic is still alive if we just take the time to notice it.

Synchronicities may rattle your analytical mind unless you realize they arise from a different kind of order, a holographic order. They are the foundation of any divination system, any oracle, and are intended to guide you through the business of living.

Quite often, synchronicities happen during dramatic times, clustering like planets around births, deaths, marriages, divorces, defeats, and achievements. A Virgo woman experienced a synchronicity concerning her father's death, but didn't realize it until weeks after he'd died. He'd spent eleven months and eleven days in the nursing home, his mind essentially gone, and had died at eleven minutes past the eleventh hour. All the elevens puzzled her until she looked in the *I Ching*. The eleventh hexagram is "Peace."

She interpreted this to mean that he had died at peace, understanding what he had been here to do and eager to move on to whatever came next.

Once you become accustomed to the texture and

feeling tones of synchronicities, it's easier to cultivate a receptive inner climate to their occurrences. Sometimes all it takes is the willingness to be open to the experience.

Creating Your Future

Right about now, you're thinking: *What? Create my future? No way. I don't have time. I have too many responsibilities right now. I don't like to meditate. I don't know how to visualize. I don't, I can't, no no no.* Turn down the left brain volume and listen up, Virgo.

Remember the story about the little engine that could? He had to make it up a hill but kept telling himself he couldn't do it, he wasn't strong enough or powerful enough. But just the same, he tried. He kept saying, *I think I can, I think I can . . .* And the more he said it, the deeper he believed it, and the deeper the belief, the more powerful he became. And he made it over the hill.

In the millennium, your success depends on the depth of your belief in yourself.

Chapter 15

Libra, the Scales

September 23–October 23
Cardinal, Air
Ruled by Venus

Libra Man

Two dates with this man and you think you know him. He's all charm, laid-back, easy to talk to, and a good listener. He loves music and may have an affinity for art and books as well. Even if he himself isn't involved in the arts, his soul is artistic. You think you know him because you stayed up most of last night exchanging personal histories then spent the rest of today at the café over on the beach, listening to music and sipping expresso and gazing into each other's eyes.

You know him through and through, right? Don't count on it.

The Libra man is often as inscrutable as Scorpio, though never as intense or as seductively magnetic. His charm is real, though, and emanates from the innermost reaches of who he is. Who knows where it comes from, charm like this, where a quick smile can turn your insides to mush in seconds flat. Be forewarned, however. He can turn that charm off and on like the proverbial faucet and it's nothing personal, really it isn't. He just needs time to weigh everything.

The scales, remember?

He has to weigh the pros and cons, the past and future, the knowns and the unknowns. He seeks the ideal balance, the perfect balance, the balance that exists at some abstract level the rest of us will never touch, much less perceive. To many people the scales that symbolize Libra represent the scales of justice. There is certainly a lot of that, a concern that justice should be served, that equality should be observed. Maybe that's why Libras make good judges. They are also scrupulously honest, saving every receipt for the tax man, claiming to the dollar and cent what they are owed, but not a penny more.

But the scales are more than any of that. Just as Virgo seeks the ideal of perfection through a relentless attention to detail, so does Libra seek balance through a constant weighing of the issues. The problem is that one day this guy is up—way up—and the next day he's way down. Back and forth it goes between buoyancy and depression. This is rarely the clinical type of depression; it's more of a surrender kind of thing, an attitude that says, *Leave me alone right now. Please. I don't want to hurt your feelings, but I need to be by myself.*

He's acutely sensitive to your feelings, but he simply doesn't know how to say no, doesn't know how to end a relationship that doesn't satisfy him, doesn't know how to back off with grace. So he doesn't do anything and hopes that everything will simply resolve itself. Once you understand this about him, you can enjoy him for who he is. A consummate lover. Delightful company. Gracious. Refined. Solicitous. And yes, a true romantic. This is the guy who likes candlelight dinners, walks on the beach at twilight, and lazy Sunday mornings in bed, all with harmonious and blissfully aesthetic surroundings.

Harmony and beauty, in fact, are two themes that run throughout his life. He needs them both. They are essential to his well-being.

As fathers, Libra men bring considerable patience and understanding to their relationships with their kids. If they have more than one child, they are fair in their affection, their honesty, their gifts, in every conceivable way. They bend over backward to be fair with their children. If one child gets a car for Christmas, so does the other. They show no favorites, even if they have a favorite. They also instill their values for honesty and fairness and really, in the end, what gift can be more precious than this?

You won't ever go wrong loving a Libra man. But he may drive you crazy with his indecision, his vacillating, his need to weigh everything. This quality makes him a formidable opponent in debates, formal or informal. After all, he's an air sign, mental and intellectual. His range of knowledge may not be like Gemini's, which tends to be vast and superfluous, but the things he knows about, he knows through and through. Just remember that when he says he loves you, he really means it. Now. This instant. This breath.

But by tomorrow, he's thinking about it, weighing the pros and cons.

Libra Woman

She's fair, that's a given.

She's unusually honest, but she may not always tell you about it.

She's smart, she can beat you at chess, she can hold her own in any male-dominated milieu. But she does it with such charm, such sublime finesse, that you're oblivious until her actions affect you.

There is something about a Libra woman that beguiles and seduces. It isn't just her sexuality, although there's some of that. It's that other worldly quality about her that people notice, the sense that she knows things and has been places that you will never experience. Quite often, it's true. Just as often, it probably isn't. The bottom line is that she creates a spell just by her presence.

Look at Susan Sarandon. Just who is she, anyway? In *The Hunger*, she seemed infinitely vulnerable and naive. In *The Client*, she played a sympathetic attorney with a checkered history. In *Thelma & Louise*, she played Geena Davis's best friend with the kind of fierce loyalty that made every woman hope for a similar best friend. In *Dead Man Walking*, she played the most convincing nun since Audrey Hepburn in *The Nun's Story*. In her daily life, she's the mother to several children, Tim Robbins's significant other, and a woman devoted to her particular causes and not afraid to speak out about them. AIDS. Human rights injustices. Libra ideals.

Ideals. Remember that word. For a Libra woman, it isn't just a concept. If her close friend is dying, she pays for a private duty nurse to tend to her friend's every need. If her son develops a sudden fear of loud noises and tells her it's because he died on a battlefield in the Civil War, she doesn't just shrug it off as fantasy. She explores it. She gets to the root of it.

But always, in the back of her mind, she's weighing everything, every gesture, every word, every nuance. She sees what you can't see. She sees because she's open to it, because deep down inside she understands that to attain true balance is to touch the fingertips of the divine.

She's a soft touch as a parent because she understands her children's perspective. She sees through their eyes, feels through their skins, hears through their ears. She can zip herself up inside someone she loves with such ease that she barely knows who she is when she disengages. And yet, always, there is a part of her that is separate, a part no one ever touches, a part that is just for herself, even if she isn't sure sometimes who that self is.

Physically, the Libra female is as tough to pin down as the Libra male. She isn't given to one particular type or another. You can't say that she's usually slender like a Gemini or that she has the thick, luxurious hair of a Leo, although she may have both. Usually, though, there's something in her eyes that gives her away, some distillation of compassion or a mischievous twinkle that lets you know you're in the presence of a special kind of spirit, an old soul.

Back to Sarandon. Who is she? Who is she *really*? She knows. But she isn't telling.

Libra in the Millennium

Okay, this is the deal, Libra. Some parts of the millennium are going to bug the hell out of you. Your need for harmony and equilibrium are going to be offended. You may not like the pace at which things in general are moving. You won't have enough time to mull, to weigh, to seek that perfect and abstract sense of balance that has been the constant theme of your life until now.

That's the bad news.

The good news is that you're entering the most interesting phase of your life, a time when every relationship you have is going to be re-defined, re-arranged, and rewritten. And guess what? You get to be the scriptwriter, the shrink, and the editor, all rolled into one. You get to wear so many hats that at times you feel like your cousin air sign, Gemini, scattered to the four winds. And thanks to Uranus and Neptune's passage through Aquarius, a compatible air sign, you ultimately flourish and come out on the other side in a new and improved version of yourself.

Energizer: The eclipse of the century on August 11, 1999, at 18 degrees Leo, affects your eleventh house of hopes and aspirations and groups to which you belong. Something that is concealed or hidden in this area now surfaces, and you must confront it and deal with it. Maybe you realize that your lifelong dream, whatever it is, will never reach fruition. Maybe you realize the opposite, that you're closer to realizing your dream than ever before.

Your friendships and group associations may change now. If these relationships don't support your creative interests and restrict your freedom of expression, then they end. The endings now, though, won't be as dramatic as they were when Uranus and Neptune joined up in your sun sign in 1993. That year was probably hellish, like being inside the walled city of Jericho as it collapsed. You released relationships and situations that no longer worked well in your life. You reinvented yourself from the ground up.

But as the millennium opens, the hardest stuff is behind you, Libra. Your personal and business relationships should be on a more or less even keel, with existing relationships contributing to your overall growth and evolution. You feel the effects on the eclipse for several months on either side of it.

Take a look at your birth chart to find out what natal house the eclipse affects. Most heavily affected are planets and house cusps that lie between 17 and 19 degrees Leo.

Catalyst: The lineup of planets in Taurus on May 3, 2000, highlights your eighth house of shared resources, taxes, insurance, and metaphysics. The Jupiter/Saturn conjunction urges you to centralize your financial affairs in some way. If you're in debt, then a home equity loan might be in order. If debt isn't the issue, you try to pull together your financial holds in some way. These may be joint holdings with a spouse or significant other. Make sure you don't owe taxes because this could be the time when the tax man comes knocking for an audit.

In 2003, with Saturn in your allied cardinal sign of Cancer, your career takes new directions. You may conflict with authority figures now—bosses, employers, perhaps even a parent or teacher. You feel your ideas and projects aren't getting the attention they deserve. Your charm, though, helps you get through this period with grace and certainty. Stick to what has been successful for you so far. Complete projects and fulfill obligations before you take on anything new.

In late September of 2004, expansive Jupiter conjuncts your sun and takes the edge off. You may be tempted to kick back and let things just take their merry course, but now is the time when a little effort goes a very long way. You may go back to school to take courses that expand your skills. Workshops and seminars bring you into contact with groups of like-minded individuals. Foreign travel is a good possibility and whatever traveling you do now broadens your understanding of yourself and your worldview.

Your creative potential runs high and strong during this period, with new ideas literally bursting forth. It may be difficult at times, though, to perceive your relationships in this same optimistic vein. You're starting to realize that you can't control every facet of your personal relationships, Libra, and simply have to allow some things to run their natural course.

Transformation: In 1995, significant changes occurred in your life that may have involved your brothers and sisters, your neighborhood, the way you communicate. Your basic thought processes changed. Blame Pluto's passage into Sagittarius. Pluto brings out whatever is hidden and buried, then collapses the old so the new can grow. Sagittarius urges you to speak your truth, even if the people around you don't like it. That makes it a difficult combination for you; all too often, you bite your tongue to keep the peace.

By the opening of the millennium, though, you should be well on your way to speaking your truth even if it upsets the people around you. This personal truth, in fact, is a vital step in your growth as an individual. It allows you to look honestly at the people in your life who may be taking advantage of you, through your need for harmony and peace. You're so capable of rationalization that in the past you've been able to rationalize just about any act of unkindness from someone you care about. But no more.

The people who have taken advantage of you aren't going to like the new you, not if they have a vested interest in you staying the way you've always been. This may become very apparent to you in January and February of 2002, when your conflicts with others at this time are likely to be heated.

Fortunately, Sagittarius is quite compatible with air, so that despite Pluto's psychic plunging, you don't feel as uncomfortable during this transit as some of the other signs. In fact, your intuition is likely to expand during the first eight years of the millennium and is one of your most valuable allies.

Pluto is sextile your sun sign at this time, an aspect that brings a certain ease into your life. So even though you're going through heavy changes, you feel okay about it. Opportunities open up, your ambitions are intense and focused. Take advantage of the moment, Libra.

Look to your natal chart for the house with Sagittarius on the cusp. Unless the cusp is at one degree, then Pluto probably transits two of your houses. What kinds of experiences can you expect? That depends on what you have buried and hidden away deep inside yourself.

One Libra man, who turned eighty-three around the same time that Pluto went into Sagittarius, had a series of shocks over the next year. His wife developed Alzheimer's, he was diagnosed with Parkinson's disease and ended up in a wheelchair, and they had to move in with one of their daughters. They sold the home they'd lived in for more than thirty years and remained with their daughter for ten months. Then they moved back to their hometown, into a retirement community, where they stayed for nearly a year, until he could no longer continue to take care of his wife. He had to commit her to an Alzheimer's unit and moved in with another daughter. After years of relative harmony and peace in his life, Pluto's transit into Sagittarius forced him to admit there are some things he simply can't control.

Pluto-type experiences aren't always negative. But they are nearly always dramatic in some way and push our lives in new directions.

Innovation: Uranus in Aquarius brings the kind of energy you can understand, Libra. The mental energy is like you. Back in early 1996, however, when Uranus went into Aquarius, you probably didn't like it at all. You prefer change that unfolds at a nice, leisurely pace, rather like a stroll in the park, and these changes were anything but. They seemed to have come out of nowhere, unexpected disruptions and upheavals that hit you in your fifth house. Maybe there were upheavals with your kids, your lover. Maybe your social life fell apart. Maybe you ran up against creative blocks.

If you didn't resist the changes, then when the millennium opens, you should be reaping the good parts of this transit—sudden inspiration, flashes of insight, innovative ideas, and creative bonuses. If, on the other hand, you're still resisting the change, then the transit simply gets tougher. It's like living in the midst of a war, with walls crumbling around you, relationships coming undone, your life in chaos.

If that's the place you've reached, then for at least one day a week for a month, clear your calendar. Lock yourself in a room, beat pillows with your fists, and scream at the top of your lungs. Get all the frustration out. Then go out and do something for yourself. Go on a shopping spree. Sign up for flying lessons. Go to the gym. Attend a concert. Don't worry about whatever is going on in your life. Just enjoy what you're doing, *be in the moment.* And when you're really there, Libra, really rooted in this instant, notice what you're thinking, how it feels. Now take this feeling home with you.

Your innovation is born from the now.

New paradigms: For the first three years of the millennium, Uranus in Aquarius keeps company with Neptune in your fifth house of creativity. What an odd couple they make. The first is a disruptive rebel; the second is a dreamy guru. Together, they create a third nameless entity that combines the best of the two. In terms of your daily life, the pair allow you to tap intuitive reservoirs that hold answers and information you need to fulfill your creative potential.

In the spring of 2001, Saturn in Gemini allows you to solidify your worldview. Hitting your ninth house, way up there above the horizon. Saturn's position brings you more into the public eye. During Saturn's two-year transit in Gemini, it's important to grasp who you are and who you are becoming so that when Saturn enters your tenth house, you're prepared for the success you've been seeking. At this time, though, it's easy to believe you know all the rules of whatever game you're playing. If you figure you've got all the answers and stop looking within, then you may be in for a rude surprise.

If you use this transit wisely, however, and pay close attention to how your worldviews are changing, then your pragmatism serves you extremely well. By 2003, you know for sure what you believe.

Truth within: With Uranus in Pisces from 2003 to 2010, the disruptions in your life tend to be of the internal variety. Nightmares with highly symbolic themes, dreams that seem vividly real, wild imaginings, odd premonitions, clairvoyant experiences, spontaneous past-life recall. This is somewhat frightening at first, but as always, the Uranian theme is don't resist, go with the flow.

The purpose of these experiences is to bolster and enrich your inner life, to inundate you with your personal truth. Then you won't be hesitant about voicing *your* opinion as opposed to the opinion you think everyone else wants to hear. You learn to say no when you mean it, instead of just backing away and letting the other person think things are fine only to find out two days later that nothing is fine—that you, in fact, have left town.

In the fall of 2004, you get some help in this department when Jupiter goes into your sun sign. All the weird inner stuff you're experiencing doesn't seem so weird now; it's eye-opening. You embrace it.

By the time Pluto heads into Capricorn in 2008, the truth you've found is put to the test, and the test usually involves issues of power. Now more than ever you should listen to that inner truth, Libra, to deepen your understanding of what's going on.

Spiritual expansion: Isn't this what the past several years have really been about? Expanding your concepts of spirituality and realizing that it has little to do with what you've probably been taught. To live a spiritual life doesn't mean you sit at the feet of a guru or that you worship your god for only a week or that you buy into whatever the latest spiritual fad may be. Rather you must integrate the small with the large, the large with the small, and attempt to live to your highest potential.

Neptune in Aquarius helps you do that. First you see the larger picture. Then you attempt to apply that larger picture to your personal life and relationships. Then you reach even farther, out beyond yourself into the global community. And at some point, you come full circle again, aware that one individual, connecting to his divine self, can make a difference in the larger world.

Self: Personally, you should be feeling like you're on a roll when the millennium opens. In the first couple of years, you're working very hard to merge your ideals with the real world. You're learning to speak up even when it ruffles other people's feathers. Even though it creates problems for you initially in your personal relationships, you're finding that it makes you feel better. Claiming your own power is the first step toward self-realization for you.

Your journey through self-discovery deepens from the fall of 2004 to 2005 and makes quantum leaps when Uranus goes into Pisces in 2004 and stays there until March 2011. Through 2010, while Jupiter travels through Pisces with Uranus, your intuition becomes a fine-tuned instrument that leads you in new directions in many areas of your life.

There will be times when you fall back on your old habits, trying to please everyone just to keep the peace. Or you say what other people want to hear because you can't bear to hurt anyone's feelings. But if you've been working consciously with your beliefs and learning to say what you really think and feel, these times are eventually reduced to brief temptations.

In the first decade of the millennium, your concern with justice and balance gradually extends to the larger world. You join with others who share your ideals and work to make a global difference.

Finances: For you, money isn't the security blanket that it is for Taurus. You like having money because it allows you to surround yourself with the fine things that you enjoy. This isn't likely to change in the millennium. Your earning ability and the ways in which you earn money, however, are likely to change.

When Jupiter goes into Scorpio in late October of 2005, it affects your second house of finances. At this time you may find that the bartering system is alive and well. Quite often, what you receive in return for a service is exactly what you needed or wanted. This is the sort of serendipitous experience that becomes common when you're living with awareness.

The financial consolidation process that you go through at the beginning of the millennium is a necessary first step in freeing up your energy. Your creativity and artistic interests play an important part in your financial affairs in 2007. Maybe you recognize a niche in the commercial market that your artistic leanings can fill. Maybe you start your own business.

You excel as a mediator, healer, or in any facet of the law. If you can bring your creative abilities into this kind of work, the financial payoff can be considerable. The most important thing to remember is to allow your intuition the freedom to speak. It is your best and most loyal ally and will lead you into new financial opportunities.

Communication: There's only one way to break a habit, Libra, and that's to deal with it consciously. So whenever you're about to express an opinion, make sure that it's what *you* really feel and believe. Check yourself every step of the way. When you do say something just to keep the peace or to keep from hurting someone's feelings, then ask yourself why you did it. What are you really afraid of? What's at the root of it?

This sort of censure may squash your verbal spontaneity for a while, but by being aware of what you say and when you say it, you ultimately break free of a pattern that interferes with your relationships. If you don't break the habit now, then the road only gets more difficult and complicated.

Pluto in Sagittarius affects your third house of communication until 2008, urging you to speak your truth. If you aren't sure at this point what your truth is, then start keeping a journal.

In Julia Cameron's insightful book, *The Artist's Way*, she recommends doing "morning pages" every day, where you write about whatever is going on in your life—issues, goals, concerns, dreams. This is an excellent way to work through any sort of habit because it makes you more conscious of what's going on inside you. Once you become more aware of the dynamics, it's easier to catch yourself before you say what you don't mean. Energy is freed up that can be channeled more creatively.

By November 2006, when Jupiter joins Pluto in Sagittarius, you should be far more comfortable communicating what you think and believe. Jupiter in its home sign makes the whole thing easier, too, and less threatening. You discover that the people who don't like your honesty are the ones who also drain your energy. They probably are the first to leave, too, which only benefits you.

Your home: If the people in your immediate environment have stifled your creativity and growth, then you either work with them to change it, speak your truth and hope they adjust to it, or the relationships end. It's that simple.

During the first decade of the millennium, your home life is likely to go through a lot of changes, particularly from 2003 to 2005, when Saturn is squaring your natal sun. You may feel at times that you're being defeated in everything you attempt. But by developing an awareness of the patterns operating in your life at this time, you can turn adversity into challenges.

And remember: the sooner you learn to say what you think and feel, the easier it all becomes.

Creative potential: This is a major area for you in the millennium. With Uranus and Neptune in Aquarius hitting your fifth house of creativity, you feel compelled to find new ways to express your creative interests and passions. Flashes of insight and heightened intuition help you do this. The more aware you are of inner promptings, the easier the process is.

Joining a group of like-minded individuals may help you clarify your creative goals. In a group setting like this, particularly if you don't know these people very well, you are tempted by your old habits to say what you think other people expect or want to hear. You quickly learn, however, that the old way doesn't work, and you either have to change how you relate to people or find another group.

When Jupiter goes into your sun sign in the fall of 2004, your creative ideas and opportunities expand beyond anything you've imagined. Everything you touch seems to turn to success, and a part of you wants to just sit back and enjoy what's happening. If you do that, however, you may regret it a year later, when Jupiter leaves Libra. The other temptation you may experience during this time is to take on everything that comes your way, expanding so quickly that you spread yourself much too thinly.

From January through mid-March of 2007, when Mercury joins Neptune in Aquarius, you have an opportunity to communicate your creative ideas. This could come through a book you start writing or through some other creative venue.

Quite often, synchronicities happen during intensely creative and dramatic periods of our lives, so pay special attention to any "coincidences" you experience now. Note the specifics of the synchronicity—where and when it happens, what it concerns, whether it involves names, numbers, or something else, and what the deeper message seems to be.

If you don't have any idea what the message is, then try to interpret it as you might a dream. Keep a notebook handy so that you can record any synchronicities you experience or even jot down ideas you might have. If it's too much trouble to write things down, then use a recorder. The point is to develop awareness of what's going on in the deeper levels of your life.

Health & work: From the summer of 2003 to mid-July of 2005, Saturn is square your natal sun. Your health may be particularly vulnerable at this time, so be sure that you're cautious about burning yourself out. Take time to evaluate what you can do to improve your general health at this time. All the usual things the experts recommend would be a good place to start: diet, nutrition, exercise, vitamins. In addition, you should try to understand the metaphoric language of illness.

Some of these metaphors are obvious. If you develop a sudden ache or spasm in your back (which tends to be the most vulnerable part of Libra's body), then ask yourself what situation or person is too much to bear. For more information on illness as metaphor, read *Anatomy of the Spirit* by Carolyn Myss and *Awakening Intuition* by Mona Lisa Schultz. Both women are medical intuitives who connect physical illness to emotional and spiritual imbalances.

When Jupiter goes into your sun sign in October 2004, your general energy and health improve. Even so, continue with any new health practices that you started in 2003.

Partnerships: This is your natural domain, Libra, and the area where the most dramatic changes are likely to take place for you. For most of your life, you've been a social creature who enjoys groups and gatherings, but only on your terms, when you're in the mood. You actually prefer the intimacy of one-on-one relationships. And yet, time and again, you have compromised your own truth because of your strong need to preserve harmony and peace. This has undermined many of our relationships.

During the first decade of the millennium, however, you find that circumstances are nudging you more and more frequently into group situations.

Sometimes your natural ability to mediate disputes and arbitrate a middle ground comes into play. Other times you are drawn to groups that share your interests and ideals, and through them, you find your true voice and the freedom to be who you are.

In fact, as the millennium progresses, you become increasingly less tolerant of relationships that don't allow you to express yourself freely. This is as true of your personal relationships as it is of your business partnerships. If you feel choked, you get out.

Spirituality: The lineup of planets in Taurus in May 2000 triggers your spiritual quest for the first decade of the millennium. All that energy touches something deep inside you and, in a sense, awakens you. The Jupiter/Saturn conjunction is particularly significant because Jupiter seeks to expand your spiritual beliefs and Saturn gives you a structure with which to do it.

Your primary spiritual focus in the millennium, Libra, is to apply your beliefs to your relationships. Once you speak your truth in a relationship and allow the other person to do the same, even if your truths differ, you realize it's okay to be who you are.

Career & profession: Ample opportunities for advancement come your way, particularly from July 2001 to the following summer, when Jupiter in Cancer hits your tenth house. From June of 2003 to mid-July of 2005, with Saturn in Cancer you face professional challenges, especially from authority figures—bosses, employers, parents. You may feel that your ideas and efforts aren't being recognized. Simply persevere and stick to what you know. Try to look at each challenge as an opportunity to learn something about yourself.

Between 2005 and 2007, the pressure eases considerably, and you're able to make tremendous headway. Just remember what you've been learning all along: say what you mean and feel. Be as forthright as possible when dealing with others.

Personal unconscious: To some extent, the challenge for all of us in the first decade of the millennium is to make the unconscious conscious. This process is especially concentrated for you, Libra, from the fall of 2007 to the end of October 2009. Saturn in Virgo makes you sure you pay close attention to any health issues that have grown out of emotions and power you have disowned.

Maintain your equilibrium, listen to your inner oracle, remain true to yourself and your truth. Then this transit is much easier to navigate, and you're able to take advantage of every opportunity that comes your way.

Tapping the Source

Synchronicities & Your Inner Oracle

The wonderful thing about synchronicities is that they always concern whatever we're focused on at the time. For you, Libra, that's likely to be your relationships and learning to communicate how you really feel and think about something.

Try an experiment. Each evening for seven days, sit quietly for a few minutes. Clear your mind. Tell yourself that you would like to tune in on an event that's going to happen the next day, then write it down. It may come to you as an image, in a word or phrase, or just as a feeling about some specific thing or person in your life. Don't worry about whether the event comes to pass the next day or the next week or whether it ever happens at all. The point of this exercise is to send a message to your unconscious that you're open to the experience. When you've done this for a week, stop writing it down. Simply give yourself a suggestion when you're waking in the morning that you would like to experience a synchronicity. Back this request with intent and desire.

The results should surprise you.

Creating Your Future

You do this daily, Libra. You do it moment by moment. The trick is to do it consciously, by developing an awareness of your deepest beliefs. Your natural intuition comes into play very strongly with any sort of conscious creation.

One man used conscious creation to find his wallet. He had gone windsurfing one day on a lake near his home and lost his wallet. He couldn't remember if he'd left it with his equipment on the grass or if it had been in the back pocket of his bathing suit. He decided, though, that this state of affairs just wouldn't do and set about to correct it.

For two days he focused on the wallet. Saw it in vivid detail, the worn leather, the items inside, and he saw it *in his hand.* On the third morning, he got a call from a man who had been fishing in the lake where he'd gone windsurfing and had hooked the wallet! It turned out this same man had been to his house the week before to find out of he needed someone to mow his lawn.

One of the best books written on conscious creation

is *Beyond the Winning Streak* by Lynda Dahl, an ex-vice president in the computer industry. If you want examples of conscious creation, Libra, read this book. She tells you how she consciously created a million dollars!

Chapter 16

Scorpio, the Scorpion

October 24–November 22
Fixed, Water
Ruled by Pluto

Scorpio Man

Even people who don't know much about astrology react strongly when they hear the word *Scorpio,* probably because the word sounds like "scorpion," the creature that symbolizes this sign. However, perhaps the power of the word makes them uneasy.

And it should. Scorpios in general are not for the meek and the mild, and the Scorpio man in particular embodies a kind of primal awareness about who he is that can be deeply intimidating. Never be frivolous with this man. If you have fun with him—and you will, many times—make sure the fun is sincere and not a front for some other emotion. Never be less than what you really are with him; he'll see through it. In fact, the best rule of thumb with this guy is to keep in mind that everything for him exists in black and white. There are no gray areas. No nuances. No lengthy rationalizations that change the essential bottom line. For both genders of the sign, life is serious business.

This is also true for people with a Scorpio moon or ascendant, although to a lesser degree. With a Scorpio moon, the intensity happens primarily on an emotional level. With the rising, the intensity seems to be concentrated in how the individual comes across to others. In any case, a Scorpio man is not to be taken lightly.

First of all, you'd better not be uncomfortable with powerful and intense emotion; this is the driving force in his life, the theme of his life, his reason for being. He *feels* to the nth degree: feels the divided loyalties in your heart, the piercing beauty of the sunset, the ringing beauty of his child's laughter. He is primal, that's the only word for it.

And this primal quality comes through in every facet of who he is. Yes, he's romantic, but it's the kind of romance that can suck you dry unless you're ready for it. He demands honesty. You must be absolutely and unequivocally honest with him because he will be that honest with you, even if he doesn't spell it out. Even if he doesn't verbalize it. Even if he waits for you to express what you feel first. To say that he's very private almost misses the point because privacy is only one facet of his personality.

His passions aren't limited. They extend to his family, his children, his friends, his creative interests. But to win his passion and his loyalty, you must first show him that you're worthy. Can you keep a secret? To say that you can is not enough; you have to show him that you can. Even then, he may not confide in you completely. There is always something that he keeps to himself, some core that you never see, much less touch.

You can always tell a Scorpio, male or female, by the piercing eyes. Their gaze is direct, penetrating, unequivocal. They look and act calm and cool, as if they didn't have a problem in the world. But inside, that intensity burns and seethes; you can see it in the eyes.

As a father, the Scorpio man is protective, stern, and has fixed ideas about how children should be raised. He instills his values in his kids from a very young age and is brutally honest about their strengths and weaknesses. In fact, he's blunt about most everything, although not in the same way that a Sagittarius is. Where a Sagittarian blurts his truth, the Scorpio thinks about it, mulls it over, then tells you.

Jealousy is easily aroused in a Scorpio man. He demands your loyalty, but don't ever think that he is bound by the same rules. If he strays, however, you probably won't know about it. He's able to maintain secrecy about his own life even under the most intimate of circumstances.

His charisma and magnetism often border on prescience. He is, in fact, quite intuitive and if he nurtures this part of his personality, can become outright psychic.

Take a good look sometime at a scorpion. See that stinger at the end of its tail? Now remember this: never cross a Scorpio man or a woman. If you do, you'll feel that sting.

Scorpio Woman

The popular image of the Scorpio woman is that of the femme fatale, a Kathleen Turner in *Body Heat*. She is seductive and secretive, passionate and alluring, and she has her own agenda. While this version of the Scorpio woman certainly exists, it isn't the whole picture.

Another type of Scorpio woman, a more highly evolved version, is Ellen Burstyn in *Resurrection*. In the movie, Burstyn loses her husband in a car accident and becomes a cripple. Her will to walk again is so strong, she eventually heals herself and discovers that she can also heal others.

A third type is Diane Keaton in *The Godfather*, the wife of a Mafia kingpin, the woman who knows the truth and tries to live with it by denying it. Each of these women experience common themes in their lives: powerful and intense emotions, dramatic experiences, strong intuitive ability, and an acute interest in the shadow side of life. Remember: Scorpio is ruled by Pluto, the mythological god of the underworld. This woman came in with a need to investigate all eighth house matters—death and dying, reincarnation, the occult.

As a friend, the Scorpio woman is as loyal as they come, once she trusts you. But in return, she expects an equal loyalty and dedication. If she calls you at three in the morning to talk, she expects you to take her call. Yes, it's irritating and inconsiderate. On the other hand, when your life collapses around you, she's your strongest ally and it doesn't matter to her how long it takes for you to rebuild your life. She'll be there.

She brings this same passionate intensity to romance, to her family, to living. In romance, she won't even look at you unless she believes you're worthy of her attention—you must impress her as someone who is as strong as she is. Once she looks, then you have to prove to her what you're made of. If you pass that test, then you may get an invitation for dinner or she may agree to go out with you. All of this is predicated on one condition, however—that you don't disappoint her. Once she's sure that you love her and that she can trust you, then all that passion comes out.

As a mother, she's devoted to her kids. Even if she's not one of those mothers who hugs you good-bye every time she heads out into her own life, she has made it abundantly clear that you are integral to her life and that she will always do anything she can to facilitate your passage from infancy to adulthood.

In the business world, she's a dynamo, every bit as qualified as the Scorpio man to attain her goals, whatever they are. She's focused on the inside and appears cool and contained on the outside, a winning combination. She may also be artistically inclined—music, art, writing, something she does with such consummate ease that it seems she has probably been studying it for years. But she hasn't.

The odd thing about the men and women of this sign is that just when you think you know them, they do something that makes you realize you have barely scratched the surface. Even if you've been married to this woman for twenty years, keep in mind that you know only the parts of her that she allows you to see. This will prevent you from ever taking her for granted, which would certainly spell the end of the relationship.

The adage about a Scorpio, male or female, is that you may hate them or love them, but you will never, never be indifferent to them.

Scorpio in the Millennium

The millennium is tailor-made for you, Scorpio, because it's going to involve change at the deepest levels of the collective psyche, which is where you do much of your best work. You aren't afraid to embrace your shadow. There are periods in your life, in fact, in which you feel you do this daily.

Much of your most difficult work was done while Pluto passed through your sun sign from 1984 to 1995. You plundered, you confronted, you were transformed. Now the rest of the process begs completion. You have to take what you learned and apply it to your life in the most honest way possible. Sounds simple, doesn't it?

Read on, Scorpio. Read on.

Energizer: The solar eclipse on August 11, 1999, brings out something in your career that has been hidden or suppressed. You may feel the effects several months on either side of the actual eclipse, sensing that something is building to a climax, but unable at first to put your finger on exactly what it is.

The closer your sun lies to the degree of the eclipse, the more deeply you're affected. Also, if you have a moon or rising in Scorpio in the middle degrees, the eclipse tends to impact your life more powerfully. In any case, the eclipse galvanizes you in a new direction in your profession or career, and ultimately, the change is beneficial even if it doesn't appear that way at first.

Maybe you've been feeling for some time that your job or your career isn't exactly what you want, but you haven't been sure how to change it. Perhaps financial obligations have prevented you from exploring other options. The eclipse may bring things to a head when your company downsizes and you're on the hit list. You may flounder for several months, locked in turmoil beneath that ever calm exterior.

Just remember, Scorpio, you possess a will that is the most powerful in the zodiac. Use it to create what you need and desire.

Catalyst: Polarity is at work on May 3, 2000, when seven planets line up in Taurus, opposing your sun. This initially creates an imbalance in your life, so that you feel like you're sitting on the side of a seesaw that's heading downward.

The Jupiter/Saturn part of this conjunction marks the end of one cycle and the beginning of a new one. The problem is that you have to get through the endings first, which are apt to leave you feeling tired and discouraged. Any relationships you're involved in that restrict your self-expression may end at this time. Ultimately, these endings benefit you, even if that's not how it feels when it's happening.

Other areas of your life flourish at this time. Professional success culminates, and opportunities for financial advancement come your way. If you're not careful, these successes can make you cocky and somewhat arrogant because you feel like you've got all the answers. You don't, of course, and in your heart you know it. Whatever problems you encounter during this one to two year period are best dealt with by looking within for the solutions.

Transformation: Transformation is your middle name, Scorpio, and it has to do with the intensity with which you live. Your life is a series of dramatic events and encounters, and this probably won't change during the millennium. What *will* change, however, is that you learn to work *with* this process rather than struggling against it. You do this by recognizing the emotional patterns that prevail in your life and probing the reasons such patterns exist.

Why, for instance, do you feel you have to control every single facet of your life and the lives of those closest to you? Is it really necessary to bring your kids' friends to the house every weekend for sleepovers, but not allow them to spend the night elsewhere? What difference can it possibly make if your assistant does the job her way instead of your way as long as the job gets done?

Pluto is in Sagittarius until 2008, so you've got eight years in the millennium to illuminate whatever is still hidden inside you and to integrate it somehow into who you are. Once you do that, you're leagues closer to fulfilling your potential.

You get a considerable boost in late November of 2005, when Jupiter goes into your sun sign for a year. You feel so great during this transit that at times you're tempted to just sit back and let the good times unfold. Instead, you should take advantage of the opportunities that come your way and try to do what you can to expand your worldview. You may want to go back to school, take workshops and seminars, or become involved with groups who reflect your passions and ideals.

Your freedom increases under the transit, too. This could translate as trips to foreign countries or trips into inner dimensions through some sort of spiritual discipline. You feel more fun-loving and playful during this transit, and even though it seems foreign to you at first, just go with it, Scorpio, and see where it leads you.

In your birth chart, look for the house that has Sagittarius on the cusp. This house is where you go through your deepest transformation for the first eight years of the millennium.

Innovation: When Uranus went into Aquarius in 1996, it squared your natal sun. Sudden unexpected events forced you to question what you were doing in some area of your life. To some extent, this process continues until Uranus goes into Pisces in the early spring of 2003.

The sudden events that ride tandem with Uranus usually happen in that area of your life where your individuality is being restricted or smothered. Perhaps it's your job. Although you like it well enough, you can't be yourself. You can't let your brilliance shine. So Uranus in Aquarius sweeps in, you get fired or laid off, and now you're free. You may also be panicked about where your next mortgage payment is coming from. This is just an example of the kinds of things that happen under this transit. If a relationship restricts you, then it may end. The point is that whatever holds you down vanishes from your life.

If you're flexible and free in most areas of your life, then the disruptive part of this transit won't be very dramatic. The disruption simply tests the stuff of which you're made.

In July 2001, you get help from Jupiter in Cancer, a fellow water sign. This impacts your ninth house, expanding your worldview and bringing you new experiences in that area, perhaps through foreign travel or people from other cultures and countries. Your creative potential is tremendous now. You have innovative approaches to old problems and are able to put many of your new ideas into action. You have a higher tolerance than usual for differences of opinion.

New paradigms: During the first three years of the millennium, Uranus shares the Aquarian spotlight with Neptune and squares your natal sun. Things may be weird for a while, Scorpio, even for you. During this transit, it's as if the cosmos asks you at every step of the way if you believe in what you're doing. You're urged to scrutinize your objectives and goals in your personal and professional lives. Anything that holds you back or restricts your freedom ends—a job, profession, a relationship.

Your natural intuitive ability deepens and helps you understand the confusion you feel around this time. You may turn to the study of metaphysics or start using a divination system that sheds light on the experiences you're having.

Part of the new paradigm you create involves how you earn money. Your avocation may become your vocation. Or you find some unique niche in the market that you know you can fill, and proceed to do exactly that. Your financial base expands as a result of this new paradigm.

Truth within: Uranus goes into Pisces in March 2003 and remains there until May 2010. Pisces, as a fellow water sign, is compatible with Scorpio; Uranus in Pisces trines your natal sun. During these seven years, many new experiences and relationships enter your life that allow you to express yourself more fully and more honestly.

The problem isn't that you lack for opportunities. As a fixed sign, though, you don't like change unless it's on *your* terms, according to *your* time frame, and *your* agenda. Uranus in Aquarius, especially during its early stages in the late 1990s, was no picnic because change was thrust on you. If you failed to give your intuitive ability full rein during that transit, then Uranus in Pisces makes sure that your psychic self finds its voice.

In late October of 2005, you get some help in this department when Jupiter conjuncts your sun. The spectrum of your worldview is expanded considerably, through people and events. These external factors seep into your subconscious and merge with all the psychic activity taking place inside you.

One way or another, Scorpio, your powerful intuition finds its rightful place in your life. And this, in turn, solidifies your personal truth.

Spiritual expansion: Neptune in Aquarius, sitting there all alone in your fourth house, initially blurs the boundaries between your early childhood and your immediate life. Old emotional patterns and memories now surface, forcing you to confront and deal with issues you would rather keep buried. But to grow spiritually, Scorpio, you need to resolve these issues and understand them in light of your life now. Once you do that, your spiritual path becomes clearer to you.

If you're still following the religion in which you were raised, you may find yourself questioning whether it fits into the life you live now or whether it answers the deeper questions that you have. These questions have always concerned you to one extent or another, but now you can't seem to just push them aside for another day. They demand answers. This is also part of the birth of your new paradigm, Scorpio, so welcome it.

Self: The fundamental lesson you learn in the first decade of the millennium sounds simple on paper. When you encounter obstacles or when things aren't going your way, you learn to let go instead of struggling to change what can't be changed. Release is a major Scorpio theme, so it's not as if you're unfamiliar with it. The difference now is that you release *consciously, willingly,* before external events force you to do so.

Remember: each sign is an archetype, the distillation of a particular type of energy. As a Scorpio, the archetypal themes that run through your life are death, rebirth, resurrection, release, and power. Katharine Hepburn is a Scorpio. So are Michael Crichton and Prince Charles. So is John Gotti.

Gotti is particularly interesting because the Mafia itself is Scorpio ruled. And from all accounts, he wielded his power in typical Scorpionic fashion—through brutality on the one hand and benevolence on the other. His wife, son, and one of his daughters are also Scorpios.

The Scorpio daughter, now a novelist, is intensely private and shuns the limelight unless she's promoting one of her novels. When she was in her late twenties, one of her brothers was killed in a tragic car accident, and shortly afterward she developed a serious heart condition. *She turned her grief inward* and then turned it outward, by establishing a charity for children with life-threatening illnesses. All of this is an illustration of how a Scorpio archetype can work in its most intense form.

In the millennium, Scorpio, your personal archetypal patterns either become apparent to you through your own inner work or they are reflected in people and situations that challenge you and force you to change.

Finances: With your usual piercing insight, you recognize economic opportunities in the millennium.

This starts early in the new century, with that lineup of planets in Taurus that all oppose your sun and compel you to look for new ways to bring home the bacon.

The traditional fields for Scorpios are financial planning and forecasting, insurance, mortician, healer, psychic, banking, investments. These traditional venues won't go away, but the millennium brings new approaches within the context of a global community.

Communication: Your deepest and most enduring communication has always been with yourself. That's going to change in the millennium, but not until the latter part of the first decade, when Pluto goes into Capricorn, hitting your third house of communication.

You feel the process long before this, though, as your own inner unfolding occurs in various areas of your life. You're working to communicate with others in a forthright manner, which will get across the intensity of your emotions.

By November of 2009, your intuitive skill should be so well developed that you're able to depend on it to guide you in the right direction, toward the right people. These people include a group of individuals who share your talents and ideals and, perhaps, even your intensity. With them, you can be yourself and through them, you learn *nonresistance* to change, Scorpio.

Your home: In the first decade of the millennium, your immediate environment undergoes abrupt and unexpected changes. Your family structure may change—a birth, a parent moves in, a child moves out, or an adult child returns. Maybe you move from one town or state to another or maybe you build onto your existing home. A parent's decline in health is sometimes associated with Neptune and Uranus in the fourth house.

However this duo affects your life, it somehow alters your deepest beliefs and ultimately connects you to the larger picture. You may find that you're reading more metaphysical and philosophical books that help you connect in a more meaningful way to people in your environment.

Again, the lesson here is release, Scorpio. Uranus is rearranging your fundamental approach to life, and Neptune is dissolving boundaries so that your intuitive ability has greater freedom.

Creative potential: Your creativity hits an all-time high when Uranus goes into Pisces in early spring of 2003 and hits your fifth house. This transit brings new opportunities, experiences, and relationships in which your creative abilities are brought fully into play. You may be attracted to or involved in new media or electronic advances. Overall, it's an exciting time for you.

Remember, though, that Uranus disrupts the areas of your life where you are the most rigid and inflexible. If your relationship with your children has been somewhat rigid until now, things change under this transit. Either they may become rebellious and hard to handle, or you will enjoy exciting and strange experiences with them.

The pursuits that you enjoy for pleasure also change under this transit. You may become more daring, more willing to take risks. Your pleasure may translate into new ways to make money.

In late fall of 2009, Jupiter joins Uranus in Pisces.

This serves as a shot of adrenaline for your creativity, romance, your relationship with your kids, and your self-expression. You no longer feel you have to hide who you are or what you think and feel. If you work in the arts, then it's likely you make more money this year than ever before in your particular field.

Your intuitive ability deepens under this transit, and you receive information through your dreams, imagination, and any sort of creative play. Your impulses are likely to be quite strong, too, at this time. They rise from the deep, intuitive layers of your psyche and are intended to nudge you in new directions, breaking up your normal thought patterns. Follow them, and you end up in the right place at the right time.

Health & work: In the health arena, the mid-eighties to the mid-nineties were difficult for you. A lot of old issues began to surface that were connected to your early childhood, sexuality, and money and power. These are archetypal themes for you, Scorpio. And when the issues and the emotions behind them aren't resolved, they tend to lodge in the area of the body where you're most vulnerable—sexual and reproductive organs and your elimination organs.

By late 1995 or early 1996, many of these old issues should have surfaced. For the last four or five years of the twentieth century, you should have worked on resolving them. If you did, then the first decade of the millennium will be a healing period in which you're able to integrate what you have learned into who you are. If you ignored the issues in the hopes that they would vanish, then you may be in for a rough period.

Your inner, emotional life is the richest of all the water signs, with intense feelings that run deeply. You need a release for these emotions—a creative outlet would be good, but a physical exercise program is even better. Best yet, combine the two. And, just for good measure, toss in five minutes a day spent in communion with your deeper self, honesty evaluating who and what you are and where you're going. In the long run, this does more for your health than the quick fix of drugs.

Your will is so strong that when you bring its full power to bear on any health problems you have, you become the medical miracle!

Partnerships: For you, life without passion is like death. That won't change in the millennium, but the way you relate to the people you're closest to is going to change dramatically.

Usually, when you're deeply involved in a relationship and things start to get bumpy, you become a bit obsessive. All of your energy seems to go into correcting whatever is wrong. In the early part of the millennium, you learn to step back, detach, and look at yourself and your behavior dispassionately. Or, at any rate, that's what you should attempt to learn.

The lesson may not be easy, but there are definite steps you can take to facilitate the process. Whenever you feel overwhelmed or obsessive, take a deep breath, hold it to the count of ten, and exhale slowly. Repeat this until you feel more grounded. Then allow your significant other the freedom to express what he or she is feeling—disappointment, anger, whatever it is. In turn, you must be honest and forthright about whatever you are feeling.

Remember that lineup of planets in Taurus in the spring of 2000? They oppose your sun in your seventh house of partnerships. You're going to feel tremendous pressure to break old patterns in this area and it has to start with *you*, not with the other person.

Spirituality: Regardless of whether you adhere to the beliefs of an organized religion or a set of beliefs that you've found on your own, your spiritual life is important to you. For about two years, beginning in the summer of 2000, spiritual issues are at the forefront of your life. Your intuitive ability is a powerful guide in this regard and leads you to the right structure for your evolving beliefs and the right venue for expressing them.

For you, Scorpio, it's all about bringing your inner and outer realities into synch with each other.

Career & profession: In the summer of 2002, when Jupiter hits your tenth house, you begin to make tremendous strides in your career. July of 2002 sets it off, with a lot of your energy going into professional matters. From July of 2005 to early September of 2007, the big payoff comes *if* you've played your cards right.

Whatever you do during this period, Scorpio, make sure that you follow your heart. Don't allow fear to undermine your goals and dreams. Take risks, listen to your intuition, and then act.

Personal unconscious: Your goal in this area is shared by all signs in the millennium: to make the unconscious conscious and to live with more awareness. The way you do this, Scorpio, is by developing balance.

From the fall of 2004 to mid-October of 2005, with Jupiter in Libra hitting your solar twelfth house, this process is facilitated in some way through an individual or a group that helps you understand the most hidden aspects of yourself.

Your health is very good at this time, which increases your energy and your drive to make visible whatever has been concealed.

Tapping the Source

Synchronicities & Your Inner Oracle

Even if you've never paid much attention to the so-called coincidences in your life, you excel at recognizing and utilizing the overall pattern of these synchronicities. This is the kind of stuff that is Scorpio's domain.

As you begin to work with your own beliefs, these synchronicities are likely to become more frequent. They make the internal visible and keep occurring until you get the message. They unfold in a variety of ways—through dreams, individuals, situations, numbers, names, books, movies. You may be browsing in a bookstore, for instance, and a book literally falls off a shelf at your feet. It *just happens* to be the very thing that answers some concern that you have. Or maybe you're on a plane, and the person sitting next to you inadvertently addresses an issue that's important in your life.

However these synchronicities unfold, they strike you at a visceral level, Scorpio, and force you to pay attention. When this starts happening, you can be sure your inner oracle is alive and well, guiding you in exactly the direction you need to go.

Creating Your Future

Conscious creation usually appeals to the Scorpio mind-set. With your will and determination, you're able to transform just about any facet of your life. You probably do it daily without even thinking about it, so just imagine what you can accomplish by working consciously with your beliefs.

One simple technique to uncover any hidden beliefs you might have is to jot down a single word or a phrase in the middle of a sheet of paper that expresses some facet of your life. Maybe the word is "job" or "my love life." Enclose the word or phrase in a small circle. Then, without thinking about it, write down everything that comes to mind as a result of that word or phrase. Jot these words around the circle, like spokes in a wheel.

If these secondary words bring to mind other words or phrases, then create a third layer. Pretty soon, you'll arrive at the innermost core of what that word or phrase means to you. This is a good way to uncover anger, grief, bitterness, power that you've disowned. You essentially are peeling back the layers of your psyche to get to the core beliefs. From this point, you can work on the emotions surrounding a particular belief.

There are many excellent books available on using visualization, affirmations, and prayer to create the future that you want. Some of the best are: *Creative Visualization* by Shakti Gawain, *Beyond the Winning Streak* by Lynda Dahl, *The Nature of Personal Reality* by Jane Roberts, *Awakening Intuition* by Mona Lisa Schultz, and *Listening to the Oracle* by Dianne Skafte.

Any of these is a good place to start creating the future you want, from your point of power in the present.

Chapter 17

Sagittarius, the Archer

November 22–December 21
Mutable, Fire
Ruled by Jupiter

Sagittarius Man

This is supposed to be the sign that spouts the truth in the new millennium, right? Well, if you've never had a dose of Sagittarian truth, you may be in for a rude awakening. It doesn't matter whether it's a Sagittarian man or a Sagittarian woman who's speaking. The man may look at you in your new outfit, eyes dropping from your face to your toes, and nod with what you think is approval. "You look terrific in that color, but maybe you should lose five or six pounds before you wear it anywhere. It's puckering in the hips. And those shoes are a couple years out of fashion, at least. But if you polish them up, they won't look too bad."

You're dying inside. You want to find the nearest rock and crawl under it. You don't know whether to sink your fist into his kisser or walk away from him and never look back. But he doesn't have a clue how you feel just then. He's simply being his usual honest self, telling you exactly how it is with not even a glimmer of understanding about how his words may affect you.

Welcome to the world of the Sagittarian man, the life of the party, the stumbling buffoon who thinks everyone is laughing at his ill-timed joke. He is the nomad who picks up and travels at a moment's notice, with nothing more in his pocket than grocery money and a sense of adventure. This is the man who thinks big, who can see the whole picture when he really wants to, and who often wanders off on tangents when he's telling you what he's *really* into.

Generally, there are two broad types. The first is the bombastic sort, the man who bludgeons you with his opinions and ideas as soon as you walk into the room. He grins a lot. He believes you find him as fascinating as he finds himself. He spouts all sorts of idealistic stuff on any number of topics—religion, philosophy, reality and illusion, foreign countries. When you manage to get a word in edgewise, he interrupts you almost immediately because he has already been there and done that. He has seen bigger cities, rafted larger and faster rivers, made more money, and taken bigger risks than you. And, oh yes, he also communes regularly with God.

Astrologers refer to this type as "less evolved." The truth, though, is that he's obnoxious.

The other type of Sag man is a Walt Disney, a Nostradamus, a Woody Allen. He may be *out there,* but he has something concrete to contribute. His mind lives within a very large framework, and he seeks to understand and communicate that framework to others. As an archetype, he is the hero who pits himself against incredible odds and not only wins the girl, but saves the universe. And he does it better than any other mortal in the history of the civilized world.

In romance, his honesty may be hard to take, but you won't ever be bored. He keeps you hopping. Literally. Today he wakes up without a quest, so he creates one, and then off he goes, galloping into the sunset with John Wayne or Han Solo. If you're there when he reaches his destination, great. If you're not, that's okay, too. He gives you your freedom. He gives you so much freedom, in fact, that you may go looking for an earth sign with whom you can share your life.

And when you're telling your friends about him years later, you remember how much he loved animals. The blustery type, however, may tend to feel that animals are an expression of himself and must, therefore, be kept in their proper places, subjugated to *his* will, *his* agenda. But the other type may bleed every time he sees a stray and may, in fact, include animal rights in his list of missions.

As a father, he also comes in two varieties. The blustery type carries his jokes with and about his kids a bit too far. "My boys are a pain in the butt," he says at dinner one night. And when one of his boys states emphatically that he is *not* a pain in the butt, the Sag father, aware of what he has said, still declares his son has been disrespectful.

The other type of Sag father is the sort that children remember with deep and abiding affection when they are adults. He's fun and adventurous, the Huck Finn of parenting. He rides the fastest roller coasters, hands waving wildly in the air as the roller coaster plunges down a sloping track, and he takes you to the most exotic places. Bali on New Year's Eve. Salem, Massachusetts, on Halloween. He teaches you courage and the importance of standing by your convictions.

Sagittarius Woman

Stand back. She's coming into the room. All eyes flit toward her. She's smiling. She's dressed to kill. She looks like all the best clichés. Then she makes a beeline for the hostess and announces that the house looks grand, but the air smells, well, odd, a bit moldy. A stick of incense should do the trick, she suggests, and pulls one out of her bag.

She's the first type.

The second type is often found among psychics, philosophers, artists and musicians, true travelers, and business entrepreneurs. Yes, they're honest and blunt, but they seemed to have learned to channel their quest into creative pursuits and very specific types of missions and ideals.

Even women with Sagittarian moons or ascendants share traits of both types. They may have a sharp, biting wit. They may hold a truth that you need to hear.

The Sagittarian woman holds her own with any man. Take the character of Rose in *Titanic.* She could arm wrestle a muscle guy and beat him. She could drink a man under the table. She could stand on the tips of her toes in her stocking feet. She competed in any arena as an equal and demanded her freedom. But she also fell in love to the depths of her soul and shot *Titanic* to the top ten list of best-selling movies.

This second type of Sagittarian woman seeks truth for the sake of truth and not because she has a personal agenda. She meets life head-on, filled with fun and play and a sense of purpose. She loves to travel, not caring where she travels; the point is the journey itself. She needs those trips, craves them. They awaken her nomadic spirit.

When she can't travel physically, then "travel of the mind" suits her just fine—a seminar, a workshop, college courses. If she gets into metaphysics, which she probably does at some point in her life, she catches on very quickly. Astral travel, clairvoyance, telepathy, past-life recall: all of it is fair game to this woman.

As a mother, this second type is the sort who rolls around on the rug with her toddlers or sneaks out into the garden with them at night to watch fireflies or an eclipse of the moon. She's fun and adventurous and encourages her kids to approach life with the same fearlessness. She may be extravagant at times with them, spending money that she doesn't have, but so what. Her magnanimous nature is infectious. Her children often grow up to be as generous as she is.

Sagittarius rules the hips, thighs, and liver. These areas are the strongest parts of their bodies and also the most vulnerable to stress. To some extent, this is true of someone with a Sagittarian moon or ascendant as well.

The Sagittarian woman has a temper, especially if you offend her sense of right and wrong or poke fun at one of her causes. She also has her own gauge for measuring what kind of person you are. One Sagittarian woman, an animal rights' activist, judges people by how well they treat their pets. To you, this may sound weird, but to her, it makes perfect sense. So don't ever tease her about her causes and never question her integrity. You will lose her quickly if you do.

Sagittarius in the Millennium

The first decade of the millennium is going to be relatively easy for you, since Uranus and Neptune are in Aquarius, a compatible air sign, and Pluto is in your sun sign. You're trying to expand your worldview and belief system, which is business as usual for you, but you're also attempting to integrate your worldview into your work, a tougher task.

You won't entirely escape the need to embrace your shadow. It isn't one of your favorite pursuits by any means, and yet it's a necessary step if you're going to harness your considerable energy and apply it to create the life you want.

From 1984 to 1995, when Pluto was in Scorpio, life may have been darker than you liked. You had to grapple with all sorts of *stuff* you had buried inside yourself over the years, and some of it wasn't too pretty. On the other hand, that phase is over now, and you, more than any other sign, have a firm grasp on the big picture of the millennium. The challenge is to fill in the details of that big picture so that you know where you're going.

Energizer: The solar eclipse on August 11, 1999, in your fellow fire sign, Leo, brings out something in your worldview, your personal belief system, that has been concealed or hidden. Whatever it is may be revealed through a foreigner or an experience with a culture other than your own.

You feel the effects of the eclipse more strongly if:

your sun sign is between 17 and 19 degrees, you have a lot of fixed planets in your birth chart, or your ascendant or moon are between 17 and 19 degrees of Leo. In your birth chart, if the house with Leo on the cusp lies between 17 and 19 degrees, then the affairs of that house are affected.

Let's say you have Leo at the midheaven (cusp of the tenth) at 18 or 19 degrees. This would mean that whatever has been hidden or concealed about your career will begin to emerge for several months on either side of the eclipse. Simply apply the meaning of the eclipse to the affairs of the house.

You feel the effects of the eclipse for several months on either side of it. Whatever emerges energizes you in a new direction that allows you greater freedom and encourages your growth.

Catalyst: The lineup of planets in Taurus on May 3, 2000, hits your sixth house of health and work. This creates an increase in your workload and responsibilities, and puts you under considerable stress. Make sure that you have some way to blow off steam during this time that doesn't involve anyone else—running, swimming, something physical.

The Jupiter/Saturn conjunction that's part of the lineup spells the end of one cycle and the beginning of a new twenty-year cycle. Be sure that you complete projects you've started before moving on to something new. Jupiter brings luck and serendipitous experiences into your work environment and urges you to be innovative and expansive. But Saturn holds you back at times, reminding you to find the proper structure.

You may feel that your ideas aren't receiving the attention they deserve. Instead of forging ahead and trying to force the higher-ups into seeing things your way (which only backfires), be diplomatic, calm, maintain your integrity. This approach pays off in the long run.

Transformation: You prefer not to see the darker side of life, which conflicts with your idealism and natural optimism. But when transitting Pluto conjuncts your sun sign, you transform at the deepest levels. Power and how you use it is one of the issues you have to deal with during the first eight years of the millennium. Think of your attitude about power as part of your shadow self, a part you need to understand, embrace, and transform.

Your best recourse at this time is to work on yourself instead of trying to wield power over others. If you're tempted to wield power, pause, step back, and ask yourself what your real motives are. Are you trying to make a point? Are you hoping to convert someone to your way of thinking? Be as honest with yourself as you are with others. Then you aren't even tempted to wield power over others.

The big picture is fine to have, but you also need to do the connect-the-dot work. Sometimes it's nothing more than thinking something through before you speak. Other times, though, the detail work requires action on your part. This is especially true from late August of 2003 to late September of 2004, when Jupiter is in Virgo. At this time you may find yourself doing things for other people without thought of compensation.

Much of your energy during the first eight years of the millennium goes into your career and profession. You feel very ambitious now, and as long as you don't allow power to go to your head, you should succeed in whatever you do.

In December of 2006, Jupiter joins Pluto in your sun sign and significant breaks come your way. You expand your business, go back to school, delve into metaphysics, or fuel your passion with concrete action. Things may go so well during that year, in fact, that you're tempted to sit back and relax. That's precisely what you shouldn't do. This year is an opportunity; seize it and run with it.

Innovation: Uranus in Aquarius may send other signs fleeing for the hills, but for you, this phase should be fun. Your fire is very compatible with the air of Aquarius, whose visionary ideas fuel your Sagittarian passion. The only problem, and it's small, is that Aquarius lies in the mental realm and is emotionally detached. This may require that you apply some Aquarian detachment to your passions, to scrutinize with your reasoning mind.

Uranus in Aquarius is also sextile to your natal sun and that usually means smooth sailing. Uranus still brings unexpected events, but they aren't as disruptive as they would be if Uranus were square or in opposition to your sun. Your optimism is obvious to others and attracts people in positions of authority. They find your ideas fresh and innovative. Virtually nothing is impossible to accomplish now *if* you can muster the ambition.

You're given plenty of opportunities to advance yourself, but sometimes you simply feel so good and so free that you would rather kick back and read or go fishing, which is probably something you haven't done for a long time. And that's the whole point of this sextile. To get you out of the rut you're stuck in so that you become aware of your own potential.

New paradigms: For the first three years of the millennium, Uranus and Neptune are paired up in Aquarius. Even under the beneficial influences, which a sextile is, this can be a strange combination. Uranus offers you the opportunities you need to take care of your external life, and Neptune awakens your compassion and spiritual ideals. Actually, though, both planets are working on your inner processes, triggering abilities that may have lain dormant for years.

During this time, which lasts until 2003, you're drawn more closely to your friends and also to larger groups of people who share your ideals. You may find yourself doing volunteer work of one kind or another. For one Sagittarian animal lover, this means volunteering for a local pet rescue league that finds homes for abused and abandoned animals. For another Sagittarian, it could mean volunteering at a soup kitchen, nursing home, or hospital. Your compassion for the less fortunate is awakened, and you *have to act on it.*

This type of work enhances your intuitive ability and brings you into alignment with your spiritual path. Surrender, Sagittarius, that's what this is about. Through surrender, your new belief system is born.

Truth within: Right about now, you're probably thinking, *Enough already. I know my truths.* After all, you've been developing and working with those truths since before the millennium started and yes, even though it's probably driving you nuts, you're trying to incorporate them into your ordinary life. Then in March 2003 Uranus goes into Pisces, squaring your natal sun, and it seems like all hell breaks loose. How is that possibly about truth within?

The answer is that first it's about challenge. You're challenged to question whether what you're doing is really what you want to be doing. Do you love your job or your career or are you just putting in time and collecting a paycheck? Are your personal relationships fulfilling or do you feel stifled? Do you really believe what you say or are you just spouting off?

Uranus stays in Pisces until mid-March of 2011. That's a long time to ask yourself these questions. So the sooner you answer them, the sooner you can feel at peace with yourself.

There are, of course, many points during Uranus's journey through Pisces where other planets come into play. One of those points is Saturn in Leo, trining your sun from mid-July of 2005 to early September of 2007. Everything in your life seems to work more smoothly during this twenty-six-month period. People you work for or who have authority over you are impressed by what you can do. You're recognized in some way for your abilities, your income is likely to rise, and you make tremendous strides in just about anything you take on.

All of this buoys your confidence and allows you to clarify how your emerging beliefs help to create your future.

Spiritual expansion: Remember the eclipse way back in August 1999 that triggered your spiritual quest? Whatever emerged then is still playing out as Neptune in Aquarius hits your third house of communication. During the fourteen years that it takes Neptune to transit Aquarius (1998–2012), you're redefining how you communicate with yourself and others. The ninth house of your worldview and spiritual beliefs comes into play because it lies directly opposite the third house. In essence, you've been preparing yourself to communicate what you really believe. Who you really are.

Now, with Neptune dragging its heels through your third house, you must be very careful to say what you mean because misunderstandings are part of this transit. If you've ignored this area of your life, then for a while you're going to feel confused about everything—what you think, what you feel, what you want. But even at this juncture, you find allies—specifically your own intuition. Expect a lot of inner nudges, synchronicities, and impulses during this time. Follow your inner oracle.

You already understand that each of us is connected to something larger than all of us. For Sagittarians, this is a given. You may differ from other people in what you call this energy—God, Buddha, a higher self, All That Is. But you know it exists, so that isn't even the issue for you. The point is that you have to synthesize your inner wisdom into who you are and then you have to relate it the larger world. The way in which you do this is your challenge, Sagittarius. And no one can tell you what that way may be.

Self: Your challenge in the millennium is to find out who you really are, what you truly believe, and what you want out of life. This quest belongs to all of us, of course, but for a Sagittarian, the quest for truth lies at the heart of what you're about.

For years you've espoused your various truths without really thinking about them. But with Pluto in your sun sign for the first eight years of the millennium, you learn to think before you pontificate. You get some help in this regard from Mars in Aquarius from late October 2001 until early December 2001. You're able to communicate what you feel and think with great clarity at this time.

Part of the Sagittarian archetype is about freedom—the freedom to do and say what you want, when you please, even if everyone else around you is saying or doing the opposite. This theme of freedom predominates from the latter part of 2006 to mid-December of 2007. Try to become more aware during this time of how your actions affect the people to whom you're closest.

Finances: Unless you have Scorpio prominent in your birth chart, you usually aren't the type who is interested in money just for the sake of money. Money is a means to an end. Money allows you to travel, to take courses and seminars. Money frees you to volunteer at the local animal shelter, to spend time with your kids, to publicize your current passion. You usually spend it as rapidly as it comes in, but you don't worry too much about it because, somehow, money is always there when you need it. That's the luck of Jupiter, which rules your sign.

None of this is likely to change in the millennium. What *will* change is your awareness that you already possess the tools to earn more than you need in a field that fuels all your Sagittarian fire and zeal. You realize the intimate of your life, including finances.

In mid-December of 2007, when Jupiter in Capricorn begins its transit through your second house, your financial base should expand. This could mean that you're earning a considerable amount of money from some creative talent or project on which you set your sights earlier in the millennium. This window of opportunity lasts until early January of 2009, then Pluto in Capricorn steps into the same house.

If you've done your inner work, you can reap considerable rewards during this thirty-year transit. If you've glossed over the inner work or ignored it completely, then you may be in for a very long haul of unpleasant transformations in the money department.

Communication: Here, the main issues are your bluntness and its lack of consideration for others, and your tendency to verbally bludgeon other people in an attempt to make them see your viewpoint. In the new millennium, these tendencies are mitigated either through your own efforts or through people and circumstances you attract. In other words, Sagittarius, if you don't do it, then external forces do it for you.

With Uranus and Neptune in Aquarius until 2003 and Neptune there until 2012, both affecting your third house of communication, you get plenty of practice in the communication department. Uranus initially disrupts your everyday routines and communications and also rearranges your thinking processes. This, in turn, redefines the way you communicate with other people on a daily level.

Neptune fogs the whole picture for a while. You feel as if you're peering through the lens of a camera that is somewhat out of focus. But if you attempt to be as clear as possible in what you say and how you communicate, the blurry effects are mitigated somewhat. The true power of the Neptune transit lies in the way it completely reconstructs your thought processes. You may develop a deep interest in metaphysical ideas now and the deeper you delve, the more intrigued you are. Your imagination soars, feeding all your Sagittarian fire, urging you to act on these new ideas.

Put these two planets together and the first three years of the millennium are a virtual powerhouse of newness and potential for you, an explosion of information, experiences, and ideas. Since Sagittarius is a mutable sign, you should be able to adapt more easily to these changes than any of the fixed signs, with the exception of Aquarius, whose millennium this is.

Your home: Okay, there's no easy way around it. If you feel that someone in your immediate environment is stifling you or somehow restricting your freedom, then the relationship may end when Uranus goes into Pisces.

If it doesn't end, then it certainly transmutes. Maybe you both have an epiphany about what the other needs. Maybe you both find someone else, but remain together for some reason. Maybe you move, and the move is mainly a distraction from the real issue. No telling how this one pans out. Free will is the operative rule here. One thing is for sure, though. Your home life is going to be unsettled after 2003.

On the other hand, your home life is unusually creative through this period of uncertainty. You feel more psychic, more in tune with your inner self. Your ideas are sharp, clear. Synchronicities that occur tend to cluster around the basic issue: can the people you love still love the you that emerges from the chaos?

By the end of 2006 or in early 2007, you've got your answers and things settle down for a while. Enjoy the peace, Sag, for it won't last long. With you it rarely does. You're too busy living with one eye on the future.

Creative potential: By the end of 2006, you've got a handle on the creative aspects of your life. You get into the college of your choice. Your paintings or manuscripts start to sell. The pet rescue league for which you volunteer hires you as a full-time employee. You find and start to live your bliss, that's what it amounts to.

This might terrify another sign, but you get right into it and may even go overboard for a while. But that's okay. This plunge is all part of the pattern and process that brings you fully into the twenty-first century.

Some of your creative endeavors involve groups of people who share your ideals and interests. This can be anything from a group of writers or artists to an animal rights' group or coworkers. The point is that the group energy helps you clarify your creative goals.

Health & work: The millennium kicks off with seven planets lined up in your sixth house of health and work. This means that stress and burnout are likely to be important components in your general health.

Sagittarians, with their tremendous hunger and passion for life, tend to overeat and overdrink when they're stressed out, so you need to watch your diet during the early part of the millennium. Cut back on fatty and rich foods, minimize your intake of red meat and alcohol, and try herbs like milk thistle that detoxify the liver. Antioxidants are also beneficial for your general health.

Since negativity in your environment can also affect your health, try smudging your home and office periodically. Sage usually works well for most situations. If your energy feels blocked, experiment with Feng Shui to strengthen the health area in your home and office.

The strongest and most vulnerable parts of your body are your thighs and liver. If you feel discomfort related to either of these areas, then you need to address the underlying emotional cause.

Partnerships: Commitment, Sagittarius, that's what you learn in this area in the new millennium. When you've been involved with someone in the past and have felt they don't support your ideals and beliefs or have felt the person was restricting your freedom of expression, you ended the relationship with no qualms whatsoever.

In July 2000, Jupiter moves into your seventh house of partnerships. This transit enhances any existing relationships you have, favors marriage in general, and also provides you with many opportunities to meet people who expand your perception about relationships. Some of these people could be from foreign countries.

By September of 2000, Saturn in Gemini has joined Jupiter in your seventh house. Others may make demands on your time now, which restricts your freedom. If these relationships demand more than you're willing or able to give, then they'll end. The problem with having both of these planets transitting simultaneously through the seventh is that one calls for expansion and the other, for constriction. But if you're honest about what you want from a relationship, you should be able to navigate this transit with a minimum of damage. Just remember: be tactful but honest.

Spirituality: Your quest for larger truths has always been at the root of your spiritual life, and that quest is only going to become more important to you in the millennium. Remember polarity? Any emphasis on one sign or house also highlights the opposite sign or house.

With Uranus and then Neptune in Aquarius, transitting your third house, the ninth house is also brought into focus. The third is how you communicate, and the ninth is your worldview. So you aren't just involved in finding your higher truths; you're concerned about communicating them and integrating them into your daily life.

Profession & career: For much of the first decade of the millennium, your focus is on the details of your career, the fine print. You're so good at seeing the larger picture, Sagittarius, that at times you neglect the small stuff and then pay for it later.

At the end of August 2003, Jupiter goes into Virgo for about a year and transits your solar tenth house of careers. At this time the detail work becomes very important. With Jupiter here, you make significant strides in achieving your professional goals and may be publicly recognized in some way for your work.

The one note of caution, however, concerns overconfidence and arrogance. This transit can make you feel so invincible that you may become overbearing about getting your viewpoint across. Just remember to practice circumspection so that you don't alienate the very people who may be your closest allies.

In the fall of 2007, Saturn transits your tenth house for about two years, and you literally harvest whatever you've sown. If you've done your homework and paid attention to all the little details along the way, then this can be a period of crowning achievement, when you make a significant impact on the larger world.

Personal unconscious: From late October of 2005 to November of 2006, your attention turns inward, toward the hidden aspects of yourself and existence in general. The whole process is easier than it has been in the past because you don't encounter those hard pockets of resistance when confronted with parts of yourself that you have disowned or buried.

Tapping the Source

Synchronicities & Your Inner Oracle

Sagittarians have an innate love and respect for the big picture, the cosmic hologram. So when that hologram speaks to you through synchronicities, you listen. The problem, though, is that you may not act on what you hear. You may just go on your merry way, figuring that your way is the only and best way.

Your challenge, then, is to acknowledge that a synchronicity isn't just the voice of the larger picture; it's also the voice of your inner oracle. If you don't understand the message of a synchronicity, don't just dismiss it. Try to interpret it in the same way that you might a dream. Who are the major players? Does the event involve names? Numbers? A current situation? What's the message?

Once you open yourself to the deeper reality from which synchronicities spring, it's impossible to ever go back to the way things were. So open yourself and use the wisdom, knowing that it's really *your* wisdom.

Creating Your Future

Once you become conscious of how your deepest beliefs create your experiences, then this process appeals to you in a big way. With your abundant optimism and focus on the future, you start having fun with it.

Set yourself a small goal at first, something simple. Maybe you're looking for a particular book that is out of print, difficult to find. Visualize yourself with that book in your hands. Create vivid details about the book—its weight, how it feels in your hands, the rustle of the paper as you turn pages. Return to this image whenever you can, making it more vivid each time. Then, after a week or so, release it. Don't worry about it. Trust that the universe will provide it.

Once you find your book—and you will—set a larger goal. Creating your future is like exercising a muscle. The more frequently you do it, the better you become at the process.

Chapter 18

Capricorn, the Goat

December 22–January 19
Cardinal, Earth
Ruled by Saturn

Capricorn Man

No one wants to think of the love of their life as a goat, the animal that symbolizes Capricorn. And yet the symbol fits the sign. No other sign is so willing to climb whatever mountain stands between him and what he desires. His ascent may take awhile, but he's surefooted every step of the way. He hopes there's a shortcut to the top, but in his heart he knows there isn't, so he just keeps climbing, making headway, driven forward by his ambition.

For a Capricorn, man or woman, ambition is the theme song. Its expression varies—president, astronaut, CEO, attorney, teacher of the year—but the theme rarely deviates. The Capricorn man seeks public recognition, if not fame, and yet he may never breathe a word about it to you. He doesn't have time to discuss it because he's too busy doing it, plotting his strategy, laying out his campaign.

Saturn, which rules the sign, makes sure he keeps

his nose to the grindstone even when he longs for a reprieve. He probably hasn't had a vacation for ten years, and yet, he hems and haws when you mention taking one. Most of the time, life is serious business for him, nearly as serious as it is for a Scorpio, but nowhere near as intense. The seriousness makes him seem older than he actually is, even when he's a kid. He often prefers the company of people older than himself, too.

Status in other people's lives impresses him, no matter what form it comes in—a beautiful home, family lineage, an important professional position. Perhaps he's impressed because it reminds him of what he hopes to attain for himself.

As a father, he's loving but a stickler for rules and regulations. He's also a disciplinarian, which his kids understand from the time they're old enough to understand. He's a bit like this in romance, too. If you're looking for the impulsive adventurous type, then you'd better look elsewhere. But if it's fidelity and a stable home life that you long for, then this guy is the ticket. Once he's smitten, it's usually for keeps.

There are always exceptions to the rule. Now and then you may come across a Capricorn man who is more of a dreamer than a doer, for whom fun is the paramount focus of his life. But if you look at his birth chart, you'll probably find an air or fire ascendant or an air or fire moon. After all, the Capricorn archetype is about responsibility and that long, steep climb over the mountain.

Capricorn Woman

One thing you can never accuse her of is laziness. When she has free moments, she fills them with something productive, something that furthers her ambitions, even if that ambition is just for today. Remember: her symbol is the goat, and she's every bit as serious about getting to the top of that mountain as her male counterpart. And she won't complain about the climb, either. She relishes the hardships as readily as she does the triumphs.

Neither gender of this sign is easy to pick out in a crowd. They come in all shapes and sizes, and can be blond, brunettes, and redheads. The latter, however, is the rarity, unless fire predominates in the birth chart. These women are generally attractive and seem to get better-looking as they age, perhaps because they come into their own as they get older. Faye Dunaway, Diane Keaton, and Mary Tyler Moore are good examples of this.

In romance, this woman tends to swing from one extreme to another. Sometimes she seems to be the most carefree person in the universe; other times a blue funk sweeps over her, and everyone around her feels it.

Basically, though, she's stable and enduring and is looking for someone who needs the same things she does. She isn't the type who can be swept off her feet. But she certainly softens when the moon is bright and the beach is warm against her bare feet. And, no, she isn't immune to being wined and dined in a gracious setting, with dinner served on china and real silver utensils placed exactly so on the linen napkins.

If she's sports-oriented, then the sport is probably something that takes her away from all that seriousness—running, river rafting, kayaking, horseback riding. She doesn't care if *you* don't participate, but don't ever try to restrict her from doing so.

As a mother, she doesn't differ much from the male of the sign, loving but sometimes reserved emotionally. She's big on rules and parameters, and if her children violate those boundaries, she's quick to punish. In dogmatic types, this punishment is physical, which leads her kids into obedience based on fear rather than respect.

Capricorns in general tend toward structured spiritual practices and beliefs, although this seems to be truer for people born in the January part of the sign. Those born in December are still close enough to Sagittarius to understand that structured religious practices and beliefs mean nothing if they aren't integrated into the totality of their lives.

The millennium holds some surprises for both types in this area. Those who are dogmatic in their beliefs may become more so, but at great expense to themselves. Those who seek to expand their spiritual beliefs may find they have to search inward before they come out on the other side, changed and whole.

Thanks to the Saturn influence, the Capricorn woman, like the man, holds a certain reverence for tradition. If Thanksgiving in her childhood home was always served with gravy, cranberries, and homemade bread, then she insists on having these items at her own table as an adult. She also creates new family traditions that her own children can carry into adulthood with them.

As a cardinal earth sign, this woman initiates action that is grounded in reality. She isn't the type to fly off to Tahiti on a whim in search of UFOs. But she might head off to an auction some Saturday morning and come home with some valuable piece of history!

Capricorn in the Millennium

The hard work is done, Capricorn. You went through your millennial trial when Uranus and Neptune conjuncted your sun sign in 1993 and threw your life into chaos. You suddenly found that your old way of doing things no longer worked well, if at all. Your habitual thinking patterns underwent a profound metamorphoses. Maybe you even learned to relax!

The first decade of the new millennium is likely to bring changes in the way you relate to and involve yourself with groups. If the Uranus/Neptune conjunction in Capricorn didn't sweep you clean of resistance to change, then the next ten years will get rid of whatever resistance remains.

Energizer: The eclipse of the century on August 11, 1999, at 18 degrees Leo, hits your eighth house. Something that has been hidden or concealed concerning joint finances, taxes, insurance, trusts, and inheritances comes to light. Whatever this is, it's something you need to know about. Since the eighth house also concerns metaphysics, it's possible that intuitive and psychic abilities you haven't been using surface in your conscious life.

Capricorns are deeply intuitive when they allow themselves to be, but the trick is to turn down your left brain's volume long enough so you can hear your inner voice. If you're a skeptic about such things now, you won't be once the millennium gets underway. Circumstances and situations occur in which your intuition comes into play. You may have an impulse to do something you've never done before, or your dreams may illuminate a concern or seem to predict some future event. One way or another, your intuition becomes stronger, more pronounced, and ushers you into the twenty-first century.

Catalyst: The lineup of seven planets in Taurus on May 3, 2000, highlights your fifth house of creativity, pleasure, and children. The Jupiter/Saturn conjunction that follows on May 28 also emphasizes your creative expression and triggers a new twenty-year cycle. Suddenly you're bursting with creative ideas, and your enthusiasm and energy attract the opportunities you need to put those ideas into action. Your output increases substantially, and you earn more money from what you create.

That's the Jupiter part of the transit. The Saturn part of it teaches you how to structure your time, how to discipline yourself, and how to enhance your creativity despite your other responsibilities. But those things are old hat to you, Capricorn.

The good news is that in August 2000, Saturn goes into Gemini and leaves the fifth house for the sixth. Your creativity goes through intense bursts of energy, and you work like the proverbial dog to make things happen. But you're happy! Hard work is what Capricorn is about, and when you're doing something you love, you work harder at it than just about any other sign in the zodiac.

If your moon or ascendant is in Capricorn, you also feel the influence of the Jupiter/Saturn conjunction. But with the moon, the effects tend to be on an emotional level; with the ascendant, it affects the self that others see, your public self.

Transformation: In late 1995 or early 1996, you may have felt that a volcanic eruption was going on deep inside you. And it was, in your personal unconscious. As the millennium opens, you've had five years of experience with Pluto in Sagittarius, moving through your twelfth house. If you've resisted all the psychological stuff that has surfaced, then you're in for a rough ride until 2008. If you've confronted the hidden and disowned parts of yourself that have surfaced, then the next eight years will be a process of integration and transformation as you weave these insights into your life.

Your work ethic is changing, Capricorn, and that's somewhat unsettling to you. Not that you're getting lazy or anything—nothing as drastic as that. You're simply integrating relaxation into your life. Quite often in the past, your work was a distraction, a way to avoid thinking about whatever was going on inside you. So when you work less, the hidden stuff comes up and you have to deal with it.

In 2003, Uranus goes into Pisces, sextiling your natal sun, and remains there until March 2011. Sudden changes occur in your life, of course, but they aren't shattering. Instead, these changes open your perceptions to new ways of thinking and being. New relationships come into your life that challenge your familiar, habitual beliefs. You may experience sudden breaks in your old relationships, and although it's painful, it's also necessary for your self-expression.

Always keep in mind that these transits reflect an internal process, an inner unfoldment toward your evolution as a spiritual being. These steps are also preparing you for Pluto's transit through your sun sign, which begins at the end of November 2008 and lasts until January of 2024. This is a powerful conjunction for you, transformative at the deepest levels. During this transit the old order of your life surrenders to the new order you've been building piece by piece.

Embrace the process, Capricorn. Trust that it's all in your best interest.

Innovation: Remember the hologram, Capricorn? If you've never understood how a holographic view of life fits into your life, then Uranus in Aquarius is going to teach you what that means. Before Uranus leaves Aquarius, you will understand how each part of your life contains the whole and that each of us is connected at the most fundamental levels.

Uranus teaches you this by disrupting any area of your life where you are inflexible and rigid, where you wear blinders. Maybe it's a job or a relationship where you feel smothered but don't want to admit it. Maybe it's the neighborhood in which you live. Look at your natal chart and find the house with Aquarius on the cusp. This will tell you precisely the area you're going to feel the impact.

Aquarians in general, however, feel Uranus's influence in the financial area. Expect disruptions and sudden reversals in your monetary affairs. The eighth house, because it's opposite the second, is also affected, which means that your shared resources are also involved. This could indicate anything from an inheritance to a tax audit.

However it manifests in your life, you have to look at the events as vehicles to a deeper understanding of the patterns that have been operating in your life. Through this understanding, a more innovative approach to earning money evolves.

New paradigms: For the first three years of the millennium, Uranus and Neptune share the Aquarian spotlight. This pair urges you to take an honest look at where you've been and where you want to go in the next ten to twelve years.

You may feel somewhat unsettled about everything in general, and when you try to zoom in on the specifics, you can't quite grasp the essence of what bothers you. This feeling is like waking from a dream that leaves you breathless or afraid but you can't remember enough of the dream to figure out why. The emotion prompts you to probe more deeply and the deeper you probe, the less vague things become. You begin to realize that your values are changing.

Since you have always identified closely with your material possessions, this realization can be very upsetting. You enjoy your display case of Lladro figurines, your Wedgwood china, your baseball collection signed by the greats, your collection of signed first editions. The problem is that the more you cling to what you possess, the more threatened those items become.

Your intuitive ability deepens during this time and attempts to guide you, if you listen and heed its advice. These changes probably won't be easy, especially if you resist. But if you trust the process, Capricorn, if you can allow yourself to step into the rushing river without throwing up a million reasons why you should not surrender, then this period is much easier for you.

Truth within: Okay, take a deep breath and hold to the count of ten, then exhale slowly, feeling each whisper of air as it leaves your lungs. Do you feel more grounded now? More centered? Good. That's exactly how you should feel when Uranus goes into Pisces from the end of 2003 to mid-March of 2011.

Now that Uranus is sextile your sun, unexpected opportunities come into your life out of seemingly nowhere. You network through new friends and groups whose beliefs are allied with yours. Your goals may have changed, but they are more in line with who you're becoming. Suddenly your life seems exciting, adventurous, and you feel more connected to everything. All the hard work you've been doing for the last few years begins to pay off.

Your thought processes are changing, and you actually like the change, Capricorn. You relish it. You may take up some form of exercise that is also a spiritual discipline—yoga, tai chi, karate. These disciplines deepen and broaden the scope of your intuition, so that you now pay close attention to flashes of inspiration, unusual and vivid dreams, even synchronistic events. You respect the information that comes to you in unconventional ways. You live closer to the core of who you are.

Spiritual expansion: Neptune in Aquarius until 2012: think about that for a moment, Capricorn. Look through that chapter on Neptune again, then interpret it in terms of your own life. What does it say to you?

The overall pattern indicates the importance of groups in your spiritual awareness, regardless of your religious affiliation. The two are really quite separate and this becomes increasingly obvious to you as Neptune makes its long trek through Aquarius.

If you have been involved in organized religion for most of your life, then you may find that organized religion is based on fear—the fear of a supreme being, the fear of what happens when you die, the fear of what will happen if you don't live according to the dictates of whatever god your religion honors. Your spiritual values, however, are based on your personal connection to the divine. The first demands that you follow someone else's rules; the second demands that you follow your own.

Self: During the first decade of the millennium, you learn to lighten up on yourself and to trust that your inner voice is a valuable source of information if you listen to it. The lessons are simple if you can just go with whatever the flow appears to be.

That isn't to say that you should toss out your goals, Capricorn. You only need to realign your thinking about how you approach them. Instead of being the person who assumes the load for everyone, try delegating responsibility at home, at work, in every area of your life so that you free up energy for yourself.

If you can do this for the first eight years of the millennium, then by the time Pluto conjuncts your sun in 2008, you're better prepared to live the structure you've been creating. Your ideas about power will also be much clearer by then, and you won't have to experience conflict with people who hold power over you or with people over whom you have power.

Part of the Capricorn archetype is about work, specifically about climbing that mountain to attain your goals. Make sure you know what you're hoping to find at the top of that mountain, then bring your considerable willpower to bear against it. As Captain Pickard in Star Trek is fond of saying, *"Make it so."*

Finances: In August of 2002, other financial resources become available to you and ease whatever financial pressure you're feeling. You're able to make significant strides financially. From the fall of 2004 through the end of October 2005, your financial gains somehow play into your career. Or perhaps your career takes off, and you reap the financial rewards. One way or another, the two are intimately connected because you are beginning to realize that all abundance begins within.

You're naturally adept at handling money and have a keen eye for spotting opportunities to make money. This won't change in the millennium. What *will* change, however, is the way you channel your moneymaking energy. You're attracted to earth-friendly companies, to entrepreneurial ventures that reflect your emerging spiritual values, and to groups of people who support your ideals, interests, and concerns.

By 2008, when Pluto goes into your sun sign, Jupiter is also there and your horizons expand considerably. Since your own values have changed, you're better equipped now to deal with powers issues related to money.

Communication: In March of 2003, Uranus goes into Pisces and stays there until the end of May 2010, affecting your third house of communication as well as your thinking processes. Your interests change—science and technology, computers, yoga, metaphysics, astrology—are some of the areas you may explore. You may take classes in one of these areas or study on your own.

These emerging interests reflect the new you that emerges as your habitual-thinking processes fall away, allowing you to perceive yourself and your life in a way that you never have before. Your intuition sharpens considerably under this transit, and you learn to listen to it and take its advice.

Your relationships with siblings and neighbors may also change at this time. You either connect with these people in a more meaningful, honest way or your relationships with them end. You simply don't have the time now to spin your wheels with relationships that appear to be obstacles to your growth.

The main thing to remember during this transit, Capricorn, is to embrace change rather than resist it. If you resist, obstacles only increase and mount to the point where change is forced on you.

Your home: Your home life and immediate environment remain fairly stable for the first decade of the millennium. There are, however, some things of which you should be aware. As your values change, your home life feels the impact of those changes. If people you live with have a vested interest in the status quo, then they may feel threatened by your thrust for growth.

The best way to handle any problems that rise in this area is to be up front about what you feel and think. If the rituals you've gone through in the past years no longer mean anything to you, then say that. If you're fed up with being the one who shoulders the bulk of the responsibility in your home, then say that, too. Try to work with the people you love to come up with other methods that are amenable to them and yourself.

The big changes in your home life begin in mid-May of 2010, when Uranus goes into Aries and hits your fourth house. But if you've been honest with yourself for the last ten years, then this transit can bring excitement and new, creative ideas into your immediate environment.

Creative potential: With the lineup of planets in Taurus in May 2000, you begin to feel a lot of pressure related to your creativity. Your abilities are now screaming to be recognized and, one way or another, they will be.

Creativity doesn't deal just with the arts; it's an approach to life, a certain perception. When it begins to emerge, it runs throughout your work, your home, the way you relate to your children and the other people you love. If you have a fondness for horses, for example, then you somehow manage to find a way to make horses prominent in your life. If you've had a book idea that you're never acted on, then now is the time to act.

In late October of 2005, other people's resources may become available to you, allowing you to embark on your creative ventures without worrying about how to finance it. This could come from a bank loan, an inheritance, a grant, or perhaps investments that pay off.

Health & work: Like fellow earth sign Taurus, you're physically strong and your body can take a lot of abuse. But even you aren't invincible. When you overwork, stress is likely to show up in your spine and your knees, the strongest and yet most vulnerable parts of your body. Saturn, which rules your sign, also rules bones and teeth, so be sure to increase your calcium and antioxidants during any period when you're putting in long hours.

From April of 2001 to early June of 2003, Saturn in Gemini hits your sixth house of health and work. In terms of your health, this indicates that you need to conserve your energy for things that *really matter.* This may be a difficult weeding process because *everything* matters to you. If you find yourself getting sick frequently during this period, then you need to realign your priorities.

As an earth sign, you're more open than other signs to your body's language. Look at health symptoms as a metaphor for something in your life that needs to be changed. If, for instance, you break bones during this transit, then ask yourself what situation or relationship are you trying to break free of?

An excellent primer on the body's metamorphic language is Louise Hay's *How You Can Heal Your Life.* Hay provides a list of ailments and diseases, gives the probable emotional cause, and an affirmation to help correct the emotional source of the illness. Even if you don't agree with everything she says, the book will encourage you to decipher the language of your body.

Partnerships: From June of 2003 to mid-July of 2005, Saturn in Cancer opposes your natal sun in the seventh house of relationships. This can be a tricky transit to get through in the relationship department. If you're in any relationship that limits or restricts your self-expression, then the relationship may not survive this two-year period. This includes not only intimate relationships, but business partnerships as well.

There may be times during this transit when your discouragement descends into outright depression. If that happens, step back, detach, and understand that it's really not as bleak as it seems. Lighten up on yourself. Chill, Capricorn, chill.

One of your new venues for relationships will

occur through groups. These people either share your interests or your goals and ambitions. Through them, you refine your personal needs.

Spirituality: Your spiritual beliefs transform gradually through the first decade of the millennium. The critical times for soul-searching occur when Jupiter goes into Leo in August 2002 and then into Virgo until September 2004. Leo affects your eighth house (metaphysics) and Virgo, your ninth (worldview). Both houses are important to your spiritual beliefs. Jupiter in the eighth urges you to expand your understanding of deeper truths, and this filters into your spiritual beliefs. Jupiter in the ninth, where it's at home, prompts you to expand your fundamental perceptions about the larger world and your place in it.

In each instance, you are challenged to fit these broader concepts into a spiritual framework that answers whatever questions you have and which works for you in your daily life.

Profession & career: The bottom line here, Capricorn, is to lighten up. It's fine to work toward your goals, but you tend to take on too much responsibility and neglect to enjoy things like a walk on the beach at sunset or going to a movie with your kids. Learn to trust the process that unfolds in your life during the first decade of the millennium. If you feel an urge to take a day off in the middle of the week to do something frivolous (like have fun), then do it. Your career won't fall apart.

In the fall of 2004 when Jupiter goes into Libra, your professional life expands and all sorts of new opportunities open to you. You're tempted to take on everything at once because you feel so confident and invincible. Don't allow opportunities to slip away, but don't take on more than you can reasonably handle. Guard against spreading yourself too thinly. This transit can bring people from other countries and cultures into your life or may indicate that you travel frequently for business purposes.

Jupiter is also square your natal sun at this time. This can cause you to feel so confident and lucky that you spend more than you should or you waste your resources on plans that ultimately go nowhere. Your self-control and discipline are tested. On an upbeat note, however, your prosperity and success in your profession is directly linked to your self-knowledge.

Personal unconscious: This period isn't as rough for you as it is for other signs. Most of your inner work in this area was done during the Uranus/Neptune conjunction in Capricorn in 1993. But there are still a few rough spots you should be aware of.

Pluto in your twelfth house demands an honest confrontation with the power you have disowned. If, for instance, you discovered rather early in childhood that any expression of anger resulted in punishment, then you may have disowned your right to express anger and turned it inward instead. Or maybe you learned that your opinion as a child didn't count, so you stopped expressing your opinions about anything. As Pluto moves through Sagittarius and your twelfth house, you reclaim your power and speak your truth.

Tapping the Source

Synchronicities & Your Inner Oracle

Even if you don't believe that a coincidence holds any special message for you, you usually recognize it, at the very least, as an "interesting anomaly," as one Capricorn put it. The trick now is to go deeper, to embrace the possibility that synchronicities hint at some deeper order in the universe, that they may be, in fact, the glue that holds the hologram together.

There are any number of excellent books on synchronicities, but for you, Capricorn, the proof lies in experience. First, you have to be receptive to the idea. Second, you must let your inner self know that you're receptive. A good step in this direction is to give yourself a suggestion before you go to sleep at night that you *are* open and receptive.

Next, pay close attention to your thoughts throughout a given day. What does the content of your conscious mind tell you about your deeper beliefs? Are your thoughts usually negative or positive or someplace in between? Do they vacillate with your moods? Probe the deeper beliefs behind negative thoughts. If you're thinking that you won't ever get a raise, for example, look for the underlying reason for such a belief. Don't you feel worthy of earning more money? Were you made to feel unworthy in some way when you were a kid?

Not every negative belief, of course, goes back to childhood. We are an accretion of beliefs that we adopt from our parents, teachers, friends, movies, and books. If you've adopted a negative belief, you can also walk away from it. This may take a little work, but you're no stranger to work. In this instance, though, the work you do is directed inward.

As you go through each day, seek to live consciously, paying attention not only to your thoughts, but to what happens around you. If you train yourself to stretch your intuitive muscles, you're more likely to experience a synchronicity. Next time the phone rings, try to guess who it is before you pick it up. With practice, your intuition will begin to provide you with the right answers.

All of this creates a fertile environment for synchronicities to happen. Once they begin to happen, keep track of them for whatever period of time suits your schedule. The more aware you become, the more frequently synchronicities occur, and the easier it is to understand and decipher their messages.

If you really don't have any idea where to begin, read *Awakening Intuition* by Mona Lisa Schultz and read Carl Jung's introduction to the Richard Wilhelm edition of the *I Ching*.

Creating Your Future

You know how to set goals. You probably do it daily in your work, your home, wherever you expend your energy. Creating your future is very much like setting goals. Brainstorm with yourself. If you could have anything you absolutely wanted, what would it be?

Draw a circle and jot your heart's desire in the center of it. Now draw lines that shoot out from the circle like spokes in a wheel. At the end of each spoke, write down something related to your heart's desire. Do this quickly, without thinking about it, whatever comes to mind. You may have a dozen spokes or several dozen. There are no correct or incorrect numbers. The point is that you're creating a powerful visualization tool, a kind of blueprint to achieve your heart's desire.

Another technique that works is to create a wish board. Cut out pictures from magazines or newspapers or other sources that depict what you desire. If you want a new laptop, cut out the make and model and glue it to the board. If you want to deepen your intuition or your compassion, then find a picture that represents that quality. Have fun with it. Pretend you're a first-grader. Do it with your kids. Then post the wish board someplace where you're likely to see it daily.

Your future is created in the same way that you create everything else in your life, by setting a goal and moving toward it.

Chapter 19

•

Aquarius, the Water Bearer

January 20–February 18
Fixed, Air
Ruled by Uranus

Aquarius Man

He looks fairly ordinary, tall or short, plump or slender, no more unusual than the people who live next door. But as soon as he zones in on you, as soon as he speaks, as soon as he's firmly in the here and now instead of off in the future somewhere, you realize he is not ordinary at all.

First, there's his approach, all the penetrating questions, as if you're some sort of specimen under his microscope that he's plucking apart bit by bit. Don't be offended, it's nothing personal. He's just trying to get a handle on what you're about. Whatever he discovers is added to the vast data bank in his head and fleshes out his concepts of the brotherhood of man.

Brotherhood: remember that word. For the Aquarian man, it isn't just a word. Brotherhood is a tangible thing, as real as the clothes on his back. His immediate brotherhood may be his coworkers, people who share his interests and passions, or it may be buddies he has known since elementary school, the old friends he hangs out with. However he defines it, these people represent his connection to the larger brotherhood, to humanity.

The real Uranian types in this sign usually have some sort of spiritual practice or belief that they follow. Rarely is this spiritual pursuit an organized religion, but rather organized in an eccentric fashion around a soul quest. One Aquarian man, for instance, followed a shamanistic path in which he ingested hallucinogenic substances while wearing headphones and listening to music. His trainer, the shaman, directed his inner quest with questions or observations intended to push the man even deeper into himself. Another Aquarian man was a practicing Catholic in his external life, but was also a practitioner of Wicca.

If you try to find a rhyme or reason to any of it, you miss the point. This man can't be pigeonholed.

As a lover, he would rather have you be his friend. He needs the companionship of a friend more than he needs a lover. Plenty of Aquarian men are married, of course, but marriage isn't what they do best. Basically, he wants a good friend with whom he can share his adventures without emotional commitment.

Dating this man is strange, no two ways about it. Forget romantic dinners. You're likely to end up in a field in the middle of nowhere, searching the skies for UFOs. He's not the physically affectionate type; the body isn't what he's about. But show him someone whose curiosity and sense of intellectual adventure matches his own, and it's a different story.

He isn't the jealous type. If you want to date other

people, that's fine. He'll do the same. Even once he commits, he's rarely possessive. As a father, he encourages early independence in his children and usually manages to impart to them his particular worldview. He generally isn't the domestic type who sticks close to home or adheres to a routine schedule.

In fact, Uranian men and women do best if they're self-employed. Their minds work in highly erratic ways, with sudden, brilliant insights that can benefit people other than themselves. Money for the sake of money is rarely their thrust in life. They enjoy money for the freedom that it gives them.

Life with an Aquarian man may not be exactly what you envisioned, but it won't ever be boring.

Aquarius Woman

There are certain rules to remember if you're dealing with an Aquarian woman. Foremost among these is never impede her freedom. If she has her heart set on spending the holidays in a Mayan ruin, then that's what she'll do. You're welcome to come along if you'd like, but if you don't, that's fine, too.

This sort of detachment can be maddening in a relationship, but you might as well get used to it because it isn't going to change. The other thing that won't change is her involvement in groups—her astrology group, her writing group, her tarot group, her travel group, her chat room group. She's a social creature to the core, but only if the social activity involves something that interests her. If you share her interests, that delights her. If you don't, that's okay, too. But don't expect her to drop her interests in favor of yours.

As a fixed air sign, she thrives at the mind level. Ideas are to her what chocolates or roses are to another woman. In this way, she's like her air sign sister, Gemini. To win her heart, you must seduce her mind. Once she commits, she's isn't likely to stray. But even when she marries you, she needs freedom to explore her interests and passions.

As a mother, she's attentive but detached and rarely overprotective unless Cancer is prominent in her chart. She's not much of a hugger, either. But what she lacks in physical affection toward her kids is compensated for in nurturing of her children's independence. She teaches them to think for themselves.

Both the Aquarian woman and the man are among the most nonjudgmental signs in the zodiac. Their friends come from every race, culture, and creed. Prejudice simply isn't a word you find in their vocabularies. So if you, as her friend, lover, or spouse, have a problem with that, then you'd better keep it to yourself.

Both genders are exceptionally intuitive. Their inner oracles hum right along, nudging them in this or that direction, feeding them information through dreams, daydreams, synchronicities. Their nervous systems tend to be highly sensitized, which allows them to "read" the energy in whatever environment they're in. But when they're overtired or stressed out, their nervous systems suffer.

The Aquarian woman is often obsessively organized in certain areas of her life and unorganized in others. It depends on her priorities. As a fixed sign, she's slow to change her opinion about anything. She, like the Aquarian man, is usually interested in technology and probably has the newest PC and software. She's a natural on the information highway and prides herself on her expertise.

This lady definitely marches to a different drummer, and it excites her when she sees other people doing the same. She's a true humanitarian who believes in equality for all and also cheers on the individual, the rebel, the revolutionary with a genuine ax to grind. She has absolutely no use for phonies and can spot one instantly. Never lie to her and never be anything less than what you really are.

Aquarius in the Millennium

This is your thousand years, Aquarius. We've been hearing about it ever since that rock musical, *Hair,* popularized the song "The Dawning of the Age of Aquarius." This is the point where the future you've embraced now becomes your present. No other sign is as ideally equipped to understand the technological and spiritual advances that are promised.

That said, however, there are certain areas you will have to pay close attention to in the millennium. You're probably thinking, *What? Me? No way. I'm ready, I'm primed.* Read on, Aquarius.

Energizer: The eclipse of the century on August 11, 1999, occurs in Leo, your polar opposite, at 18 degrees, and affects your seventh house of partnerships. Something that has been hidden or concealed in one or more of your relationships surfaces at this time, which you must confront and deal with. This information or event pushes you in a new direction in your partnerships with others.

You may feel the effects of the eclipse for several

months on either side of it. Its influence is felt most strongly by people with a lot of fixed signs in 17 to 19 degrees. If, for instance, your natal moon in Leo is at 19 degrees, right smack on your midheaven, then the eclipse brings some hidden facet in your profession and career to light. Since your moon is involved, your emotions would be affected in some way.

Catalyst: The lineup of seven planets in Taurus on May 3, 2000, highlights your fourth house—your home, immediate environment, one of your parents, your early childhood. Your responsibilities at home and with your family seem enormous at this time, almost overwhelming. Old childhood issues may surface, or you may have to deal with one of your parents in some way.

The Jupiter and Saturn part of this lineup conjunct on May 28 and square your natal sun. The Jupiter part of this transit is usually good. Your family expands—a birth, adoption, or a parent moves in with you. You may also add onto your existing home or buy a larger home. In general, your home life and immediate environment offer opportunities for inner growth and evolution as well.

Be careful that you don't get cocky and arrogant, particularly with people who have authority over you. Even though you feel enormously lucky now, conserve your resources and watch what you spend.

The Saturn part of this equation is touchier. Saturn really chafes at your Uranian nature for freedom, Aquarius. And now, as it squares your sun, you find it difficult to deal with people who have authority over you. Instead of charging into battle, step back and use your wonderful Aquarian mind to change the situation. You probably do this all the time and don't even realize it.

One Aquarian woman visualizes the way she wants a situation to be, then sets an arbitrary time for herself later in the day when she will "switch probabilities." By perceiving the future as merely a wave of probabilities, she then uses her considerable willpower to pull in the probability that she wants. She doesn't always get it, but that never daunts her optimism. Next time, she simply tries harder.

While Jupiter seeks to expand, Saturn restricts, and it seems the two are working counterpoint to each other. On a deeper level, though, Saturn brings structure to the new experiences that Jupiter ushers into your life.

Transformation: In 1995, when Pluto entered Sagittarius, your group associations as well as your ambitions and dreams began to undergo a major transformation. If you were involved in groups at that time, then your interest in them may have waned. Maybe you quit them and joined groups that reflected your emerging interests.

Now, as the millennium opens, you have some clear ideas about how Pluto in Sagittarius is working in your life. It is sextile your natal sun, which usually denotes ease and opportunities that may come to you by working with groups of like-minded individuals. This group work enhances your creativity and clarifies your goals, dreams, and ambitions.

Perhaps you have always dreamed of writing and selling a screenplay. Now is the time to join a local writers' group, take workshops and seminars about screen writing, and generally steep yourself in the creative and technical process.

One Aquarian man had a deep interest in UFOs and had a story idea that he wanted to expand into a book. Although he wasn't a writer, he connected with a book packager who found the ghostwriter for the project. They worked out a lengthy proposal, and the book packager sold the idea to a major publisher.

But because Pluto in Sagittarius plumbs the psychic depths and urges you to speak your truth, this Aquarian man realized that a ghostwriter's voice would not be *his* voice, regardless of how close the collaboration was. So he decided to write the book himself, even though he wasn't a writer. Sagittarius can sometimes be overconfident, a bit puffed up, and may take on more than it can handle. This was the case with the Aquarian man; the book has yet to be written.

This is just one way in which Pluto in Sagittarius can manifest. Your free will molds the energy, not the other way around. *You* are the scriptwriter.

In late October of 2005, Jupiter goes into Scorpio and affects your tenth house of profession and careers. This brings expansion, luck, and success in professional matters, and may also bring your creative work into play somehow. Your self-discipline is important at this time and saves you from the excessive pride that sometimes accompanies this aspect.

Innovation: Uranus in Aquarius is like coming home for you. The energy is high-pitched and quick, brilliant and abrupt. Since Uranus went into Aquarius in 1996, your life has undoubtedly gone through sudden, unexpected changes in the areas where you were most inflexible and rigid. You also have experienced freedom from any situation or relationship that limited your freedom of expression.

As the millennium opens, this general trend continues, although by now you should know that your primary obligation during this period is to yourself. Your freedom, your self-expression, your growth. Anything Uranian in nature has always appealed to you, of course, and Uranus going through its home sign only increases that interest. Any of these areas may seize your interest now: astrology, computer technology, science, metaphysics, certain types of alternative healing methods. You're also focused on expressing who you are and doing it as honestly as possible.

With Uranus in Aquarius, many of your group associations may occur over the Internet. As we progress further into the millennium, in fact, the Net is likely to become even more important in connecting people through the virtual global community.

Your best ideas now may come to you while you're in an altered state, so pay attention to your dreams, daydreams, and whatever images come to you when you're relaxed. If you meditate, pay attention to recurring images and themes.

For about a year, beginning in July of 2000, Jupiter in Gemini highlights your creativity, children, and the things you do for pleasure. Jupiter is also trine your sun at this time, deepening your creative potential and giving you the self-confidence you need to tackle things you've never done before.

New paradigms: The pairing of Neptune and Uranus in your sun sign for the first three years of the millennium is a strange combination, even for you, Aquarius. Some days you may not know how you feel about anything. You see the world enveloped in a thin fog that prevents you from seeing anything clearly. But other days, you're hooked right into the universal flow, connected to something much larger than yourself. *You get the message.* Then you wake up the next day and wonder what you were so excited about. What message? What flow?

The fulcrum shifts again and again during these three years. Your emotions may seesaw from high to low, back and forth until you realize that your new paradigm is based, in part, on recognizing your emotions. On letting the emotions run fully through you. This isn't easy for an air sign to do, and it's especially difficult for an Aquarian. You have always prided yourself on your cool detachment and your visionary intellect. What you realize, however, is that emotions are as vital as intellect. Both must be acknowledged and balanced.

Truth within: When Uranus goes into Pisces in March 2003, your group involvements may take a new turn. Instead of being a part of the group, you may lead groups in some way, bringing your knowledge to other people. In this way, you maintain the individuality that you prize so highly and yet also contribute to the larger collective.

Uranus stays in Pisces until May of 2010. During this time your intuition makes quantum leaps and so does your idealism. Make sure, though, that you stay grounded and rooted firmly in the present moment. In fact, for a few minutes a day, practice sitting still, in the zen of the moment. In these moments your inner truth shines.

Spritual expansion: This is the ultimate purpose of Neptune in Aquarius. First, it works to break down the boundaries between you and others, the ego defenses, the mind games. That's usually when confund physical fatigue come into the picture. But begin to perceive the larger truths, the confusion and fatigue usually vanish and your imagination clicks in. Your compassion is stirred and compels you to reach out to others. And it's in this reaching that your spiritual expansion begins.

During Neptune's fourteen-year transit through your sun sign, you may have to sacrifice something important in your life for something else that is equally important. At times it may seem that you don't have any choice in the matter, that the choice, in fact, is made for you through external circumstances. But this is only part of Neptune's illusion. The truth is that you always have a choice but simply choose to believe otherwise.

Ultimately, Neptune in Aquarius nudges you to expand spiritually on a personal level, then urges you to reach out to others in the same spiritual vein.

Self: Your challenge in the millennium is to retain your connection to humanity and the larger world while developing a deeper awareness of your emotional needs and your emotional intelligence.

The millennium opens with both Uranus and Neptune in your sun sign. This dual conjunction to your sun urges you, on the one hand, to break free of any relationship or situation that restricts your freedom, and yet on the other hand, you're deeply confused about what this freedom actually entails.

To know what the freedom entails, you first have to pinpoint what or who makes you feel restricted. If it's a relationship, how does it restrict you? If it's a situation such as a job, do you have other options? Take an honest look at your life situation, then visualize the changes you would like. This simple exercise often serves to make you acutely aware of what you have created in your life—and what you must release to go forward.

Remember: the changes that Uranus brings into your life happen abruptly and unexpectedly. The equivalent is an explosion. The good thing about it, though, is that you can adjust rather quickly and move on. Neptune doesn't work that way.

Neptune's effects are far more subtle and gradual, due in part to its much slower movement through a sign—fourteen years versus the seven that it takes Uranus. Where Uranus disrupts, Neptune dissolves. In this case, it dissolves your ego boundaries, so that initially you feel confused, puzzled, disturbed. Since the sun represents your vitality, you may also go through periods where you feel lethargic and heavy, as if you weighed five hundred pounds.

With your ego quieter than usual, your emotions have greater freedom and rise like high tide, often inundating you with their power. Not surprisingly, transcendental experiences happen during Neptune/sun conjunctions. Your compassion and your capacity to love deepen under this conjunction, but you may also be somewhat gullible.

Finances: For you, money is merely the manifestation of energy directed in a particular way. You aren't particularly interested in amassing wealth just to have money. For you, it's a vehicle to freedom. If you want to run off to Bali for a week to immerse yourself in native customs, you don't have to worry about putting it on Visa. If you want to update your computer, you do it and toss in all the software trimmings. This isn't likely to change in the millennium. But the way you earn money and your values in general may change when Uranus goes into Pisces in 2003 and begins its transit through your second house of money.

This can mean sudden financial windfalls or sudden financial disaster. These are the two extremes, and the way it plays out for you depends on your attitudes, will, and how inflexible you are in this area. Say you've been buzzing along for the last five or ten years, raking in money at a job you aren't crazy about, but have been reluctant to leave because the pay is so good. During this transit you'll probably either quit the job or get fired. One way or another, Uranus disrupts the status quo and coerces you to grow.

The opposite may also be true. If you've been struggling to establish a business you love, but are barely balancing the books, then Uranus provides the break you've been hoping for.

All disruptions start within. But with Uranus in Pisces, that "within" assumes very definite qualities. Maybe you dream that you're growing organic vegetables and herbs in the South Seas. Silly dream, isn't it. After all, you're happy doing what you do. But when the dream repeats itself time and again, you begin to pay attention. *You become receptive.* So you start dabbling in organic gardening in your backyard. Pretty soon neighbors and friends are requesting your herbs and vegetables. Then they're buying them. And before you know it, you have a full-blown business and are faced with a choice. Do you stay with your job or do you take that leap into the unknown?

The choices you make now affect your joint finances when Saturn goes into Virgo in September 2007, Pisces' polar opposite, the eighth house versus the second. Before you make your choice, be sure to listen to the promptings of your inner oracle, Aquarius. It won't steer you wrong.

Communication: This really isn't a big deal for you in the first decade of the millennium. When you have something on your mind, you say it. You may not say it with the bluntness of a Sagittarius, but you get your point across.

What's going to change, though, is the way you communicate your emotions and the venue in which you do that. The Internet isn't just a place where you cull information; it's also a meeting place, the virtual equivalent of a block party or your neighbor's living room. The Internet is where you meet people. Some of your closest friends are people you have never met face-to-face. Or they are people you have met first over the Internet, in chat rooms or on bulletin boards or through e-mail.

In the fall of 2004, when Jupiter trines your natal sun, these types of contacts become even more important to you. You reach out emotionally through the virtual world, to connect with people who share your interests and worldview, and you connect emotionally. Some of these people may be from other cultures and countries and, in some way, your association with them expands your own communication skills. You're able to delve more deeply into your feelings.

Nora Ephron's take on this, *You've Got Mail,* could be the end result.

Your home: Reread the catalyst section, which details the ramification of the planetary lineup in Taurus and the Jupiter/Saturn conjunction. If you have your natal chart, look for the house that has Taurus on the cusp. That house represents the area of your life where you're going to feel overwhelmed for a while.

Creative potential: From the end of June 2000 to mid-July 2001, Jupiter in Gemini impacts your fifth house of creativity and forms a trine to your natal sun. In August 2000, Saturn joins Jupiter. This spells a period of creative adventure and innovation. Everything you do now seems to succeed and some sort of public recognition for your creative work is likely at this time.

Your goals strengthen and your creative vision expands. People who hold authority over you are impressed by your work and ideas and smooth the path for your success.

The powers that be, however, may challenge you and your work sometime between mid-July 2005 to September 2007, when Saturn opposes your natal sun. If you've done your homework, the opposition won't be such a big deal. You simply move ahead, keeping your own counsel, patiently biding your time.

Health & work: The Saturn opposition to your natal sun can create health problems if you aren't particularly attentive. Avoid taking on any new responsibilities for this two-year period and instead, focus on finishing what you've already started.

You benefit from periodic respites to conserve your energy—long weekends where nothing more is required of you than lounging on a beach and sipping margaritas; a day here and there where you do something entirely for yourself; pampering yourself with whatever makes you happy. Visualization and affirmations help in situations where you feel burned-out and overburdened. Or you might try what the Aquarian woman did earlier in this chapter; "pull in" the wave of probability that fits the future you want.

Partnerships: The eclipse in Leo in August 1999 launches a partnership theme for you in the first decade of the millennium. Whatever has surfaced in your relationships as a result of the eclipse is an insight that you carry with you into other partnerships.

In August 2002, with Jupiter in Leo, your existing partnerships expand and new relationships enter your life that somehow broaden and deepen your worldview. People from other countries and cultures may play a vital part in your life at this time. This period lasts for about a year. Then, in mid-July 2005 when Saturn enters Leo, your relationships are tested. This transit can stress your marriage or relationship with your significant other. But if you confront problems head-on and honestly attempt to work out your differences, the relationship strengthens.

Spirituality: The Aquarian age is tailor-made for you in this department. Your spiritual beliefs and how you practice them are already integral to your daily life. You attempt to live your beliefs to the best of your ability, and that won't change in the millennium. The challenge, however, is for you to have such a firm handle on your beliefs that you can begin imparting them to others.

You may be ready to do that when Jupiter moves through Libra from late September 2004 to late October of 2005, impacting your ninth house. If you have writing abilities, this would be an excellent time to put them to use. If you want to teach, plan a strategy on how you might go about doing this. The Internet may prove to be one of your most valuable tools during this phase, allowing you to connect to large numbers of people who share your ideals.

Profession & career: Your spiritual pursuits play right into your profession. Once Jupiter moves into Virgo, hitting your tenth house, you begin to refine your methods, paying closer attention to the details. In other words, if you're writing a book about your spiritual beliefs, are you going to write a how-to or a personal story? Or are you going to combine elements of both? Or perhaps your beliefs are best expressed through some sort of divination system. The point is that you now define your methods and apply this technique, whatever it is, to the larger picture.

Personal unconscious: At the end of December 2007, Jupiter in Capricorn moves through your twelfth house. The content of your unconscious mind becomes much easier for you to access now and you won't meet much if any resistance to it. You have many opportunities to expand and deepen your spiritual understanding, and your compassion for others runs at an all-time high.

In January 2008, Pluto goes into Capricorn, hitting your twelfth house. If you've taken advantage of the Jupiter transit, this one won't be as dramatic as it might be otherwise. Any power that you've disowned throughout your life or any behaviors and emotions that you were taught were "bad" are going to surface now. Essentially you're cleaning out the psychic garbage that has accumulated throughout the years and must use what you find as opportunities for growth.

Tapping the Source

Synchronicities & Your Inner Oracle

This is an area you love. If you're like most Aquarians, you easily recognize and interpret a synchronicity when it happens to someone else. But you may have trouble interpreting the experience when it happens to you. The problem isn't the metamorphic language; it's that you doubt your interpretation because it applies to your own experience.

To build your confidence, interpret your dreams for a week and take note of the various symbols and language that your unconscious uses in dreams. Keep track of recurring symbols and themes. If you have the time, make a personal glossary of the symbols. Then apply these to a synchronicity when it happens.

If your dreams include animals, there might be one that appears repeatedly. Maybe you even think of this animal as your "guardian creature." Post pictures or photographs of this animal in your work area to remind your conscious and unconscious mind that the animal is an important symbol for you. Chances are, the animal somehow will work into your next synchronicity.

You can do this with virtually anything that is important to you in your daily life. By making these symbols visible, you're giving yourself permission to explore this area of your own psyche.

Creating Your Future

This is an area where Aquarians also excel. The future is your venue. Every day you're faced with choices. Should you go shopping or get that chipped filling fixed? Should you take the cat to the vet or take your son to soccer? With each choice you make, one set of probabilities opens up and another set closes off.

One of the best visual depictions of probabilities is the movie *Sliding Doors*. In one probability, the heroine doesn't get through the sliding door on the train she needs to catch. In the other probability, she does. The movie follows both tracks and shows what she discovers and lives through in both probabilities. A page-turning novel that deals with this idea is *The Man Who Turned into Himself*.

If you're unsure how to go about using conscious creation to create what you want, reread the section earlier in the chapter about the Aquarian woman who "pulls in" wave probabilities. Then observe a group of children as they play. Quite often the kids make up the script as they go along, talking about it and revising as they go along. Kids, in fact, seem to know how to pull in wave probabilities without even knowing what they're doing, and they do it through their intent and passionate desires.

During a Thanksgiving presentation at an elementary school, one child got up in front of her class to talk about the things in her life for which she was grateful. Included in her list were her animals. "I'm grateful for my hamsters, my three cats, and the dog I'm going to have very soon."

That she would have a dog very soon was news to her parents.

Less than two weeks later, a friend of the girl's asked if she and her family would be interested in a golden retriever that she had. The dog's family had given it to the county school system because one of their kids had developed asthma. The friend's father trained dogs for the county to sniff out drugs in high school lockers, and the golden had flunked the course. So they took the dog, and the girl got her wish.

It's all in the magic of belief, Aquarius.

Allow your intuition to guide you in this process. You won't take long to get the hang of this. An exercise that engages your intellect, your intuition, and your zeal is your kind of thing.

Chapter 20

Pisces, the Fish

February 19–March 20
Mutable, Water
Ruled by Neptune

Pisces Man

Physically, there are two types of Pisces individuals—the whale and the dolphin. The first tends to be physically large both in height and in weight. He looks awkward when he walks, as if his feet are too small for the rest of him. The dolphin type is more graceful, at home in his body. This type has great feet, an example of nature's perfect symmetry.

Both types have incredible, liquid eyes that are probably a startling color, quite large, and the focus of his entire face. These are the kind of eyes you can get lost in, especially over a romantic dinner somewhere, just the two of you sitting in the candlelight. There is a lot of that with a Pisces man.

This guy, after all, discovers and relates to the world through his emotions and his imagination. Romance is high on his list and he is, in fact, the prototypical romantic, willing to do whatever is necessary to win the woman he loves. There's another kind of

Pisces man, though, who romances his imagination, swept along in its rich blue waters. Albert Einstein was this type.

The Pisces man isn't ambitious in the conventional sense of the word, not unless he has a Capricorn moon or ascendant. He enjoys money, but has no burning hunger to be rich just to be rich. If he speculates in the stock market or in investments, he usually goes with his gut. As a Neptune-ruled sign, his intuition is so highly developed that it runs through him like a river; it's not something he has to think about.

Something of the actor is in this man. This may develop when he's a kid, and his feelings get hurt. He's so sensitive that even from a young age he absorbs the moods of the people around him. He's a psychic sponge, and all too often the sponge part of it fails to discriminate between positive and negative influences. As a result, his times alone aren't just important to him, they're vital to his emotional and physical well-being. He should strive to stay away from people whose general dispositions are negative because he'll absorb the negativity.

Psychic ability is evident in many Pisceans, male or female, possibly manifested as clairvoyance, mysticism, or strong gut feelings. At the very least, this man explores metaphysics at some point in his life and may have an interest in reincarnation, astrology, spirit communication, and other similar topics.

Like Aquarius, he accepts people as they are, without prejudice or complaint. He asks only that you do the same for him. He finds this ready acceptance in children, who enjoy him as much as he enjoys them. He's the sort of father who takes the kids to the beach, river rafting, snorkeling, scuba diving, sailing. As a water sign, water sports appeal to him. Physically he benefits from drinking large amounts of water.

Since Pisces rules the feet and the lymphatic system, the Pisces man melts when you massage his feet. He also benefits from foot reflexology. As a Neptune-ruled sign, his physical ailments may be difficult to diagnose at times.

The symbol for the sign, of two fish swimming in opposite directions, describes an indecisiveness that is often apparent in Piscean individuals. This usually manifests as an emotional ambivalence that drives other people crazy. His indecisiveness may be as obvious as an on-again, off-again relationship in which the fish proclaims his undying love one day, then avoids you the next. Blame it on the war between his head and his heart.

The Pisces Woman

She's as enigmatic as a Scorpio woman, although much softer about it, and as sentimental as Cancer. Those dreamy, liquid eyes of hers turn heads on street corners and if she notices the attention, she doesn't show it. Among female Pisceans, the whale and dolphin analogy also holds true. But with both types, there is a part of her which is always distant, separate, traveling the celestial highways of her imagination.

Back on Earth, this woman is sometimes found working behind the scenes in large corporations or in institutions. Her deeply compassionate nature attracts her to the health and medical fields, to psychology and counseling, or to metaphysics. Many Pisceans are exceptionally artistic and gravitate to industries like film, theater, fashion, the arts and writing, and publishing.

Like the male Pisces, this woman is a true romantic, the type who falls in love with love. When she's not in love, in fact, her life may not seem as bright and vivid and certainly not as interesting. But she also needs her downtime, her solitude, periods of respite from the outer world when her imagination soars to almost mystical heights. If she's robbed of that solitude, then she, like the male Pisces, turns her energies inward and may seek escape through alcohol or drugs.

Women who have Pisces moons or ascendants often possess a transcendental quality that hints at depths the rest of us will never touch, much less perceive. The Pisces-moon types frequently display emotional ambivalence, particularly when it comes to relationships or marriages. The typical Pisces-moon type that's locked in a dead-end marriage carries on complicated arguments with herself about why she should leave and why she should not leave. The bottom line is that she leaves when she's so miserable she simply can't stand it anymore.

As mothers, these women often share deep psychic connections with their children that allow them to understand what their offspring feel even when the kids themselves don't know what they feel. Their compassion embraces all the travails and challenges of childhood and adolescence—shyness, awkwardness, dating and acne, hurt feelings, and broken hearts. The Piscean mother is always there to pick up the pieces and put Humpty-Dumpty back together again.

The Piscean woman is as emotional as the man. Her emotions tend to show themselves during stressful periods of her life, and it's usually some unrelated event that triggers what she's feeling. She might cry uncontrollably, for example, at the memorial service for a person she hardly knew, thus releasing pent-up sorrow over some situation in her own life.

As an archetype, Pisces represents the end of an evolutionary cycle, in which the ego-self is transcended and unity with a larger self or divinity is achieved. However, several types of Pisces exist within the archetype. The first type, male or female, is caught in the martyr or victim loop, where unity is attempted through sublimation to another's needs. This type would be the mother who gives up her own needs and desires for those of her kids. Then, later in life, she resents her kids or herself for the sacrifices she made. The second type subordinates her ego through service to others, but does it with an open heart, out of pure compassion. The third type, which fits most Pisceans, is a combination of the first two. Regardless of which type you know, the Pisces woman is always more complex than she appears to be.

Liz Taylor is probably one of the best examples of the Piscean archetype. First, look at her violet eyes; they're pure Pisces. Then look at her life. She has been in the spotlight since she was a child actress (Neptune rules the film industry), has been married eight times, twice to the same man (Pisces romanticism), has gone through various addictions (Neptune and escapism) and numerous health problems. Then she transcended all of it by becoming one of the most visible and vocal spokespeople for AIDS awareness.

In the early part of her life, she exemplified one expression of the Piscean archetype; in the latter part of her life, she exemplifies the other.

Pisces in the Millennium

In the new millennium, you learn to bring your considerable wisdom and intuitive ability into alignment with your profession and career. You become more adept at protecting yourself against influences that, in the past, you've absorbed from the people in your immediate environment. You have the opportunity to express the full range of your imagination and emotions. Sounds like paradise, doesn't it?

The one caveat is that you have to learn to take care of yourself before you take care of others. This may be difficult for you to do and sounds contradictory to the Aquarian message. But it's vital that the boundary between you and other people doesn't blur to the point where you don't know who you are. You already have a deep connection to humanity, and to contribute fully to the global community that emerges in the new millennium, you need established parameters between self and others.

Energizer: The eclipse of the century on August 11, 1999, occurs at 18 degrees Leo, in your sixth house of health and work. As a mutable sign, it won't affect you as much as it does the fixed signs, unless you have a moon or ascendant in Leo, Scorpio, Taurus, or Aquarius that falls between 17 and 19 degrees.

Something in your health or work that has been concealed or hidden comes to light now, which you have to confront and deal with. Possibly something as simple as a habit intensifies that you've neglected to break—smoking, eating desserts, drinking—and now have to break. It might involve a coworker or a boss whom you have disliked without apparent reason and now you understand why.

You're likely to feel the effects of the eclipse for several months on either side of it. To find out which area of your life is specifically affected by the eclipse, look at your natal chart and locate the house with Leo on the cusp.

Catalyst: The lineup of seven planets in Taurus on May 3, 2000 forms a sextile to your natal sun and highlights your third house of communication. This house also includes siblings, neighbors, and your fundamental-thinking process, as well as routine travel and daily activities. You're going to feel that the petty details of life are consuming all your time and energy, and for a while, that's exactly what's happening.

Your responsibilities in this area increase as you approach the Jupiter/Saturn conjunction later this same month. With both of these planets sextile to your sun, your timing is important. Take advantage of any opportunities that come your way. Even something that lands in your lap that doesn't seem like much of an opportunity should be explored because it may prove to be better than you think.

Your thinking definitely expands. You're able to see the entire forest now, not just the proverbial trees. Your perception in and of your daily world is expanding. You may take workshops or seminars that broaden your consciousness, or you may go back to school to improve your skills. Some of the attitudes you've held as inviolate now begin to fall away from your life or they expand into something else.

This is a great time to make plans for the future, Pisces. You're able to think in bigger terms now, to conceptualize where you're going and what you want to achieve. You may be publicly recognized by people in authority.

Transformation: Around the end of 1995, you began to experience certain conditions and situations with an underlying theme about power—your power over others, their power over you. Blame Pluto in Sagittarius, squaring your natal sun. This aspect can trigger the beast of ambition in virtually anyone and also can bring out parts of yourself that you need to heal.

By the opening of the millennium, you've had four years of experience with this aspect. You should know by now whether you've become the beast of ambition and power or whether you're trying to heal issues revolving around power. This transformative process can be painful if you resist and instructive if you don't. Either way, though, you change dramatically and fundamentally during this time.

You get help, of course, from some other transits. From July of 2001 to the end of July 2002, Jupiter is in Cancer, a fellow water sign, and trines your natal sun. Your creativity takes off. You're able to tap creative reservoirs in yourself that you may not have known existed. Your physical energy and health are also good at this time, which feeds into your creative well.

The first few years of the millennium, in fact, are preparing you for Uranus's transit through your sun sign in 2003.

Innovation: This phase may not feel very innovative for you, Pisces. Feelings you would rather not know about may surface, but take heart. All of us have at least one or two phases like that in the millennium. Uranus's transit through Aquarius from

1996 to mid-March of 2003 hits your twelfth house of the personal unconscious.

This happens to be Pisces' native home, but the fact that Uranus is going through it indicates that things may happen more abruptly than you like. At times the inner disruptions may feel like volcanic eruptions. Old attitudes and beliefs suddenly rise up, waving flags and flapping their arms, demanding that you deal with them, understand them, and then release them. Since the twelfth house deals with institutions, you may come up against some of your beliefs through nursing homes, prisons, hospitals, Alzheimer's units, and any similar place.

In traditional astrology, this house also represents "hidden enemies." But this is a kind of insidious term that implies ignorance on your part, and that simply isn't the case. Your deepest beliefs are at work here. While it's true that some of those beliefs may not be apparent to your conscious mind, they are still *your beliefs* and attract certain types of experiences. If those experiences include so-called hidden enemies, then it behooves you to make your deepest beliefs conscious and to work hard to change them.

Once you do this then Uranus's passage through your twelfth house becomes innovation in its purest form, enabling you to draw on your inner wisdom to put your ideas out into the larger world.

New paradigms: This one comes about when Uranus and Neptune share the same sign. You already know that Uranus's role in Aquarius isn't going to be anything to write home about, Pisces. Fortunately, Neptune rules Pisces and the twelfth house and is generally more compatible with your basic nature regardless of what sign it's in.

As a pair in the same sign, though, they're the odd couple that somehow find a plateau where they can tolerate each other's differences. While Uranus disrupts your old ways of thinking, Neptune prompts you to look very deep and to ask profound spiritual questions. This is something you do a lot of routinely, Pisces, but Neptune makes sure that you do it in terms of your entire life, not just a segment of your life.

Therapy may be one way of exploring this transit. To have someone else's perspective helps, but it must be the right someone. You have to feel that you can talk honestly about whatever your unconscious kicks up. If a therapist goes against your nature, then maybe a close friend is helpful at this time. If a friend doesn't fit the bill, then start talking into a tape recorder. Or write down what you feel.

Julia Cameron's book *The Artist's Way* might appeal to you simply as a device for organizing your thoughts. She recommends "morning pages" as a way to get in touch with whatever you feel, good or bad, artistic or mundane. There is something about seeing your thoughts on paper (or a computer screen) that makes an impact.

Regardless of what technique you use, the point is to make the unconscious conscious. By doing so, your new, emerging belief systems become readily apparent to you.

Truth within: Finally. You're getting closer to home now, Pisces. You're Goldilocks emerging from the woods and standing in front of the house where the three bears live. Should you go in or simply walk on? You go in, of course, but mostly out of curiosity, because you want to know *what's there.*

That's how this transit is for you. What are you really made of? If mysticism is your game, then this is the time when you really get into it. If you feel most spiritually satisfied through an artistic expression, then this is when you produce exquisitely, with brilliance and insight. Whatever your particular slant, you begin to live who you are, without apology, without sacrifice.

And how can that possibly be bad, Pisces?

Spiritual expansion: Fourteen years. In the cosmic scheme of things, it's spit in the wind. But if you live to be eighty-four, it's one-sixth of your life. That's Neptune in Aquarius. If you reach even further, to when Neptune goes into your sun sign, add another thirteen years, and you have more than a quarter of a century. So if you're hoping for a picnic in the millennium, Pisces, forget it. You're in for the long haul. Until the spring of 2025, in one form or another, you'll hear Neptune's song.

Dive deep, it says. Enjoy the ride. And if you don't come out as a guru, you'll know, at the very least, who you are and what you believe and why you're here and where you're going. Most of us will not discover this much in a lifetime.

Self: You're at Sea World in California, the granddaddy of marine theme parks, watching the dolphin and whale show, when suddenly you begin to feel nauseated. By the time the show is over, you're so dizzy you can barely stand.

This is how your "psychic sponge" may work at times in the millennium, absorbing the energy around you. Although this is a negative example, the same principles are at work when you're with a group of like-minded individuals and absorb their collective creative energy.

With Uranus conjuncting your sun sign from late 2003 to March of 2011, you're more sensitive psychically. Use some sort of protective technique when you're in a crowd of strangers so that you don't absorb whatever psychic stuff is in the air. This doesn't have to be anything elaborate. You can focus your intent on protection, or simply envision yourself surrounded by a white light.

Uranus conjunct your natal sun also brings a magnetic quality to your personality that attracts the right opportunities and people to further your creative and professional goals.

Finances: For about a year, beginning in the fall of 2004, Jupiter in Libra opens doors to other people's resources. Maybe something as mundane as your mortgage or bank loan comes through or something as significant as an inheritance.

However this plays out, it would be in your best interest to pay off any outstanding credit-card debts you may have. If you're the type of Pisces who loves to spend, spend, spend, then now is the time to set up a budget and try to stick to it. If you're the other type of Pisces, who is generous to a fault, learn to be generous with yourself first and follow that parental adage: save ten percent of everything you earn.

In 2008, when Pluto sextiles your sun, your goals—financial and otherwise—may undergo a significant change. Your natural compassion and altruism may find suitable outlets in fields such as health, medicine, and the arts.

When Jupiter trines your natal sun from October 2005 to November of 2006, your financial situation improves significantly. You may spend a lot of money, too!

Communication: With the lineup of planets in Taurus on May 3, 2000, and the Jupiter/Saturn conjunction in Taurus, communication is a priority for you in the new millennium. Specifically, this means that instead of keeping your hunches and intuitions to yourself, you tend to share them with other people now, even if those people may not approve.

Your basic thought process and your perceptions are changing, which alters your relationships with siblings, neighbors, and people you encounter in your daily life. By speaking your truth, Pisces, you're stepping out of the shadows. You're on some sort of quest and even if the nature of that quest isn't always clear to you, your intuition is your strongest guide and ally. Trust it.

Your home: Your self-restraint and discipline are tested for the first three years or so of the millennium. It begins when Jupiter in Gemini squares your natal sun, then continues with Saturn squaring your sun. This creates some friction in your immediate environment with parents, significant others, even with bosses and employers. You should exercise patience during this time and remain alert for synchronistic hints that nudge you in one direction or another.

Unresolved childhood issues may surface that you have to deal with and understand. If you try to ignore these issues, then they manifest in situations that you attract or through other people who reflect the issues. The whole point of these transits, Pisces, is to weed the inessentials or outdated beliefs and relationships from your life.

Creative potential: You're going to love this part of the millennium. From June 2001 to mid-July of 2005, your creative energies are running high and fast. Your ideas are original and innovative and your output astonishes and impresses people who have authority over you. Your intuition rides tandem with your creative ability at this time and nudges you in directions that benefit you. Apparently you're consistently in the right place at the right time.

Be careful, however, to fulfill any obligations and responsibilities that you assume during this period. Try not to take on so much that your energy is scattered.

If you have children, your relationship with them improves significantly.

Health & work: Once you learn to protect yourself psychically, your general health is likely to improve because you won't be as prone to picking up other people's emotional baggage. For about two years, though, from September 2007 to the end of October 2009, Saturn opposes your sun and stresses your physical vitality.

Before the opposition begins, be aware of the needs of your physical body. Set up a regular exercise program, be sure that your diet is nutritious, and find some sort of physical outlet that also satisfies your spirit. Since you have a natural affinity for water, daily walks along a beach might be in order. If you don't live near a beach, then at least get outside in the fresh air.

You benefit from a diet rich in seafood and should drink eight to twelve glasses of water a day just to keep your body flushed of toxins. Your feet are the most vulnerable part of your body, so treat them well, Pisces, and they'll always take you exactly where you need to go!

In the work arena, the Saturn opposition seems to bring challenges from every direction—bosses, coworkers, clients. They argue with you, they don't appreciate what you do, they are generally cantankerous. But if you've laid the foundation earlier in the millennium and have proven yourself to the higher-ups, this period won't be nearly as stressful as it could be. Just hang in there and know that this, too, shall pass.

Partnerships: Say what you mean and mean what you say, Pisces. That alone goes a long way toward mitigating any problems you have in the relationship area. Your emotional ambivalence in your most intimate relationships is often just an excuse to sidestep a situation you've created. Instead of avoiding it, deal with it by being as honest as possible without hurting the other person's feelings.

Even in your partnerships, however, it's important to maintain a psychic boundary between yourself and the other person. This keeps you from merging with the other person's energy or from taking on their psychic garbage. In business partnerships, the same caution applies.

Spirituality: This is always an important area for you and becomes even more so as you move through the first decade of the millennium. The trick is to maintain your spiritual equilibrium by avoiding extreme or fanatical religious movements. By integrating your spiritual beliefs and your deep compassion into your profession and career, you avoid the fanatics and are better able to bring about change in the larger world.

From October 2005 to November of 2006, your

spiritual orientation expands and you may begin teaching what you know and what you're learning to other people.

Profession & career: You usually aren't the type for power trips. But with Pluto square your natal sun until 2008, you may surprise yourself. Your ambition may rear up and bite you in the hand, Pisces, and if it does, tread very carefully during these eight years. Ambition itself isn't the problem; it's how you go about achieving what you want that may create difficulties.

Even if your ambition doesn't overwhelm you during these eight years, power issues arise in your dealings with other people. The whole point of this transit is to make you more aware of how you wield power over others or how they wield power over you.

During the Saturn opposition from September 2007 to October 2009, don't attempt to push your own agenda in the professional arena. You meet too much resistance if you do and end up feeling as if you're continually banging your head against a wall that simply won't yield. Be patient, bide your time, and work diligently at whatever you do.

Personal unconscious: Your challenge in this area is to make the unconscious conscious so that you can harness the full power of your innate psychic ability. You, like your fellow water signs, have all the tools you need to do this. Pay close attention to your conscious thoughts, to your dreams, to what you say in casual conversations. By honing in on your deepest beliefs, you're able to work with the beliefs that no longer work for you and create beliefs that are more in line with the new, emerging you.

This is an ongoing process for you, Pisces, that intensifies as Neptune approaches a conjunction with your sun in February of 2012. Even though the second decade of the millennium is beyond the scope of this book, this Neptune transit through Pisces is worth mentioning. Your compassion, psychic ability, and your concern for conditions in the larger world deepens. This is when you can truly make a global difference, Pisces, *if* you've done the required inner work for the first decade of the millennium.

If you've tried to ignore your intuition and neglected to develop this side of your personality, then this transit brings a lot of confusion to your life.

Tapping the Source

Synchronicities & Your Inner Oracle

A synchronicity speaks to you in the language of dreams, Pisces, a place that is as familiar to you as your own skin. You already know that such occurrences are actually the voice of your inner oracle, but even so, you don't always pay attention to the message or follow the advice.

For a set period of time, work with the messages that come through synchronicities. Do it in a spirit of adventure, as a sort of test to see if there's anything to any of it. Then sit back and watch your life change and your understanding deepen.

One exercise that works well with most water signs is to watch how the Piscean archetype works in your own life. This requires a certain detachment about your own actions, but can be enormously revealing about who you really are and where you're going.

Listed below are some of the attributes of the Piscean archetype:

1) Intuitive, mystical, "gut feelings"
2) Vivid imagination
3) Escapism through alcohol, drugs, food
4) Deep compassion for others
5) Torn between free will and letting events take their own course
6) Romantic, idealist
7) Adaptable
8) Deep connections to inner self through dreams, imagination, fantasy

If you don't keep track of your dreams and try to interpret them, then now is the time to start. A lot of information comes to you through dreams, and if you begin to work consciously with them, this process is speeded up. Your journey through life is intensely focused on self-discovery, Pisces, and that means delving into your private, deepest self to discover who you really are.

If you're a reader, there are several books you may want to read during this test period that will deepen your experience: *Listening to the Oracle* by Linda Skafte, *Awakening Intuition* by Mona Lisa Schultz, and *The Artist's Way* by Julia Cameron.

Creating Your Future

Despite your intuitive and often mystical nature, using your beliefs consciously, to create your future, may not be something you've ever seriously entertained. To get the hang of it, Pisces, start with something small.

Maybe you're hoping to get a week off at the time of year that is busiest for your company. Instead of worrying about what your boss is going to say or instead of not requesting the week at all, spend a few minutes each day envisioning yourself at the locale where you want to go. Do this as vividly as possible and repeat it until the visualization is so clear you feel it inside you. Then envision yourself talking to your boss about it. Again, make this visualization vivid.

When you feel completely comfortable with both visualizations, make some gesture that confirms your belief that you'll get the week off at the time of year you want. Buy something you might need on the trip. Then try it out on your boss.

To bolster your confidence in this process, read Shakti Gawain's classical book, *Creative Visualization.* Belief, Pisces. It all boils down to belief.

Afterword

Everyone has an opinion about what the millennium will bring. Scholars make educated guesses based on past cycles; psychics and astrologers make predictions based on broad patterns that they perceive; and the rest of us go along from day to day, hoping it won't be as bad as we may believe. But the bottom line is that none of us really *know.*

If, however, the future is created from moment to moment, through choices each of us makes, then let's try to make choices that help others as well as ourselves. If we are to create a future that is really the Aquarian vision of equality and humanity for all, it must begin with each one of us, in our individual, daily lives.

So the next time you're tempted to tell off your meddling neighbor or a coworker, bite your tongue and ask yourself why you've attracted this person or experience into your life. *What's the message?* If you've got chronic allergies or get a dozen colds a winter, take a look at your beliefs. Do you believe that "everyone gets three colds a winter"? If you're in debt, if you're lonely, if you're locked into negative patterns in a relationship, ask yourself what beliefs led to this situation. Do you believe in your worth as a human being?

At every turn in our lives, we have opportunities to grow and evolve so that we may realize our fullest potential. There's no time like now to begin the journey.